P9-CLE-734

LINCOLN CHRISTIAN COLLEGE AND SEMINARY

The Cultural Dictionary of the Bible

The Cultural Dictionary
of the Bible

John J. Pilch

A Liturgical Press Book

 THE LITURGICAL PRESS
Collegeville, Minnesota

Cover design by David Manahan, O.S.B.
Photograph by Sonia Halliday Photographs.

PHOTOGRAPHS AND ILLUSTRATIONS
Corel Photos: 16, 17, 18; in L. H. Grollenberg, O.P., *Atlas of the Bible,* Nelson: 114; Jeffrey Hutson, O.S.B.: 42; Liguori Publications: 90; The Liturgical Press archives: 24, 28, 44, 56, 83, 149, 175, 180, 182, 185, 188; Robin Pierzina, O.S.B.: 54, 101, 137; Hugh Witzmann, O.S.B.: 57, 69, 107, 126, 186.

Scripture quotations are from the Revised Standard Version Bible, with adaptations. The Old Testament, © 1952. The Catholic Edition of the Old Testament, incorporating the Apocrypha, © 1966 by the Division of Christian Education of the National Council of the Churches of Christ in the United States of America. The New Testament © 1946. The Catholic Edition of the New Testament, © 1965 by the Division of Christian Education of the National Council of the Churches of Christ in the United States of America.

The author in preparing this dictionary has relied on the original Hebrew and Greek texts of the Bible.

Copyright © 1999 by The Order of St. Benedict, Inc., Collegeville, Minnesota. All rights reserved. No part of this book may be reproduced in any form or by any means, electronic or mechanical, including photocopying, recording, taping, or any storage and retrieval system, without the written permission of The Liturgical Press, Collegeville, MN 56321. Printed in the United States of America.

	2	3	4	5	6	7	8	9

Library of Congress Cataloging-in-Publication Data

Pilch, John J.
    The cultural dictionary of the Bible / John J. Pilch.
       p. cm.
    Includes bibliographical references.
    ISBN 0-8146-2527-4 (alk. paper)
     1. Bible–Dictionaries. I. Title.
BS440.P653   1999
220.3–dc21
                                                        98–7101
                                                         CIP

In loving memory of my wife,
JEAN PETERS PILCH
(1936–1997)
the first reader of these articles,
which made her eyes dance
with enthusiastic excitement,

and with gratitude to her parents,
MRS. SAMMIE PETERS LONG

and

THE LATE MR. SAM ANTHONY SCAMARDO,
who brought this "gift of God"
into the world

100235

Contents

Acknowledgments

The articles in this volume are revisions of previously published materials that appeared in *The Bible Today* from 1993 to 1997 and in *PACE (Professional Approaches for Christian Educators)*. The following are the original articles that appeared in *PACE:*

"Jews and Christians: Anachronisms in Bible Translations," *PACE* 25 (April 1996) 18–25.

"Scripture, Culture and Catechesis," *PACE* 19 (March 1990) 189–192.

"Who Killed John the Baptist?" *PACE* 19 (April 1990) 216–219.

"Secrecy in the Gospel of Mark," *PACE* 21 (February 1992) 150–154.

"'I do not know the man!' Deception and Lying in the Bible," *PACE* 21 (January 1992) 111–114.

"Separating the Sheep from the Goats," *PACE* 21 (April 1992) 215–218.

"A Spirit Named 'Fever,'" *PACE* 21 (May 1992) 253–256.

Preface

This collection of previously published articles has been revised and arranged in the format of a cultural dictionary. By "culture" I understand a system of shared interpretations of persons, things, and events. These interpretations belong to specific time-and-space frames and are endowed with emotionally anchored meaning. People in a given culture share strong and common feelings about the meanings they attribute to persons, things, and events. The entry on SHEEP AND GOATS is an excellent illustration.

Since each article discusses a variety of persons, things, and events under its title, the Contents presents a more comprehensive, alphabetized list of these subjects for ready reference. For example, no single article treats "translation" concerns as a major topic. Such questions, however, are treated within the articles JEWS AND CHRISTIANS, SICKNESS, and ABBA, which also discusses the appropriate translation of SHALOM and SALT. In the Contents, uppercase references identify complete articles; lowercase references list some of the related topics treated in the articles.

The list of basic resources at the end of this volume presents a representative selection of dictionaries, atlases, and similar books to which a beginner might turn in order to gain additional or supplemental information on each topic. The bibliography at the end of each entry for the most part reports the social scientific sources (Mediterranean anthropology, psychological anthropology, medical anthropology, and the like) that gave me an important insight into the distinctive, Middle Eastern cultural world of the Bible. Teachers, preachers, students, and others might find these particularly useful or interesting. Those readers who are dismayed by these references can skip them without any disadvantage. The nuggets of wisdom offered by these references are incorporated into each article.

I wish to express special thanks to my long-time friend and biblical colleague at Notre Dame University, Prof. Jerome H. Neyrey, S.J., who suggested the dictionary format for these articles. This Cultural Dictionary can serve as a companion or sequel to my three-volume series, *The Cultural World of Jesus Sunday by Sunday* (The Liturgical Press, 1995).

May these reflections continue to contribute to a growth in understanding of and appreciation for the Mediterranean personalities who wrote the books and populate the pages of the Bible.

JOHN J. PILCH

Georgetown University
Feast of St. Francis of Assisi
October 4, 1998

ABBA

Increasing numbers of ethnic minorities in the United States make the need for multicultural education a pressing concern. A 1989 Census Bureau report notes that Blacks constitute the nation's largest minority at 28.9 million. Hispanics number 17.7 million, and the category "other minorities," which includes Asians, Pacific Islanders, American Indians, Eskimos, and Aleuts, is tallied at 7.3 million.

Ordinarily, multicultural education centers around the challenges faced by teachers from a majority population instructing learners from a minority population. Because the United States population is still predominantly white and English-speaking, multicultural specialists usually inform white Anglo[-Christian] educators about the characteristics and needs of ethnic minorities, and then provide them with strategies for communicating information to different ethnic groups of learners. The same challenge exists for preachers, teachers, and Bible students who seek to understand the Bible as a document from the ancient Mediterranean world and then communicate it to people in other cultures.

Something that has been largely overlooked in multicultural religious instruction, however, is the fact that the Good News itself poses a cultural challenge to any believer who does not share the Mediterranean culture in which that Good News originated. For more than two decades now, biblical scholars have been analyzing the Scriptures from this fresh cultural perspective with very rewarding and stimulating results. Here are a few of these refreshing insights.

WORDS, WORDS, WORDS

Over the last twenty-five years, words like *Abba* and *shalom* have become a normal part of the vocabulary of most Christians. Our Judaic ancestors in the faith would be proud that their non-Judaic descendants have learned a few words of the Hebrew language. At the same time, they would likely be embarrassed that these same descendants fail to realize some basic things about "words, words, words."

1

Words in isolation do not convey meaning. Language scholars and ordinary people realize, for example, that the English word "fire" has a different meaning in each of these sentences: "A raging fire burned our home down." "My favorite golden oldie is 'Baby, Light My Fire!'" "My brother-in-law got fired last week." "My dad fired up the engine, and our boat headed out of the harbor."

These different meanings of "fire" derive from our culture, our social system. Without a knowledge of the mainstream United States culture or social system, a foreigner assigned to translate these sentences into another language would not gain much help from an English dictionary alone. The same would be true of a believer trying to read the Bible in the original languages and feeling confident that a Hebrew or Greek dictionary is all that is needed.

ABBA

Many preachers and teachers have taught learners that *Abba* is an Aramaic word that means "Daddy." Jesus used it as a special, tender, and loving way to address his heavenly Father. Some scholars even suggested that *Abba* developed from infant babbling, just as the word "Mama" did. The great scholar Joachim Jeremias is almost singlehandedly responsible for promulgating this understanding, which has been repeated without question or doubt in thousands of classroom lectures at all levels from graduate school through seminary to elementary classes.

Imagine the shock when in 1988 the venerable, veteran language scholar James Barr published a fresh review of the evidence and concluded that *Abba* was not a childish expression comparable to "Daddy," but rather a more solemn, responsible *adult* address to a father. He further pointed out that the word could be either Hebrew or Aramaic, and if Jesus used it, a scholar would be hard-pressed to prove that that word is central to our total understanding of Jesus.

Barr's linguistically solid conclusions can be easily validated by recalling that the only time *Abba* occurs on Jesus' lips in the Gospel record is in Mark's report of Jesus' prayer in Gethsemane: "Abba, *Father . . .* remove this cup from me; yet not what I will, but what you will" (14:36). The Greek word following *Abba* is correctly translated "Father." There is a Greek word for "Daddy" *(pappas)*, but Mark did not use it.

Moreover, the painful context in which Jesus prayed and used this formal address to his Father tallies well with our understanding of child-rearing in Mediterranean culture. Physical punishment was routine and common. Read Proverbs 13:24; 19:18; or 23:13-14 for advice on this topic. Recall Sirach's exhortation: "Beat his ribs while he is young, lest he become stubborn and disobey you" (30:12).

Recall how the author of the Letter to the Hebrews motivates his listeners to bear the suffering God sends: "God is treating you as sons; for what son is there whom his father does not discipline?" (12:7, but read verses 1-11 for the complete picture). A mark of mature manhood in Mediterranean culture was the ability to endure without flinching any and all physical punishment meted out. The author of the Letter to the Hebrews found that quite normal.

Mark portrays Jesus as a perfect, adult Mediterranean male, who prayed for his Father to remove the physical threat to his life but submitted to it without debate. Mark also notes that Jesus hung on the cross from the third hour (15:25) to the ninth hour (15:34) and only then shrieked out, just before he died (15:37). The centurion's admiration of the manner of Jesus' death could be interpreted, among many other things, as an admiration for what others would later call "machismo" in this culture (15:39).

This reflection on the social world in which the word *Abba* means "Father" (rather than "Daddy") demonstrates how culture fleshes out the meaning of a word. Fathers are a universal fact of human life, but each culture experiences "father" in a different way. American Bible readers must be very careful not to insert an American understanding of "father" into the Mediterranean world of our ancestors who populate the pages of our Bible.

SHALOM

After his adultery with Bathsheba, King David summoned her husband, Uriah, back from the war and asked him literally about the *shalom* of Joab, the *shalom* of the soldiers, and the *shalom* of the war (2 Sam 11:7)! Though etymologically the Hebrew word *shalom* means "completeness," "wholeness," "soundness," David is quite simply asking, "*How goes it* with Joab, the soldiers, and the war?" This is one illustration of *shalom* used in salutations or basic inquiries. Other examples would include Genesis 29:6; 37:14; 43:27; 1 Samuel 16:4; 25:6; 29:7.

A recent scholarly study of the word *shalom* has listed at least eight different meanings or interpretations of the word in the Hebrew Bible. Clearly, the numerous nuances of this Hebrew word are so rich that there is hardly any single word in any modern language that can capture its meaning. As a result, presenting the radical meaning of this word as "wholeness" is rather unfounded, and the standard stress on this interpretation is misinformed.

Specialists have repeatedly cautioned Bible readers not to lift words or sentences out of their literary context. They have urged instead that readers pay careful attention to the context in which words and sentences appear. In this instance, language scholars would remind readers to also pay attention to the *social* or *cultural context.* Words in any language simply do not have one-to-one equivalents in any other language. The Hebrew word *shalom* means "peace," but it has at least seven other meanings. Just as with the English word "fire," culture determines the meaning in each instance.

SALT OF THE EARTH

After introducing his sermon with the Beatitudes, Matthew's Jesus says to his disciples: "You are the salt of the earth" (5:13). Americans, with their concern about high blood pressure, think of salt (with a sense of guilt!) as a flavoring in foods. Italian Americans may think of salt in its capacity to preserve foods such as *baccalà.* For first-century Palestinians, salt brought to mind a stove.

The Arabic word for "oven" *(arsa)* suggests that the Hebrew and Aramaic word for "earth" might carry the meaning of "oven" too. Specifically, the word describes an oven familiar in many cultures of the world—an earth oven, a clay oven. Perhaps Jesus can be more correctly understood to have said: "You are [like] salt in the earth oven!"

Knowing that the Aramaic word might mean "earth, dirt, ground" *and* "earth or clay oven" is not enough. One needs to know how such an oven "works" in the Mediterranean world. The fuel used in this oven is not wood (which wasn't plentiful in ancient Israel) or charcoal, but camel and other animal dung, of which there is a steady and abundant supply in that region.

One of the household duties a young girl must learn while growing up is how to collect this dung, mold it into patties, and prepare it as fuel by salting it and letting it dry out in the sun. At the base of the oven itself, a block of salt is placed as a kind of catalyst for the dung-patty fuel. Therefore, in all the "salt" passages of the New Testament, salt is presented in its function as an aid to making fires burn rather than as a seasoning or preservative agent.

"You are the catalyst (salt) in the earth oven. But if the catalyst (salt) has lost its catalytic ability (saltiness), how shall its catalytic ability (saltiness) be restored? It is no longer good for anything except to be thrown out and trodden under foot by human beings" (Matt 5:13). The block of salt on the oven floor eventually loses its ability to "fire" the fuel, but it can still serve as a solid footing for an otherwise muddy road. Salt never loses flavor, but it can lose its fire-stoking ability. How fitting, then, is the very next image: "You are the light of the world."

"For everyone will be salted for the fire. Salt is good, but if salt looses its catalytic ability, how will you restore that? Have salt in yourselves (= be a catalyst), but be at peace with one another" (Mark 9:49-50). This reflection follows naturally upon mention of the hell-fire in verse 48.

"Salt is good, but if salt has lost its catalytic ability, how will that be restored? It is good neither for the earth oven nor for preparing fuel cakes ('for the dunghill'). People just throw it away" (Luke 14:34-35). This statement on salt continues a preceding reflection on discipleship and the need for disciples to see projects through to completion.

"I came to light the oven ('set fire in the earth oven')," says Jesus. "How I wish it were already kindled" (Luke 12:49). He then notes that his presence does not bring peace as much as it divides loyalties (father against son, etc.) of suffocatingly tight-knit, extended Mediterranean families. Note also what kind of *shalom* Jesus is talking about here.

Of course, it is important to know what a word means, but perhaps it is even more important to know the cultural connotation of a word. This is very obvious in the case of the three words examined here: *shalom, Abba,* and *salt.*

SOCIAL CONTEXT: CONFLICT-PRONE CULTURE

How does this understanding of "salt" contribute to a better appreciation of the New Testament and its Mediterranean cultural context? Experts describe Mediterranean culture as "agonistic," that is, Mediterranean people are conflict-prone. Recall how often Jesus is involved in a conflict in the Gospels and how often the disciples in Acts of the Apostles find themselves in court.

This tendency toward conflict is a natural consequence of the core values of Mediterranean culture: honor and shame. Every person is presumed to be honorable and spends a lifetime guarding, protecting, and maintaining that honor. The ongoing cultural "game" concerned with honor consists of "challenge and response." Individuals challenge the honor of their equals in hopes of shaming them (catching them off guard, unable to make an appropriate response), and thereby increasing their own honor. Such persons are truly "catalytic"; they enjoy lighting fires.

Consider the scenario in Mark 7:1-23. Pharisees and scribes (a group in competition with the Jesus group) have a *grievance* against Jesus' disciples, who ignore Pharisaic, that is, non-Torah, traditions about "how" to eat ("wash hands up to the wrists before eating"). Some make a difficult four-day journey from Jerusalem just to encounter and spy on Jesus. They *challenge* him about this violation of "their" norms and thus initiate conflict with him.

Jesus now must answer fittingly to preserve his honor. He replies with an insult ("you hypocrites"), a biblical quote from Isaiah, and a counter accusation ("you replace God's command with human tradition") with proof (the *corban*). Then Jesus brings the crowd into the scene to witness his shaming putdown of the Pharisees and his "non-answer." (The Pharisees are concerned about *how* the disciples eat; Jesus answers about *what* one eats.) Because honor is a public claim to worth *and* a public acknowledgment of that claim, the crowd is essential to Jesus' success. Presumably they are impressed with his ambiguous reply ("parable") and give him a "grant of honor," settling this dispute for now. (Jesus' disputes were not ultimately settled until his death, when God himself "honored" Jesus by raising him from the dead.)

Inside, Jesus gives a private explanation of this "parable" to his disciples, something he does throughout the Gospel (see Mark 4:34b). The significance of these private explanations is that Jesus is clearly building his own following, one that stands in conflict with the Pharisees' outlook on life.

Notice, therefore, how integral to this conflict-prone society is the understanding of salt as a critical element in making fires burn. Jesus' advice in Mark 9:49-50 to remain "salty" (yield no ground; defend your honor; challenge the honor of other groups) but at peace with one another (don't waste energy challenging one another, as in Mark 10:35-45, when two of the Twelve want higher places or more honor than the other ten; focus instead on the *competing group*!) is well-advised strategy for a fledgling movement challenging traditional and established factions.

CONCLUSION

Interpreting the Bible respectfully is a cross-cultural enterprise for all readers. Those whose ethnic heritage does not derive from the Mediterranean area face the challenge of respecting the cultural differences between that part of the world and other countries. The core Mediterranean values of honor and shame (public experiences) are not as central in mainstream American culture as guilt (a private and internal experience). Conversely, many Mediterranean languages have no word for "guilt" as understood and experienced in America.

Those whose ethnic heritage does derive ultimately from one of the countries bordering the Mediterranean also face the challenge of recognizing that common Mediterranean values, beliefs, and practices assume a variety of expressions in these many countries. Mexican-Americans, for instance, whose culture derives ultimately from Spain, recognize that the kind of stove Jesus describes in the Gospels sounds very similar to the *horno* so familiar in the southwest United States and Mexico. Multicultural understanding can be deeply enriched with the discoveries and insights provided by the social-scientific approach to interpreting the Bible.

FOR FURTHER READING

Barr, James. "*Abba* Isn't 'Daddy.'" *Journal of Theological Studies*, n.s., 39 (1988) 28–47.

Malina, Bruce J. "A Conflict Approach to Mark 7." *Forum* 4, no. 3 (1988) 3–30. For a complete picture, see also the articles on Mark 7 by Jerome H. Neyrey, S.J., and John J. Pilch in this same issue.

Pilch, John J. "Preparing Salt for the (H)earth." *The Catechist's Connection* 1, no. 2 (October 1984) 1–3.

_____. "Your Abba Is Not Your Daddy." *Modern Liturgy* 16 (February 1989) 26.

ANGER

As the *sherut* pulled slowly out of Manger Square in Bethlehem onto the road to Jerusalem, a woman balancing a basket on her head stepped in front of the vehicle as she began to cross the road. The driver stuck his head out the window and began shouting at her, the veins in his neck swelling, his face turning deeper shades of red. The woman paid no attention but continued her slow walk. A man sitting at the base of the wall across the way began shouting back at the driver in equally shrill tones. The exchanges continued until the woman no longer blocked the way. Abruptly the shouting stopped. As the driver moved the vehicle slowly forward, he turned to us in the back seats and said in lilting English: "Look, look at the hillsides. Aren't they beautiful? Aren't they just gorgeous? Have you ever seen such beauty? A lovely sight indeed."

While the fabled cabdrivers of New York City might be able to match this scene, some differences come to mind. This native New York passenger in the *sherut* that day prayed that the angry exchange would not escalate to violence. It didn't! More surprising yet was the driver's sudden and complete shift between contrasting emotions. Such a mercurial temperament would be an impediment to getting, much less keeping, a job in the West.

Commentators attribute Jesus' disruptive actions in the Temple to anger (Mark 11:15-19 and parallels). Some call it "holy anger" or "righteous indignation," yet none of the passages mentions any emotion. Was the emotion so obvious that none of the evangelists bothered to identify it explicitly? Did witnesses think that Jesus was angry? Insights from cultural psychology and Mediterranean anthropology can help modern believers gain a fresh understanding of this event, of anger, and of other emotions in the Bible.

EXPRESSING EMOTIONS

Western psychology tends to believe that English-language words for emotions describe universal states of feeling. Since they are considered to be biologically rooted, emotions are the same for all human beings but are expressed differently. In contrast, experts in cultural psychology focus on differences *and* similarities in emotional meanings across cultural groups. Anger, fear, and sorrow seem to be more similar than different across cultural groups. Still, the differences should not be minimized, because emotions carry different, sometimes even contradictory, meanings in different cultures and are expressed in different ways. In general, men in the West keep their emotions hidden and controlled. In the Middle East, men are more openly emotional, even with other men (for example, Judas kisses Jesus in public in Matthew 26:49); they do not have to justify their emotions and emotional attachments (Phil 1:7-8) and value spontaneity in feeling and action.

The spontaneity with which Jesus disrupted normal and necessary Temple activity is culturally understandable and laudable. What is puzzling in this scene is the lack of appropriate reaction from his disciples or friends. When a person's spontaneous activity might result in damage to self or others, that person's relatives, friends, or disciples should restrain the culprit before damage is done. After being restrained, this person would protest innocence. "How could this happen? I know better. I don't know what came over me." Amazingly, no one tried to restrain Jesus. Immediately afterward, power-wielding authorities sought to destroy him (Mark 11:18; Luke 19:47).

BASIC QUESTIONS

Specialists ask four basic questions when analyzing emotions across cultures. How does the meaning system define an experience as an emotional one (e.g., anger) rather than some other kind (e.g., heartburn; high blood pressure)? What particular emotional meanings (e.g., "happiness," "honor") are brought into play in different ethnic groups (Americans; ancient Judeans) and in different temporal-spatial regions of the world (the United States, ancient Palestine)? To what extent is the experience "emotionalized" (e.g., anger) rather than "somatized" (e.g., red face; flared nostrils) in different ethnic groups and places? Finally, how are these emotionalized or somatized meanings learned, acquired, and triggered?

THE MEANING SYSTEM

On its face, Jesus' disruptive behavior in the Temple was very shameful. Honor, the core value of this culture, prescribed behavior appropriate to persons, places, and things. The Temple was God's dwelling place among human beings. One function of the Temple was to gather tithes and offerings to support Temple personnel, who in turn were to redistribute the surplus to the needy. Too often Temple personnel retained the surplus for their own use.

What would this latter experience have produced? A condition such as high blood pressure? An emotion such as anger? The widow whose self-impoverishment for the sake of the Temple Jesus lamented did not seem angry (Mark 12:41-44; Luke 21:1-4). She seemed to prefer compliance rather than defiance. Was Jesus angered by what he observed? It's not clear in the report.

It is plausible that each experienced shame. The widow, by definition of lower status in society, was forced to lower her status still further by self-impoverishment. Jesus, and perhaps the widow too, was ashamed of the shameless leaders whose perverse teachings forced this woman and others into culturally disapproved self-abasement. This and similar memories could have triggered Jesus' disruptive action in the Temple.

Above these scenes loomed God, whose honor Jesus perceived to be compromised, if not entirely challenged. One can draw this plausible, cultural conclusion from Jesus' allusions to Isaiah (56:7) and Jeremiah (7:11), who similarly perceived God to be dishonored or shamed by those who turned the house of prayer into a den of robbers (Mark 11:17 and parallels).

The Hebrew Scriptures report numerous instances where God perceived personal dishonor and in true Mediterranean fashion sought vengeance for this disrespect (Lev 26:14-39; Deut 32:39-42; Ps 94:1-7; Ezek 35:12-15; Mic 5:10-15; and others). Modern readers call this *lèse-majesté* (English: "lese majesty," a violation of personal honor and a crime of high treason in honor-based culture). "I will spend my fury against you and my rage at you shall subside; I will grow calm and not be vexed any more. Because you did not remember the time of your youth and were not in dread of me in all these matters, see, I am holding you to account for your ways—declares Lord YHWH" (Ezek 16:42-43, Anchor Bible translation; compare 5:13). "Venting" emotions (see RSV) is not a strategy for redressing affronts to honor. God and Jesus do not vent their emotions. Cultural values suggest that Jesus' experiences in the Temple primarily stirred his sensitivity to blatant dishonor where honor was due. Anger in this context is different from anger in Western culture.

EMOTIONAL MEANING

A value essentially consists of an idea or concept that is bonded with an emotion or feeling. Honor and shame are concepts *and* emotions. In cultures in which these are core values, everyone is socialized into a range of feelings and emotions that accompany the concept. A compliment or word of praise causes one's chest to swell, evokes a smile, engenders positive feelings. To be identified as an honorable person stirs a distinctive feeling recognized as "honor." The experience of "felt shame" can destroy control of one's sphincters, cause fainting, or stir rage.

To perceive that God's abode was being dishonored, disgraced, and disrespected would stir the powerful feeling of positive shame in Jesus. Positive shame is a concern for maintaining the requirements of honor, and utter revulsion for its transgression. His disruptive action was an effective measure for restoring respect due to God because it was more than an emotional outburst. Commentators correctly identify Jesus' action as a prophetic symbolic action, that is, an action that effectively set irrevocably in motion God's will for the here and now. Jesus acted on behalf of God to put an end to this dishonor once and for always.

"EMOTIONALIZED" OR "SOMATIZED"

In the contemporary West, anger is perceived primarily as an internal experience, an emotion that also has bodily expression: the raised and trembling voice, the red face, shaking or quivering limbs, and the like. Even when the visible, physical, accompanying effects disappear, the abiding emotion still plays havoc with the blood pressure.

The non-introspective Middle East, in contrast, tends primarily to somatize experiences. The Hebrew words translated as "anger" are illustrative. The key word is "nose" (or "nostrils" in the plural). Of course, the nose is the organ of respiration, and anger affects both the nose and breathing. Thus a person described literally in Hebrew as "short of nose" (Prov 14:17) or "short of breath" (Mic 2:7; Exod 6:9) is impatient or angry. In contrast, a person "long of nose" (Prov 14:29) or "long of breath" (Eccl 7:8) is patient and slow to anger. "The LORD, the LORD, a God merciful and gracious, long of nose (= slow to anger)" (Exod 34:6).

In anger, the nostrils become distended and breathing is hard. Often the Hebrew literally speaks of a burning nose (Gen 30:2: Jacob's nose burned against Rachel = Jacob's anger was kindled against Rachel). Gradually the burning spreads its heat and red color from the nose to the entire face and affects the eyes (Mark 3:5). Another Hebrew word for anger means "outpouring" and probably describes the unrestrained stream of words to express one's anger. Yet another Hebrew word means "splintering," plausibly describing the actions of a person driven by anger to shatter, smash, and splinter whatever is in the way.

Only John's reference to Jesus' "making a whip of cords" (2:15) suggests that Jesus' feeling of positive shame may have stirred him to anger of the "splintering" variety. John's citation of Psalm 69:9 (compare Ps 119:139) to provide the motive for Jesus' actions adds further insight. "Zeal for your house has consumed me, and the insults of those who insult you have fallen on me." The Hebrew word for zeal etymologically means "intensively red," describing the color of the face of a person experiencing this emotion. "Ardor" is a good English translation. Zeal or ardor gives rise to various feelings: love, hate, jealousy, fury, disturbance, strong passion, and emotional commitment to the honor of people (2 Sam 21:2) or of God (Num 25:10-11). As Phinehas was driven by zeal to redress the offended honor of God (Num 25:1-18, esp v. 11), so John's Jesus was perceived by his disciples to be driven by zeal to redress God's honor, besmirched by Temple personnel and their practices (John 2:17).

LEARNING REACTIONS

How are these meanings learned, acquired, triggered? The advice in Proverbs and Sirach contains meaning-making elements that crop up in daily personal conversations and interactions. "Make no friendship with a man given to anger, nor go with a wrathful man, lest you learn his ways and entangle yourself in a snare" (Prov 22:24-25). Such collective wisdom guided day-to-day behavior in ancient Israel and socialized young and old alike in the proper ways of interpreting people and situations and the proper and improper cultural responses.

Traditions about prayer, fasting, the Temple, and the like would be another source through which one learned the "emotionalized" or "somatized" behaviors proper to each experience. "I was glad when they said to me, 'Let us go to the house of the LORD!'" (Ps 122:1). The pleasure experienced by people living in harmony is compared to oil running down Aaron's beard (Ps 133:1-2). These joys seem to be somatized. History suggests that the name and the person "Herod the Great" stirred negative emotions: fear, hatred, distrust, and more. Daily discussion would reinforce such responses. Children learned the bodily expression of these feelings from their elders. Thus does culture set the triggers.

Thus Jesus' disruptive action in the Temple was a complex response involving a number of elements he absorbed from his culture: a prophetic symbolic action against a venerated and cherished institution, a feeling of positive shame, and very likely other emotions like anger.

CONCLUSION

Americans are fond of analyzing biblical events and characters from a psychological perspective. Yet Third World researchers caution that Western psychology is a monocultural science. It is so rooted in Western values as to be misleading and often useless for understanding other cultures. Cultural psychology helps Bible readers and interpreters to recognize the complexity of emotional experience and expression in the Middle East. It is so distinctively different that in this perspective one meets these ancestors in the faith again, as if for the first time.

FOR FURTHER READING

Lutz, Catherine, and Geoffrey M. White. "The Anthropology of Emotions." *Annual Review of Anthropology* 15 (1986) 405–436.

Pilch, John J. "Psychological and Psychoanalytical Approaches to Interpreting the Bible in Social-Scientific Context." *Biblical Theology Bulletin* 27 (1997) 112–116.

Schweder, Richard A. "The Cultural Psychology of the Emotions." In *Handbook of Emotions*, ed. Michael Lewis and Jeannette M. Haviland, 417–431. New York and London: The Guilford Press, 1993.

CLOTHES

Sirach, the Hebrew sage, lists clothing along with bread and water as basic necessities of life (Sir 29:21). Jesus, the Galilean teacher, tells his followers not to worry about clothing, food, or drink (Matt 6:25-34). Are clothes a basic necessity of life or not? Which particular article of clothing is a necessity? Why? Where? Would Jesus agree or disagree? Reading the Bible in its Middle Eastern cultural setting places these questions in proper perspective. Clothing in that culture is a necessity of life, but for reasons far different than those a Western reader might expect.

IN THE BEGINNING

According to the traditional story in Genesis, clothes were not initially a necessity of life. Adam and Eve were naked and not ashamed (Gen 2:25). Only after disobeying God did they become aware of their nakedness and decide to sew fig leaves together as aprons for themselves (Gen 3:7). This new awareness struck in the man a fear of God: "I heard the sound of you in the garden, and I was afraid, because I was naked" (Gen 3:10). After declaring the consequences of the disobedience for the three characters in this scene, God made garments of skins for the man and woman (Gen 3:21).

This story has many interpretations. Anthropology offers yet another one. In all cultures, clothes play a role in binding people together. By independently crafting fig-leaf loincloths, the man and woman not only distance themselves from the Creator but also from each other. In contrast, by crafting skin garments for the couple, God confirms a continuing personal bond with each, while the gift of clothes from a common donor binds the couple to each other. This is one way of understanding the first couple's clothes as a necessity of life.

CLOTHING MATERIALS

Among hunter-gatherer peoples and Middle Eastern Bedouins, animal skins constitute the basic article of clothing, with the hair or wool worn on the inside. Mention of tents in Genesis 4:20 suggests that the skill of weaving was probably learned and honed very early in history. The ideal material for tents is haircloth woven from black goats' hair, which is waterproof and almost indestructible (Exod 26:7; Song 1:5). Sackcloth was also made of this material (Isa 20:2).

Camels' hair was woven into a brown cloth from which a prophet made a mantle (Zech 13:4; Matt 3:4; Mark 1:6). Sheep wool was also woven into cloth and made into garments (Lev 13:47). Long known in Egypt, linen and cotton were used by the Israelites at least since the Exodus (1 Chr 4:21; Exod 28:5-6). The Torah forbade wearing clothes made of wool and linen woven together (Deut 22:11) because these materials derived from two different orders of creation: animal and plant. Purity requires that distinctions should not be blurred and boundaries should not be trespassed.

ARTICLES OF CLOTHING

Scholars list five basic articles of clothing mentioned in the Bible. It seems that men and women both wore the same five articles, though some scholars claim that there were differences between men's and women's clothing. The prohibition against wearing any article of clothing of the opposite sex (Deut 22:5) suggests that the differences may not have been easily discerned. It is less plausibly a reference to transvestism or cross-dressing.

Tunic. The garment worn closest to the skin was the tunic. It was sometimes called the inner garment or undergarment and was made by folding a piece of material lengthwise in two, sewing it down the side but leaving openings for the head and arms. Assyrian monuments depict Jewish prisoners wearing short-sleeved tunics.

The tunic was ordinarily made of linen material and sometimes of wool. It seems that both women and men wore the same kind of tunic (Gen 3:21; Song 5:3), though special tunics like those of the priests designated status (Exod 28:40; Lev 16:4).

The patriarch Jacob loved Joseph more than any other of his children and demonstrated this by making for him an ankle-length tunic with sleeves that reached the wrists (Gen 37:3; the Septuagint mistranslated a difficult Hebrew word and called this tunic a "many-colored" coat). As is always the case with clothing, this special kind of tunic did more than cover the body. It was ordinarily worn by royalty (see 2 Sam 13:18), a point not lost on Joseph's brothers. The rest of the story is familiar.

Tabitha (Dorcas) made tunics and cloaks for widows in the community (Acts 9:39), though clothes-making in this and many cultures was not exclusively a woman's task (see Exod 35:35).

Cloak. This garment was a loose-fitting coat, sleeveless or with short sleeves, that was worn over the tunic. The cloak was strong enough to carry all sorts of things (Exod 12:34; Judg 8:25; 1 Sam 21:9). It protected against heat and rain in daytime and served as a "sleeping bag" at night. For this reason, a cloak given to a money-lender by a borrower to guarantee repayment of a loan had to be re-turned to its owner before sunset (Exod 22:26-27; Deut 24:12-13).

A cloak was used as a sheet to cover the drunken Noah (Gen 9:23). Ruth put on a cloak to visit Boaz (Ruth 3:3). Crowds threw their cloaks on the ground as a carpet for Jesus (Mark 11:7-8). An ill woman in search of healing touched the blue fringes on Jesus' cloak (Matt 9:20). On the day of reckoning, a disciple ought not go back for the cloak (Matt 24:18).

Is the cloak or the tunic one of the absolute necessities of life in the Middle East? No matter which article was demanded by a plain-tiff or a thief, Jesus urged his followers to give the other up as well (Matt 5:40; Luke 6:29).

Belt. Also called a girdle or sash, the belt was worn around the waist by men (1 Kgs 2:5) and women (Isa 3:24). Some were made of leather (2 Kgs 1:8; Matt 3:4), others were woven (Prov 31:24) and had an ornamental fringe or tassel. The belt could cinch either the tunic or the cloak, making the upper part of the cloak into a kind of pocket or purse (Matt 10:9). Sometimes a sword was tucked in the belt (John 18:10). Similar to the belt was the loincloth (Jer 13:1-11),

Two Palestinian men, each wearing a kaffiyeh.

or ribbons worn by women (Isa 3:20), especially brides (Jer 2:32).

The phrase "to gird one's loins" describes a tightening of the belt, indicating that one is ready for action, for example, travel (Exod 12:11) or combat (Jer 1:17).

Head-covering. In this in-stance as in the preceding, the bib-lical and related data is seldom clear. At the very least, headgear protected against sun and sand. One kind of headdress was worn by both men (Isa 61:3, 10) and women (Isa 3:20). The basic head-covering was a simple cloth draped or wrapped around the head and held in place by a headband, sometimes forming a turban (Job 29:14). Actually, the headband symbolized masculinity and was never worn by a woman. Priests wore special headgear for ceremonial duties (Exod 28:39). Related to a head-covering is the veil, a distinctive article of clothing for women intended to cover the face in certain circumstances. It was definitely required in the presence of a stranger (Gen 24:65), though some veils permitted the face to be seen (Song 4:1, 3). It too protected against sun and sand.

Footwear. Sandals seem to have been the ordinary footwear throughout the biblical period. The sandal consisted of a simple sole of leather or wood attached to the foot by straps or thongs (Gen 14:23; Isa 5:27; Mark 1:7). Texts indicate that women sometimes wore fancy sandals or even slippers (Ezek 16:10; Jdt 10:4; 16:9).

The significance of going barefoot depended upon specific circumstances. If one was forced to do this, it was clearly a sign of humiliation (Job 12:19). If one did

Sandals are a common foot covering in the Holy Land.

it voluntarily, it would signify a deliberate and intentional setting aside of cultural rules, a legitimate and respected determination to be "out of bounds," as was permis-sible in grief (2 Sam 15:30) or mourning (Ezek 24:17, 23).

Summary. There are many variations and expansions on these five basic articles of clothing. For instance, extensive contents of a lady's wardrobe are identified in Isaiah 3:18-24. Contemporary Bible resource books list still other items. For the most part, these traditional resources adopt a functional view on how clothes might be a necessity of life: they provide protection and privacy, they signal gender, status, etc.

ANTHROPOLOGY OF CLOTHING

Besides serving the practical purposes just mentioned, clothing also, and perhaps even more importantly, serves other, notably symbolic, purposes. Anthropologist Jane Schneider's in-depth investigations demonstrate how cloth in many cultures has furthered the organization of political and social life. This is evident in various domains of meaning in which people use cloth and clothing. Schneider's model and the insights it generates shed fresh light upon some familiar biblical texts.

Moslem women in the Jerusalem marketplace near Damascus Gate.

Domain of manufacturing cloth. This domain is dominated by the spinners, weavers, dyers, and finishers of cloth. The process that surrounds the manufacture of cloth makes it an analog in many cultures for the regenerative and degenerative processes of life. Cloth connects human beings to one another and to ancestors and future progeny.

Weaving. Of the basic elements in the weaving process, the warp, or vertical element, is interpreted as masculine, while the weft (woof), or horizontal element, is interpreted as feminine. Just as both genders collaborate in generating new life, both elements of weaving combine in generating cloth.

Many people believe that weaving skills derive from God and are transmitted through dreams and revelations. This seems to have been true of the Israelites too (Exod 35:30-35). By respecting and acting in accord with this divine inspiration, the clothmaker reactivates, as it were, the spiritual connection between God and the resultant clothes.

A seamless garment, that is, one that has an endless warp, is considered sacred by many world cultures. The endless warp represents unbroken threads of kinship and descent going all the way back to the Creator. People believe that continuous weaving transmits a spiritual force, and cutting a seamless cloth challenges or denies that idea and incurs divine displeasure. Perhaps this explains why the soldiers at Jesus' crucifixion determined not to divide his seamless garment (John 19:23-24).

This same understanding of the Deity's role in the manufacture of cloth highlights the significance of God's making skins for the first couple (Gen 3:21). Whereas their disobedience distanced them from God, the Deity's manufacture and gift of clothes for them restored the bond between Creator and creatures.

Dyeing. In classical Mediterranean cultures, dyeing was a demanding and arduous process, easily monopolized. Purple came from a glandular secretion of the whelk mollusk, a kind of snail, which was finished and sun-dried near Tyre. The Phoenicians were experts in making this dye, and the country names *Phoenicia* and *Canaan* in their respective Greek and Hebrew mean "purple dye." This is a bluish purple (hyacinth), the color prescribed for tassels on the corners of cloaks (Num 15:38).

The Bible also mentions a reddish or fiery purple (Prov 31:22; Exod 26–27) and scarlet (a dye made from the dried bodies of certain female insects: Gen 38:28, 30; Song 4:3). Once a cloth was dyed scarlet, it was nearly impossible to bleach it out (see the point Isaiah makes of this in Isa 1:18). This was the color of the Roman military mantle placed on Jesus as a mock king (Matt 27:28).

These three colors are mentioned repeatedly as elements of priestly garments (Exod 28), gifts to the Lord (Exod 35), curtains for the tabernacle (Exod 36), the screen (Exod 38:18), etc. Professors K. C. Hanson and John H. Elliott have pointed out that these colors have long been considered powerful protection against the "evil eye" in the Mediterranean world. Anyone involved in the sacred mysteries would be especially certain to wear such colors to prevent displeasing and protect against potentially hostile spirits. Jesus was familiar with this cultural belief (Matt 20:15; Mark 7:22; Luke 11:33-34) and, like everyone else, wore the traditional blue color for protection (Matt 9:20; Num 15:38).

Domain of clothes. Cloth used as dress or adornment reveals (Exod 28:1-4) and conceals (Gen 38:13-30) identities and values. It is emblematic of age, sex, rank, status, and group affiliation. The priest on his way from Jerusalem to Jericho in Jesus' parable faced a serious dilemma (Luke 10:30-37). The thief's victim whom the priest encountered was "half dead," so it was impossible to determine his social group (Judean, Samaritan, or other) from his accent. The victim was also naked, so no clue to his social group could be read from his clothes. For example, male cloaks discovered in Israel by the archaeologist Yigael Yadin were made of white or yellow wool, with reddish-brown or blackish-blue notched bands woven into the fabric. Some cloaks had stripes of the same color as these notched bands at the neck opening.

CONCLUSION

Further anthropological reflection on clothes in other domains of meaning (e.g., bestowal and exchange; investiture and rulership ceremonies) would help a Western reader better understand why Sirach and the ancients considered clothes a necessity of life. It had less to do with privacy and protection from the elements than with many other dimensions of human life considered by the ancients to be equally important. The spiritual dimension of clothes seems to have loomed very large in their minds.

FOR FURTHER READING

Brock, S. "Clothing Metaphors as a Means of Theological Expression in Syriac Tradition." In *Typus, Symbol, Allegorie bei den östlichen Vätern und ihren Parallelen im Mittelalter: Internationales Kolloquium, Eichstätt 1981*. Eichstätter Beiträge 4. Ed. M. Schmidt and C. Geyer, 11–38. Regensburg: F. Pustet, 1982.

Edwards, Douglas R. "Dress and Ornamentation." *Anchor Bible Dictionary* 2:232–238.

Stillman, Yedida K., and Nancy Micklewright. "Costume in the Middle East." *MESA Bulletin* 26 (1992) 13–38.

Thompson, Wesley. "Weaving: A Man's Work." *Classical World* 75 (1982) 217–222.

Weiner, Annette B., and Jane Schneider, eds. *Cloth and the Human Experience*. Washington and London: Smithsonian Institution Press, 1989.

COINS

Western Bible readers often try to calculate the modern equivalent of coins in the New Testament, such as the denarius (Matt 20:2) or the stater (Matt 17:27). This is almost impossible because the grades and weights of these coins varied, even when newly minted. The best one can do is to become familiar with the relative equivalencies of coins in the ancient world in the hope of appreciating what the biblical text communicates.

Actually, the Hebrew Bible does not generally refer to coins when it mentions money. Abimelech paid restitution to Abraham for Sarah with sheep, oxen, male and female slaves, and a thousand pieces of silver (Gen 20:14-16). These were actual pieces or slices of silver and not coins.

When did coins come into existence? What kind were they and what purposes did they serve? This article reflects upon the various coins of the ancient world mentioned in the Bible and other information necessary for understanding coins.

DEFINITIONS

According to those who study coins, money is anything that serves as a medium of exchange, a store of wealth, or a measure of status. Money is always invested with a quality of desirability. Thus sheep, goats, birds, grain, oil, wine, and other such commodities served and continue to serve as money in many cultures.

Coins are a form of money. Strictly speaking, the essential defining characteristic of a coin is that it expressly or implicitly show the authority by which it was issued and which guarantees its acceptability as a means of exchange. Upon returning from Babylonian Exile, Ezra (8:27) gave to the leading priests, among other things, twenty gold bowls worth a thousand darics. The daric was a Persian gold coin weighing 8.4 grams and was first minted by Darius I, who ruled between 521 and 485 B.C.E. It depicted the Persian king shooting a bow. This confirms scholarly opinion that coins were not used by the Hebrews as a medium of exchange in Palestine until after the Exile.

BEFORE COINS

Prior to the invention of coins, payments were made according to the weight of precious metals, mainly silver. In fact, the Hebrew word most often translated "money" is literally "silver." Scales or balances became an essential part of daily life, because they were the means for weighing out the various pieces of precious metal (Ezek 5:1; Isa 40:12; Ps 62:9; Job 6:2).

The major concern, of course, was that the balances be accurate or just. Ezekiel 45:10-12 reminds the people to have honest balances and equivalences (see also Lev 19:36; Job 31:6; Prov 16:11). Warnings against "false" balances (Prov 11:1; 20:23; Mic 6:11) indicate how difficult life is when everything hinges on dyadic relationships in which partners use a personal scale and weights rather than standards established and enforced by a central government.

WEIGHTS AND MEASURES

The Bible doesn't offer specific insight into the earliest standards of weights and measures. It refers simply to "pieces" or "shekels." The Hebrew verb *shakal* basically means "to weigh" and "to pay," and the noun *shekel* designates a conventionally established unit of weight. No inscribed talent or mina weights have been found in Palestine, but shekel weights have been discovered and are widely divergent between and within every system.

The ancient world knew several systems for weighing, the two most prominent being the Babylonian (which was based on sixty) and the Egyptian (which was based on ten). The Babylonian system was already in place by the end of the third millennium B.C.E. In this system, one talent was divisible into sixty minas, and a mina was divisible into sixty shekels. Each system possessed simultaneous "light" and "heavy" standards that also seem to be reflected in the Bible.

Abraham purchased the field of Ephron in Machpelah by weighing out four hundred shekels of silver "according to the weights current among the merchants" (Gen 23:16). Experts believe that according to the Babylonian standard, which lasted until the Hellenistic period, a silver shekel equaled 8.25 grams. This seems to be the "light" or common shekel weight.

The "heavy" weight appears to be reflected in the "shekel of the sanctuary" (Exod 30:13; 30:24; 38:25-26; Lev 5:15; 27:25) or the shekel "by the king's weight" (2 Sam 14:26). In other words, anything (e.g., taxes) measured by the heavy standard would be greater than anything measured by the light standard.

Even so, Amos describes merchants of his time who planned to "make the ephah small and the shekel great, and practice deceit with false balances" (8:5). Even when true coins emerged later in history, they still varied greatly in weight, and the sizes ranged from eight millimeters to forty millimeters in diameter. This variation made money-changers an essential part of daily life and commerce.

COINS

Coins were first minted in Asia Minor, very likely by King Croesus of Lydia around 650 B.C.E. They were small globs of electrum, an alloy of silver and gold, with a design on one side and a punch mark on the other. The design was the head of a deity, and the stamp or punch mark made them legal tender. These coins bore no inscription and did not circulate widely. Croesus later struck silver and gold coins to supplement or expand the supply of electrum.

Some experts think that merchants may have originally invented coins because they obviously facilitated commerce and simplified so many aspects of life, such as paying and receiving taxes, providing for Temple maintenance, and much more.

YEHUD COINS

The first true coins ever struck by local authorities of Judah in Palestine were the Yehud coins. They were minted in or near Jerusalem sometime after 400 B.C.E., under Persian authority, and have been found almost as far south as the Egyptian border. Judah was a province of a Persian satrapy ("across the river") that included Syria, Phoenicia, Palestine, and Cyprus.

Reflecting Greek influence, these coins portray the head of Pallas Athena facing toward the right on the obverse, and an owl with an olive branch and the Aramaic inscription *yhd* (Judah) on the reverse. Since the denominations are fractional, these coins probably supplemented the larger silver coins from Tyre (the shekel), Sidon, and Gaza. A study of the Yehud series of coins suggests that some of Judah participated in two revolts against Persia and suffered defeat. Having been introduced into the country, coins now had to play a major role in rebuilding the destroyed economy of the region.

NEW TESTAMENT COINS

In first-century Palestine, the Greek and Roman monetary systems coexisted, and coins of both systems are mentioned in the New Testament. The silver drachma was the basic unit of the Greek system, generalized by Alexander the Great (332/331 B.C.E.). The woman with ten drachmas searched for the one she lost and rejoiced when she found it (Luke 15:8-10). The drachma was roughly equivalent to the Roman denarius in commerce ("light" system), but in official payments it was calculated to be only three-fourths of a denarius ("heavy" system).

The drachma was worth six obols (not mentioned in the Bible), which in turn was worth eight coppers *(chalkoi)*. In Matthew (10:9) and Mark (6:8) Jesus forbids wandering missionaries to carry copper in their purses, though the word does not refer specifically to this coin.

Ancient coin showing Antiochus IV Epiphanes, Syria, 2 c. B.C.E.

Roman coins began to circulate in Palestine after Pompey (106–48 B.C.E.) and were widely used under Herod the Great, who modified the coins. His bronze coins were inscribed in Greek, utilized pagan symbols (shields, helmets, eagles, etc.), recorded a date, and were intended to supplement larger coinage, like the denarius. The denarius was the basic unit in the Roman system. This silver coin or its equivalent was the average daily wage in first-century Palestine (Matt 20:1-16) as well as the poll tax (Matt 22:15-22; Mark 12:13-17; Luke 20:20-26). The disciples estimated that it would take two hundred denarii worth of bread (Mark 6:37) or more (John 6:7) to feed the large crowd that had gathered to hear Jesus.

The value of the very costly ointment an unnamed woman used to anoint Jesus was estimated to be worth more than three hundred denarii (Mark 14:5). Matthew's Jesus tells a shocking story about a servant who was forgiven a debt equivalent to six hundred thousand denarii (ten thousand talents) but was unwilling to forgive a fellow servant a debt of one hundred denarii (18:23-25)!

The denarius was divided into ten (later sixteen) asses (see Matt 10:29; Luke 12:6), and the as was divided into four quadrants (Matt 5:26), a copper coin which was the smallest in value in the Roman system. In first-century Palestine, the Roman procurators minted such coins between 6 and 66 C.E. Jesus lamented the widow's self-despoiling gift of two copper coins (lepta, which equal one quadrant) to the Temple (Luke 21:1-4; Mark 12:41-44) because she was misled by the scribes, who "devour the estates of widows" (Luke 20:47; Mark 12:40).

The shekel, a silver coin minted in Tyre or Antioch, was worth four denarii. The thirty pieces of silver that Judas received for betraying Jesus were very probably shekels of this kind (Matt 26:14-16).

COINS AND SYMBOLISM

Much more can be said about ancient coins and their equivalences, but Westerners should not overlook the symbolic role, sometimes called the propaganda value, of coins in first-century Palestine. Since 90 to 95 percent of the population were peasants who lived at a subsistence level, specialists suggest that the various coins of small denominational value had greater symbolic than commercial significance. The coin could not purchase much, but it did remind the possessor of the ruler's identity and values or virtues desired of citizens and subjects.

In 37 B.C.E., when the armies of Herod began to attack Jerusalem, Mattathias Antigonus struck a coin at half the weight of other issues depicting a seven-branched menorah. The coin contained his name in Hebrew on one side and the Greek phrase "belonging to King Antigonus" on the other. The message: Do not allow the Temple menorah to fall to Rome and Herod, its puppet king!

Several imperial coins minted from the time of the Roman emperor Trajan (98–117 C.E.) and extending to Emperor Maximian (286–305 C.E.) depicted the emperor's image on the reverse and an *Orante* figure on the obverse. Very frequently the word *pietas* appears near the figure. These were "propaganda" coins to remind the possessor who the emperor was and that *pietas* was owed to him. Though translated as "piety," this Latin word is more properly understood as filial devotion. It describes a virtue that characterizes the obedience, submission, and respect that a child ought to show to a parent who provides it with security.

Clearly, through this coin the emperors recommended that citizens and subjects extend similar devotion, obedience, and submission toward them, the empire, and the gods. Subjects should consider their ruler as a father figure, that is, a patron to whom a client was indebted for all the "good things" of life.

The image of the *Orante* was also common in Roman burial places, but it began to appear in Christian catacomb paintings around the year 180 C.E. Examples can be seen on a sarcophagus at Santa Maria Antiqua in the Roman Forum and on a mural at the House of Saints John and Paul near the Colosseum in Rome. It is the figure that appears most frequently in catacomb art.

Christians, therefore, were very consciously transforming a pagan symbol and its meaning, familiar to them from propaganda coins, to serve their own purposes. Inspired by Jesus' statement in Mark 3:31–35, Christians perceived the group of believers who clustered around Jesus as a family. Paul routinely relied on kinship terms like "brother in Christ" or "sister in Christ" to describe the members of the Church. The pagan *Orante* figure, the symbol of "piety," a family value, became for Christians a symbol of their new, fictive family, the Church.

CONCLUSION

This brief survey of coins in the ancient world opens yet another small window into the biblical world. It helps a modern reader gain a better appreciation for life and values in that time and place and also highlights the symbolic meaning of money, which is perhaps more important than its purchasing power.

FOR FURTHER READING

Betlyon, John W. "Coinage." *Anchor Bible Dictionary* 1:1076–1089.
Kreitzer, Larry J. *Striking New Images: Roman Imperial Coinage and the New Testament World.* Sheffield: Sheffield Academic Press, 1996.
Scott, R.B.Y. "Weights and Measures of the Bible." *The Biblical Archaeologist* 22 (1959) 22–40.
Snyder, Graydon. *Ante Pacem: Archaeological Evidence of Church Life Before Constantine.* Macon, Ga.: Mercer University Press, 1985. Chapter Two: "Early Christian Symbols, VII. The Orante," pp. 18–20.

COSMETICS AND JEWELRY

In the epilogue to the story of Job, God restores all that his faithful servant had lost, including his seven sons and three daughters. "The first [daughter] he called by the name Paloma, the second he named Cassia, and the third Cosmetique" (Job 42:14). The late Father Bruce Vawter invented these pretentious pseudo-names to capture the spirit of the original Hebrew: Jemimah ("dove"), Kezia ("cinnamon"), and Keren-Happuch ("container of kohl").

In the ancient Mediterranean world, cinnamon and kohl served as perfume and a cosmetic. When water is scarce, as it was in the ancient Middle East, how often can people bathe or do laundry? Do they have a high tolerance for foul odors? Were perfumes or cosmetics actually deodorants or substitutes for frequent ablutions and fresh laundry? A review of pertinent biblical texts through the lenses of Middle Eastern culture enriches a reader's understanding of these passages.

POWDERS

Kohl. The Hebrew name of Job's third daughter, Keren-Happuch, is literally "horn of kohl." This substance is a fine, black powder that served as a pigment with which Israelite women darkened the edges of their eyelids to make their eyes look larger and brighter. It is similar to antimony, a black or orange-red crystalline compound used as a pigment in fireworks and matches. The Arabic word for this substance is *kuhl*, from which the English word "alcohol" derives. Spanish alchemists used this word *(al-kuhl)* to describe the extremely fine powder and highly rectified spirits.

The Bible never speaks kindly of women who used kohl. Jezebel painted her eyes and adorned her head in her proud and defiant effort to thwart King Jehu, who killed her husband and sought her life too (2 Kgs 9:30). The postexilic editor of her story presents the Phoenician princess Jezebel as an object-lesson for Israelites against marrying foreign women, a strong sentiment in his era. Jeremiah

(4:30) and Ezekiel (23:40) note that faithless Jerusalem and Judah resort to this same ineffective strategy to fend off impending doom.

Cinnamon. The Hebrew name of Job's second daughter, Kezia, is a kind of cinnamon also called cassia. This powdered bark comes from a tree native to Southeast Asia whose buds, leaves, and twigs all have a cinnamon smell. Sometimes the twig of a sweet-smelling plant or flower was carried in the hand. Cinnamon was imported (Ezek 27:19) for use in making perfumes (Prov 7:17-18), anointing oils (Ps 45:8), and spices (for aromatics, not for food: Song 4:14).

It is difficult to explain why Job's daughters, who were nameless in the prologue, receive names in the epilogue. The two names associated with cosmetic powders probably serve simply to underscore their singular beauty (Job 42:15).

OTHER COSMETICS

The Bible mentions various cosmetics, including perfumes, balms, gums, myrrh, ointments, and salves among other items. Some were used to beautify the hair and the skin. Others served as deodorizers or fumigants.

Alabaster perfume container.

Perfumes. The Song of Songs mentions miscellaneous perfumes that are also listed elsewhere in the Bible.

Nard (also **spikenard:** Song 1:12; 4:13-14) is a scented perfume or ointment that was imported from the Himalayas in alabaster boxes. In the New Testament, Jesus was anointed with nard by a woman while he reclined at dinner (Mark 14:3-5; John 12:3-5). Judas' observation that it could have been sold for more than three hundred denarii (approximately a year's wages? See Matt 20:2) indicates its precious value.

Myrrh is an Arabian gum resin that exudes from the bark of a tree. In powdered form, it was used as a sachet between the breasts (Song 1:13; see also 4:14; 5:1) or to freshen beds (Prov 7:17). Men used myrrh in powdered form to freshen garments (Ps 45:8) and in liquid form to perfume the beard (Song 5:13) or as an anointing oil (Exod 30:23; Ps 133:2), including preparing the dead for burial (John 19:39).

Frankincense (Song 3:6) was the resin most commonly burned to produce fragrance or fragrant smoke. Other popular fragrant resins were myrrh, bdellium (Gen 2:12), galbanum (mixed: Exod 30:34; alone it had an unpleasant odor and was used as a repellent to keep away snakes and gnats), and gum (see Gen 37:25).

Frankincense derives from trees native to South Arabia, Somaliland, and Abyssinia. Israel imported it from Saba in South Arabia (Isa 60:6; Jer 6:20). The Song of Songs depicts the procession of a king accompanied by billowing clouds of fragrance from the burning of frankincense, myrrh, and all kinds of exotic powders (3:6). The Magi brought Jesus three kinds of incense: frankincense, myrrh, and gold, which were burned on the golden altar (see Heb 9:4; Rev 8:3; 9:13; Luke 1:11).

Perfumers. Scholars of the ancient Mediterranean world observe that this culture was very fond of fragrance. Indeed, perfumers constituted a category of specialists. Bezalel, associated with the tent of meeting, seems to be the first perfumer mentioned in the Bible (Exod 37:29). The royal household also had perfumers (1 Sam 8:13), a position held by female servants. By postexilic times, perfumers were a recognized guild (Neh 3:8) that was drawn from priestly families (1 Chr 9:30). Their chief task was to compound and dispense incense and aromatic oils for use in the Temple and for cosmetic, medicinal, and embalming purposes.

Recipes. The Lord gave Moses a recipe for anointing oil that included liquid myrrh, sweet-smelling cinnamon, aromatic cane, cassia, and olive oil (Exod 30:22-25). He also gave a recipe for incense, combining sweet spices, stacte (or storax, a kind of sap), and onycha (a substance from a marine shellfish) with galbanum (a yellow or greenish-brown gum resin), sweet spices, and pure frankincense, seasoned with salt (Exod 30:34-38).

Both the oil and the incense were holy, that is, reserved for use only as specified by the Lord in conjunction with the tent of meeting. Anyone using it for another purpose was to be ejected from the community (Exod 30:33, 38).

Concluding reflection. Science indicates that each human being has a catalogue of more than fifty thousand different smells stored within the brain. Because of this sense's direct connection to the limbic system and the hippocampus in the brain, scents and aromas easily stir memories stored there. The Sage associated friendship with fragrance: "Oil and perfume make the heart glad, but the sweetness of a friend is better than one's own counsel" (Prov 27:9). The smell of the various incenses that accompanied the high priest in the Holy of Holies later rekindled the memory of that spirit-to-spirit encounter.

JEWELRY

In the ancient Middle East, ornaments and jewelry served basically as amulets, that is, as charms or talismans to ward off evil or protect against the evil eye. Originally, a mark or a tattoo served this purpose (see Gen 4:15; Ezek 9:4-6; Rev 14:1). Eventually these protective marks were replaced by objects that could both repel and cast a spell (see Song 4:9). The objects included arm bracelets (Ezek 16:11), nose rings (Gen 24:47), signet rings (Song 8:6; Jer 22:24), neck chains, and earrings among others.

Earrings. In ancient Israel, the most common shape of the gold earring was an oblong-style loop. Specialists call this "lunate," because it resembled a crescent moon. It went through the earlobe to the back, where the broader side could be seen. The lunate earring also resembled the upturned horns of bovine animals, and there is a long-standing association of these two shapes in the ancient Near East. When describing earrings, Ezekiel (16:12) uses a peculiar Hebrew word related to other words that refer to bovine animals, e.g., the calf, the heifer, and cart drawn by cattle.

Cultural anthropology suggests a pertinent explanation for the association of lunate earring and upturned horns and the function of both amulets as protection against evil. Societies that depend primarily upon animal husbandry for economic livelihood regard spirit aggression as the predominant or secondary cause of human illness. Members of those societies seek to protect themselves against spirit aggression with amulets and specific colors: blue and red, whether in cloth or in precious stones (see the description of the high priest's garb in Exodus 28 and 39).

Garlands. Ezekiel 16:12 notes that the Lord placed a beautiful crown on the head of the woman symbolizing Jerusalem. The Sage describes parental instruction as a "garland for the head" (Prov 1:9) and adds that wisdom will place a "fair garland" on the head of the one who respects her (Prov 4:9).

Here again these garlands were successors to, and may well have continued to function as, protections against evil. Jewish scholars trace the origin of phylacteries (mentioned only once in the Bible: Matt 23:5!) to the custom of wearing protective amulets on the head. The Hebrew texts that recommend wearing the words of the Lord (between the eyes) on the forehead use a word meaning "bands," which were very likely the predecessor of the phylactery (see Exod

13:9, 16; Deut 6:8; 11:18). Wearing such objects on the hand or around the neck seems to find echoes in Proverbs (3:3; 6:21; 7:3).

Other Jewelry. A well-known passage in Isaiah (3:18-21) lists an array of jewelry, much of which is mentioned nowhere else in the Bible. Professor Elizabeth E. Platt of the University of Dubuque Theological Seminary proposes a fresh translation that sheds new light on this passage:

> [18]In that day the LORD will take away the finery of the ankle bangles, and the sun- or star-disks, [19]and the crescents, the drop pendants, and the necklace cords, and the beads, [20]the garland crowns, and the armlets (or foot jewelry), and the sashes (or girdles), and the tubular "soul cases," and the snake charms, [21]the signet rings, and the nose rings.

Other translations read "perfume boxes" in verse 20, where Professor Platt translates "tubular 'soul cases.'" These were cylinders with papyrus whose writing was intended to repel misfortune or sickness. Other translations report "amulets" where Professor Platt specifies "snake charms" (see Jer 8:17). In antiquity, women often carried serpent figure charms in their hands, just as Arab women prior to Mohammed wore golden serpents between their breasts.

Professor Platt's translation choices are confirmed by the position taken in this article that jewelry served primarily as protection against evil.

Because Isaiah introduces this passage by commenting that the women of Zion are haughty in gait and bearing, "mincing along as they go, tinkling with their feet," many commentators thought he was criticizing women for their vanity and extravagant fashions.

Professor Platt points out that only four of the thirteen jewelry items are associated with women in the Bible: ankle bangles, beads, sashes or girdles (see Jer 2:32), and nose rings. Eight of the other items relate more fittingly to men of high rank. Women may have worn them or a female version of them, but they were not exclusive to women. In a ninth-century relief, for example, King Assurnasirpal II is depicted wearing star-disks. The prophet, therefore, appears to be criticizing people in high office for their abuse of power and their collusion in social injustice.

CONCLUSION

"In all the land there were no women so beautiful as Job's daughters," writes the author of this biblical book as it comes to a close (Job 42:15). The text suggests that they used cosmetics to enhance their beauty, and it is tempting to think that they also used varieties of jewelry, including gold and silver, for the same purpose. While this is quite possible and plausible, it is also likely that they used the jewelry as amulets to ward off the kind of misfortune their father Job was somehow unable to escape by his piety alone.

FOR FURTHER READING

Matthews, Victor H. "Perfumes and Spices." *Anchor Bible Dictionary* 5:226–228.
Platt, Elizabeth E. "Jewelry, Ancient Israelite." *Anchor Bible Dictionary* 3:823–834.

DANCE

According to Luke 9:7-9, the death of John the Baptist was an open and shut case. Herod the tetrarch had John the Baptist beheaded. The longer reports in Matthew 14:1-12 and Mark 6:14-29 add other characters and events that only confuse the matter. Even a careful reading and comparison of the three reports leave many puzzles, and group discussions are frequently colored by details from modern films with no basis in the biblical record.

For instance: "When Herodias's daughter came in [to Herod's birthday party] and danced, she pleased Herod and his guests" (Mark 6:22//Matt 14:6). Who can remember this dancer's name? Can anyone describe the dance she performed? Those who read the texts closely and carefully know that these answers are not in the biblical text. A rereading of the complete story in Mark 6:14-29, Matthew 14:1-12, and Luke 9:7-9 prompts everyone to wonder: Where did we learn the details we have inserted into this story?

HIGH AND LOW CONTEXT LITERATURE

Comic strips and the Gospel stories are examples of "high context" literature. Authors who write for readers of their own culture leave out many details because they can safely and correctly presume that their intended readers can supply what is required to get the point. The author and the readers share a common culture and common understandings. One "Frank and Ernest" comic strip presented the two characters standing amid ancient ruins. Frank speaks: "I've been an archaeologist for thirty-seven years. Nobody knows the rubbles I've seen." The words are easy to understand, and the majority of American readers will grasp the reference to the Afro-American spiritual "Nobody knows the *troubles* I've seen." Knowledge about slavery in the United States, about the songs of the slaves known as "spirituals," and about this particular spiritual is so familiar to Americans that this comic strip does not need explanatory footnotes. But would a foreigner learning the English language be able to interpret this strip correctly without help? Would a grammar, dictionary, or encyclopedia help?

Such "high context" literature is quite different from "low context" literature. If you have ever read the fine print on your credit card agreements or contracts for buying a car or a home or any insurance policy, you have experienced "low context" literature. Such documents leave nothing to the imagination. Every possible eventuality is anticipated and identified. Any lawyer can explain what is written there even if the ordinary lay person can't.

The evangelist assumes that his readers know the name of Herodias's daughter and the precise identity of this Herod (a common and repeated name in that family!) and many other cultural details. While his contemporary readers certainly knew these details, we don't. We must go beyond grammars, dictionaries, and encyclopedias and seek additional information from ancient history and cultural anthropology. At the same time, we must refrain from inserting our culture and our culturally conditioned imagination into our biblical texts.

ANCIENT HISTORY

Ancient historians like Josephus and modern studies of such works tell us that Herod the Great, a Judaic puppet king appointed by Rome, lived from approximately 73 B.C.E. to 4 B.C.E. (Jesus was born in 6 B.C.E., before this Herod died). Herod the Great had ten wives (successively, not simultaneously), with whom he had many children. After his death in 4 B.C.E., Herod the Great's kingdom was divided among some sons, one of whom, Herod Antipas, was given Galilee and Perea to rule.

Herod Antipas ("that fox" of Luke 13:31-32) dominates the Gospel stories and is involved in the death of John the Baptist. Only Mark calls him "king" (perhaps mistakenly or perhaps because people viewed him as such). The other evangelists call him "tetrarch," meaning "one of four rulers," but this title generally indicates a status lower than that of a king and an ethnarch.

Herod Antipas first married a daughter (whose name we do not know) of the Nabatean King Aretas IV in order to assure protection against hostile raids on his territory. Later he married Herodias, the wife of his half-brother Herod (not Philip, as misidentified in Matthew and Mark), forcing the daughter of Aretas (his first wife) to return to her father. Herodias already had a daughter, Salome, who was very likely the one that danced for Herod Antipas's birthday party.

Herodias herself was the daughter of Aristobolus (and Berenice), a son of Herod the Great and Mariamne I (his second wife).

Aristobolus was a half-brother of the Herod whom Herodias first married and a half-brother of her second husband, Herod Antipas. In both instances Herodias married a half-uncle. Ideally, in that culture she should have married one of their sons, a first cousin. John the Baptist criticized both this improper marriage partner and the adultery before the marriage.

History is not a strong suit with Americans. The history of the Herods is particularly confusing because so many members of that family bore the same name. Notice that even Matthew and Mark confused them. Yet without some knowledge of the history of Jesus' time, the Gospels are impossible to interpret. That is why the basic Catholic method of Bible interpretation is called the "historical-critical" method. Without an accurate historical understanding, so-called "spiritual" or "theological" interpretations are meaningless. But history alone is not enough.

MEDITERRANEAN CULTURE

Specialists called cultural anthropologists (those who study and compare different cultures), and particularly Mediterranean anthropologists, help fill in many details that are reported or presumed in "high context" biblical stories but escape the historical-critical method of studying these reports. For instance, most of us very likely imagine Salome's dance for Herod and his guests to have been like belly-dances we have witnessed at ethnic festivals or carnivals. Yet these modern dances are primarily for entertainment and do not have the same function as the dances of Mediterranean antiquity and of contemporary Mediterranean peasants or the Bedouins.

Space. In the Mediterranean world, all reality is divided and classified as male and female. Space is similarly divided: in general, the public arena is male space; the domestic arena is female space. Dancing is intended primarily for private, female space, that is, in the home. The primary audience for this dancing, therefore, is the nuclear family or female guests, both kin and non-kin. The Middle Eastern family of antiquity was quite extended. It included the male head of household (the patriarch) and his brothers, married and single, and all their children, including married sons and their families. Because the most highly desirable marriage partner for a man was his father's brother's daughter—that is, his paternal uncle's child, a first cousin—such marriages made this large extended family quite a tight-knit group. (Herodias should ideally have married Antipas's child, her first cousin, and not her half-uncle Antipas.)

At the same time, this large family was very private. Only a prostitute would dance before male non-kin or in the public domain.

Matthew's report (14:6) that Salome danced before the company gathered for Herod's birthday party could be interpreted as a family affair. In that case, Salome is portrayed as an "honorable" woman, since explicit, sexual, exhibitionist behavior such as dancing was permitted in the culture but was restricted to the nuclear family or an all-female setting.

Mark's report (6:21-22) that Salome danced before Herod's guests, including "his courtiers and officers and the leading men of Galilee," portrays Salome as a "shameful" woman who violated the cultural rules governing female sexual behavior and honor. An honorable woman would have refused to dance before such a totally inappropriate audience.

Honor and Shame. Honor and shame are the core cultural values of the Mediterranean world, both ancient and contemporary. Honor is a public claim to worth *and* public acknowledgment of that claim. Shame is a lack of sensitivity to one's honor, a carelessness in guarding and maintaining it. These notions permeate the Bible from beginning to end and are absolutely essential for an accurate understanding and interpretation of the text.

Following the cultural division of all reality into male and female, honor is linked with the male, and shame is linked with the female. Men can protect themselves, but women are considered vulnerable and require vigilant protection from their men (father, brothers, spouse).

Some man (spouse, father, brother) was expected to keep Salome on the right track. That her stepfather, Herod Antipas, allowed her to dance before his courtiers and officers and leading men of Galilee marks him as a clearly dishonorable man. He had no sense of propriety, he was shameless. That her mother, Herodias, did not stop her from dancing in such company confirmed the shamelessness the mother had already exhibited by being unfaithful to her husband Herod and then marrying his half-brother Herod Antipas. In Mark's version, therefore, the dance reflects a lack of honor or shamelessness on the part of Salome, Herodias, and Herod. In Matthew, however, the dance context seems honorable.

The Dance Itself. Four things are explicitly displayed in the dance: female sensuality, beauty, ability to dance, and gold. Bellydancing is intended to be flirtatious, entertaining, and fun. An all-female audience can appreciate these qualities as much as a male audience can.

The dancer's eyes are ordinarily downcast, and the hair is often used as a drape or a foil. Recalling that ideal marriages are between first cousins, and that dancing is intended primarily for the nuclear family members, a dancer can safely display sensuality and beauty to this audience in hopes of facilitating her acceptance by an arranged marriage partner. There was no courtship or dating in that culture as we know these practices in our culture. Moreover, since the primary purpose of veils is to guard women from the gaze of male non-kin, the use of veils in a dance in the presence of kin serves a sensual rather than a cultural purpose.

Belly dancing also requires great skill. The dancer must be in firm control of arm movements, which should encircle the torso in order to display her best jewelry. At the same time, the dancer must be adept at rotating the hips a full 360 degrees at various speeds, while the torso must be shaken in a lineal fashion. The combination of these contrasting movements of pelvis and torso is quite a skill.

Lastly, notice that an equally important feature of the dance is to display clothes and jewelry. The dancer positions herself before sections of the audience so that they might inspect her attire, especially her gold. Since it is a woman's task to contribute to the "honor" of the men in her life (honor is a family or group virtue), displaying the gifts that have come from men is an effective way to do just that.

Gold is given to women on all occasions. It is not only a mark of deepening affection, respect, concern, and protection by male kinsmen, but the gift also becomes legally the woman's. No one, not even her kinsmen, may remove it without her permission. Recall the photographs of Mediterranean brides you may have seen in which the bride is wearing a "chain" or "cluster" of coins. This is her wealth and security as well as a mark of honor-status. This dance is essential to an honor and shame culture.

Role of the Mother. Surely the reader has noticed that a presumably adult female dancer has pleased the king and been offered a reward, but she turns to her mother for a suggestion! In Mediterranean culture, a woman has no standing until she bears a child, especially a *son*. Salome the unmarried adult is no better than a child still dependent upon her mother (and male kin).

The power a Mediterranean mother wields over the children is truly awesome. Boys are reared exclusively in the women's world until puberty. Yet, even after they move into the adult male world, they are still subject to the will and manipulation of their mothers. Recall how the mother of James and John attempted to persuade Jesus to give her sons places of honor in his success (Matt 20:20-28). Remember also how Jesus' mother and brothers came to take him back home because people were saying he was "beside himself," that is, out of his mind, crazy (Mark 3:20-35). Clearly these mothers expected to be heeded or obeyed by adult males.

Girls never escape the women's world, even after they are married. Women are always with other women and the children as a group. Women socialize young girls into their proper roles, and women as a group enforce the cultural expectations of women regarding veiling, a female sense of shame, knowing one's place (private, female space), etc.

Salome had no will of her own. She turned to her mother for advice when her stepfather, Herod Antipas, offered her whatever she wished. Mark explicitly notes that "*Herodias* had a grudge against [John], and wanted to kill him. But she could not . . . ." The man whom Herodias could manipulate, her husband Herod, could kill John, but Mark's Herod feared John as a righteous and holy man.

HEROD'S OBLIGATION

Why was Herod unwilling and/or unable to change his promise or go back on his word? Binding oneself by an oath in that culture was serious business. The commandment prohibited calling on the Lord to witness the truth of something "in vain" (= false swearing; see Exod 20:7). But by the first century of the Common Era, people had figured out ways to wiggle out of commandment obligations (see Mark 7 and the *corban*). Herod certainly knew these strategies. Why did he not use them?

The factor that actually forced him to keep his word was the "guests." The Mediterranean world is a very public place. Privacy is impossible. Herod gave his word with an oath to Salome in public, in the presence of his guests: the extended family (Matthew), his courtiers, officers, and the leading men of Galilee (Mark). To go back on his word would have been shameful. It would also have crippled his effectiveness as a ruler. If a relative could not count on Herod's word (bad enough), how could non-kin—all his subjects—hope for better treatment (worse yet)? Herod's hands were tied.

CONCLUSION

Who, therefore, killed John the Baptist—Herod? Herodias? Salome? The guests? The culture? All of the above? Do Matthew, Mark, and Luke suggest different interpretations? A knowledge of history and cultural anthropology helps readers to unravel some of the mysteries in these biblical reports.

FOR FURTHER REFERENCE

"Family Matters: The Role of the Family in the Middle East." Encyclopedia Britannica Films, X0, 4004; 25 min.

Hanson, K. C. "The Herodians and Mediterranean Kinship." Parts I, II, III. *Biblical Theology Bulletin* 19 (1989) 75–84; 142–151; 20 (1990) 10–21.

Witherington, Ben, III. "Salome." *Anchor Bible Dictionary* 5:906–907.

DEATH

Demographers estimate that the population of first-century Palestine was probably around 250,000. Geographers observe that the country was approximately the size of contemporary New Jersey. Modern-day visitors to Jerusalem are awed at the sight of the numerous tombs that cover the entire east side of the Kidron Valley. How many people are buried here? Were the dead buried in coffins? Is it true that they were buried vertically to save space? Did they ever run out of burial space?

During the Stone Age (25,000 to 3,800 B.C.E.), the dead were generally buried in the ground (inhumation). By the Bronze Age (3,800 B.C.E.), a diversity of practices appeared. Archaeologists have discovered small burial containers resembling houses or shrines, cist graves (tombs made with stone tablets), and ossuaries (stone bone-containers) that were placed in cave tombs.

PLACE OF BURIAL

In the patriarchal period (Middle and Late Bronze Ages) and even later, people were buried where they died. Miriam was buried in Kadesh (Num 20:1); Aaron on Mount Hor (Num 33:39); Moses in the valley in the land of Moab opposite Bethpeor (Deut 34:6). Often the corpse was buried near a tree. Rebekah's nurse, Deborah, was buried under an oak below Bethel (Gen 35:8). Rachel was (most likely) buried at Ephrath near Ramah in the territory of Benjamin, north of Jerusalem (1 Sam 10:2; Jer 31:15), and not near Bethlehem, as stated in Genesis 35:19, a mistaken gloss on Ephrath. Jacob marked the place with a stele (Gen 35:20). The bones of Saul and his sons were buried under the tamarisk tree in Jabesh (1 Sam 31:12-13). The tree may have been reminiscent of divine presence (Gen 21:32-33) or immortality (Gen 2:9).

Still, multiple burials in family caves were the prevalent practice. Abraham the resident alien purchased the cave at Machpelah from Ephron the Hittite (the "people of the land") to bury his wife, Sarah (Gen 23:1-20). Before dying, Jacob charged his sons to bury him in this same cave, which by this time was also the resting place of Abraham, Isaac, Rebekah, and Leah (Gen 49:29-33).

BURIAL WITH THE FAMILY

The importance of a family burial place to our ancestors in the faith demonstrates that the core value of kinship and family-centeredness that dominated life in Mediterranean culture also characterized its burial customs. In general, it was important to be buried with one's family in the family tomb, as illustrated by the patriarchs. The family tomb of Joshua was in Timnath-serah, in the hill country of Ephraim, north of the mountain of Gaash (Josh 24:30). Samuel was buried in the family tomb at Ramah (1 Sam 25:1a; 28:3a).

Saul initially was not buried in the family tomb (see above), but David felt duty-bound to rectify this condition (2 Sam 21:12-14). The recurrent phrases "gathered to his people" (Gen 25:8; 35:29; 49:29, 33) and "slept with his fathers" (1 Kgs 2:10; 11:43; 14:31; 15:8; etc.) reflect a belief that family bonds extended beyond death. Not to be buried with one's family was a calamity surpassed only by the shame of not being buried at all (1 Kgs 14:11; Isa 14:20; Jer 16:4; 22:19; Ezek 29:5; Eccl 6:3). This latter fate was reserved for sinners (Deut 28:25-26).

BURIAL OUTSIDE THE CITY WALLS

The common custom was to bury the dead in tombs outside the city walls. The one exception to this custom appears to have been the burial of the kings of Judah. Though the Deuteronomic historian tells us that David "slept with the fathers" (1 Kgs 2:10), the fact is that he did not. David and his ancestors were presumably from Bethlehem (1 Sam 16:1-13), but David was "buried in the city of David," Ophel (1 Kgs 2:10). This was a Jebusite city that did not belong to any tribe, so David made it his capital city in 997 B.C.E. (2 Sam 5:6-9) and installed the ark of the covenant there too (2 Sam 6). During the Herodian and Byzantine periods, Ophel ridge was within Jerusalem's city walls.

What would be the significance of burying kings within the city, that is, among the living? Scholars are not agreed about this, but one plausible reason may be that kings were the people's conduit to God. Prophets delivered their messages primarily to kings and not to ordinary people. The tomb of the king, therefore, might have had the significance accorded later to holy men like Akiba. Here people obtained guidance, advice, answers to some of life's problems, and the like. These tombs were recognized as places of revelation.

East of the Old City of Jerusalem, these burial markers are part of an old and large cemetery on the Mount of Olives.

BURIAL CUSTOMS

As one might expect from a high-context document like the Bible, there is precious little information about burial customs in ancient Israel. It seems that the eldest son or closest relative present closed the eyes of the deceased at death (Gen 46:4). Jacob and Joseph were embalmed (perhaps more correctly, mummified) quite likely because this was the customary practice in Egypt, where they died (Gen 50:2-3, 26). Otherwise, embalming was not customary among the Israelites. Only in the Hellenistic period do we read of an anointing of the body associated with its burial (Mark 16:1 and parallels).

Families and professionals (see Jer 9:17) lamented the deceased person. King David's decision to lament while his stricken child was sick but to cease lamenting when the child died seems unusual (2 Sam 12:15-23) but is quite intelligible from a Middle Eastern cultural perspective. Fasting, lamenting, and mourning (i.e., weeping, rending garments, cutting hair, and the like) in the Bible are protest strategies calculated to stir another person (often a person of power or means) to action (see the Beatitudes: Luke 6:20-21). David sought to stir God to rescue the young child, the offspring of his adulterous union with Bathsheba. When the child died, David recognized that he had failed to persuade God to save the child's life. The protest strategies served no purpose now. Instead of lamenting, David sought to comfort himself and Bathsheba and hoped that God would bless their union with a new child. God did not disappoint them.

THE HELLENISTIC PERIOD: BENCH TOMBS

In the Hellenistic period, "bench" tombs located near the family patrimony were also common. The St. Étienne tombs north of Jerusalem preserve some fine examples. In general, such a tomb consisted of a central court surrounded by burial chambers, each of which contained waist-high "benches" on which to place a body. To make room for new burials, skeletal remains and other objects were relocated to a repository (a pit) in the center of the room or under a bench. Pottery and other objects found in the tombs were placed there sometimes for the deceased, but more often for those who visited the tomb for cultic or other purposes.

THE BURIAL OF JESUS

Accounts of the death and burial of Jesus reflect the cultural beliefs and practices of that day. People lamented him (Luke 23:27, 48; see also Luke 8:52). Jesus' body may have been washed (Acts 9:37) before Joseph of Arimathea, a disciple, wrapped it in a linen shroud and placed it in his own new tomb, hewn in the soft limestone rock (Matt 27:59-60). Friends came to the tomb after the Sabbath intending to anoint the body (Luke 24:1).

Joseph of Arimathea's tomb may have been a family tomb or perhaps a "personal" tomb, if one interprets Matthew's description of him as "rich" to indicate social prestige. It was part of the intricate cemetery complex that surrounds the walled city of Jerusalem.

ROLLING STONE TOMB

The entrance to this sort of tomb was sealed by a circular, disk-like stone that was set into a groove carved in front of the rectangular-shaped entrance to the tomb. The stone could be rolled in one direction or the other to seal or open the entrance. Even a small-sized stone, e.g., four feet in diameter and six to eight inches thick, would be difficult if not impossible for one person alone to roll away. The stone served to protect the contents of the tomb from thieves.

Still, the fact that Jesus was buried in the tomb of a stranger, even though one well-disposed toward him, added insult to injury, as it were. Jesus was not interred among his ancestors, like the patriarchs. He did not "sleep with his fathers," nor was he "gathered to his people." Moreover, no one sought to rectify this situation for him as did David for the bones of Saul.

SECONDARY BURIAL: OSSUARIES

Something else of significance must be included in the story of Jesus' death and burial, namely, plans for his secondary burial. Though not mentioned in the high-context document we call the New Testament, the practice of secondary burial was very common in the first century C.E. Joseph's tomb would have had niches (about 6.5' x 25.5" x 22"), called in Hebrew *kôkîm*, in which a corpse was placed and would remain for about one year. This was the official mourning period. When the flesh had rotted, the bones would be gathered and placed into a stone bone-box called an "ossuary." The name or names of the deceased whose remnants were thus gathered would be inscribed on the box. This practice made it possible for the same family tombs to be used for many generations.

In her book *Seeing the Lord*, Professor Marianne Sawicki shares interesting insights about the cultural beliefs surrounding late Second Temple burial practices involving these bone-boxes. Judaic sources reflect the conviction that a person's evil deeds somehow derived from and permeated the flesh. Only when the flesh was entirely rotted would these deeds be eradicated.

When the year had passed, the mourning period ended with the relatives gathering up the bones into the ossuary or simply piling them up with the bones of related ancestors. The ossuaries of the Bronze Age were shaped like little houses, but in the Hellenistic pe-

Dating to perhaps the first or second century A.D., these ancient ossuaries were discovered on the Mount of Olives, Jerusalem, near the Church of Dominus Flevit.

riod they were oblong boxes about 22 inches long, 12 inches wide, and 10 to 16 inches high. The length of the box approximated the length of an adult thigh bone.

INTERPRETING SECONDARY BURIAL

Professor Sawicki notes that the ossuary resembled the box used for storing scrolls. Since it was a widespread Judaic belief in the first century that human bones retained the personality, one could imagine these longer bones to be scroll spindles ready for new material on which God would write anew. It was also possible to imagine these bones as parts of a loom on which God would weave a new body. Inkwells and spindle whorls discovered in excavated tombs lend a high level of plausibility to such scenarios for interpreting ancient artifacts.

These cultural insights shed new light on the death and resurrection of Jesus. By raising him from the dead and not allowing his body to decompose, God declared a favorable judgment upon the words and deeds of Jesus. This judgment contrasts with and overturns that negative judgment of the authorities who put him to death.

In summary, the funeral practices of both the Old and the New Testament reflect the group-centered nature of Mediterranean culture. Just as Mediterranean dyadic personalities needed others to shape their identity in life, so in death family ties remained unbroken by burying deceased family members in the same family tomb. While Joseph's magnanimous offer to bury his master's body in his personal tomb was honorable and noteworthy, the fact that Jesus died away from his hometown and was not buried in the family tomb can be interpreted as the ultimate disgrace of his shameful end.

Yet this dark picture of the final days of Jesus' life would be totally wiped out by the brilliance of Jesus' resurrection from death by his Father. A modern believer can appreciate this now all the more from a clearer understanding of secondary burial in Jesus' world and the theological significance of his being denied this opportunity. The better acquainted we become with the cultural world of the Bible, the better sense we can make out of so many of our puzzles in reading this ancient book.

FOR FURTHER READING

Hachlili, Rachel. "Burials." *Anchor Bible Dictionary* 1:785–794.
Kennedy, Charles A. "Cult of the Dead." *Anchor Bible Dictionary* 2:106–108.
Sawicki, Marianne. *Seeing the Lord: Resurrection and Early Christian Practices*. Minneapolis: Fortress, 1994.

DECEPTION AND LYING

As a youngster in pre-Vatican II parochial school, I learned that it is never permissible to tell a lie, even if that lie could somehow save the whole world. Later in graduate school, my moral theology professor said: "If it were possible to save the whole world by telling a lie, my suggestion is: 'Tell the lie!'" Perhaps the fact that my moral theology professor had lived and taught in Rome, a Mediterranean city, for the greater part of his theological career helps to understand his opinion.

The core value and greatest personal wealth in Mediterranean cultures is honor. In Mediterranean cultures, a person or group that loses honor is as good as dead. Secrecy is a legitimate cultural strategy for maintaining and safeguarding honor (see Secrecy). When secrecy fails, it is equally legitimate to resort to deception and outright lies in order to protect or gain honor. Saving the world would be an honorable accomplishment; hence lying could be a legitimate strategy for achieving that goal in a Mediterranean view of things.

Deception and lying are strategies for restricting the public flow of information over a period of time. The ability to control the dissemination of information is a mark of power and a sure guarantee of retaining personal or group honor. Experts in Mediterranean culture have identified eight kinds of deception employed in the service of honor. Here are biblical examples of these honor-saving and honor-gaining strategies.

CONCEALMENT OF FAILURE

Certain deceptions are intended to cover up the failure of an individual or group to live up to the highest ideals or requirements of the social code. Anthropologists presented Jesus' parable about the two sons (Matt 21:28-32) to contemporary Lebanese villagers (without Jesus' final question) and asked for their assessment. The villagers unanimously agreed that the son who told his father he was going to work in the field though he actually did not do so was the truly honorable son. He gave his father a respectful answer and told him what he wanted to hear. The son who refused to go but later went anyway was viewed as acting shamefully. His public refusal of his father's exhortation was an insult to the father and a challenge to parental authority. The villagers would not abide such blatant dishonoring of a father by a son.

In the Mediterranean world, appearances are more important than reality. The first son lied to conceal his failure. It is important to recognize that Jesus did not ask the "honor" question but rather: "Which of these did the will of the father?" Even contemporary Mediterranean natives would agree with the judgment given by Jesus' contemporaries. Jesus' question, however, is not the first one that comes to the Mediterranean mind.

CONCEALMENT OF UNINTENTIONAL FAILURE

Sometimes people fail despite their best efforts, but even this must be covered with a deception because one's honor is at stake. The lawyer who asked Jesus about eternal life (Luke 10:25-29) expected to trick Jesus. In the Mediterranean world, every question is viewed as a challenge. It must be answered even if one does not know the correct answer. (Contemporary natives prefer to give tourists erroneous directions rather than admit that they don't know where a place or monument is located. Ignorance is shameful; the appearance of knowing is honorable.)

Jesus resorted to one of his favorite strategies and responded with a counter-question and an insult. "How do you *read*?" Surely an expert in the law can read! And the lawyer fell into Jesus' trap, because he showed that he knew the answer to his question. He correctly cited Leviticus 19:18. His pretense and deception were unmasked; Jesus had publicly shamed him.

But since the lawyer did not intend to fail, he quickly countered with another challenging question whose answer he already indicated that he knew when he cited Leviticus 19:18 about the identity of a true neighbor. This second question therefore was another deception, a lie, a pretense of ignorance, intended to cover his unintended failure to trap Jesus with the first question.

FALSE IMPUTATION

Sometimes it is necessary to attack the honor of another in order to save one's own honor. In our modern world, this strategy is: the best defense is an offense. In Jesus' world, the attack took the form of a lie of false imputation. According to John's Gospel, opinion about Jesus was divided (7:12-13). In dialogue with Jesus, Judeans made a claim to honor (John 8:39). Jesus challenged their claim (8:39-40). The Judeans made a further claim to honor (8:41). Jesus offered an insulting response: "You are children of the devil, and you lie like your father who is the father of lies" (8:44). To save what remained of their honor, the Judeans accused Jesus of being a Samaritan and of having a demon (8:48), both of which charges they knew were false but which they leveled anyway to tarnish Jesus' honor.

AVOIDING QUARRELS OR TROUBLE

In cultures in which honor is the core value, quarrels can easily escalate to violence that could result in someone's death. Since no one really ever wants a quarrel to reach this point, deceptions and lies are often pressed into service in order to avoid a quarrel or escape trouble, both of which can besmirch honor and lead to violent consequences.

After Jesus' arrest, Peter hung around outside the courtyard to learn what would happen next. A servant girl publicly associated Peter with "the Galilean," but he denied it "before all" and denied even knowing what the girl was talking about (Matt 26:70). Another servant girl made a similar charge, and Peter once again lied, confirming it with an oath: "I do not know the man" (Matt 26:71). Leviticus 19:12 forbade calling upon God to witness a lie.

Finally the bystanders pointed out that Peter's accent betrayed him. In response, Peter lied once again and cursed himself (see Ruth 1:15-18 for the nature of this curse) while repeating his oath that he spoke the truth. Peter's triple, bald-faced lie was clearly told in this instance to avoid trouble. He feared that he might be subjected to a fate similar to that of Jesus and preferred to lie rather than speak the truth and accept the consequences.

It is also possible to view Peter's lie as an attempt to cover his unintentional failure. Earlier in the evening during the supper, Jesus indicated that all will desert him in his time of need. Peter vehemently denied this. "I will never fall away . . . . Even if I must die with you, I will not deny you" (Matt 26:33-35). But in the darkness and confusion surrounding Jesus' arrest in the garden, Peter fled with the others. He had failed to keep his boastful claim! Those who arrested Jesus and who planned his arrest knew that Jesus was not alone in the garden. Gossip spread the knowledge to others. Peter's choice was to admit his failure to be a loyal disciple or to protect his honor by lying about his relationship with Jesus. He chose the latter to cover his failure as a disciple.

FOR GAIN, SOMETIMES MATERIAL

Honor in the Mediterranean world is also reckoned in part by material possessions. But this culture also believes that all material goods are limited in quantity and already distributed. "There is no more where this came from." Hence it is shameful to increase one's possession in this culture because the suspicion is that one has stolen the goods. How, then, can one increase goods? By cheating on a deal or by pretending to be cunning and shrewd.

The story of Naboth's vineyard is illustrative (1 Kgs 21). The vineyard is the basis of Naboth's honor rating in his society. He was duty-bound not to relinquish the vineyard. The king's offer to purchase or make an exchange for it was actually improper and shameful, but the king was hoping that Naboth would be swayed. When Naboth refused to yield, the king was shamed. Having been caught acting shamefully, the king wanted to die!

The king's wife, Jezebel, came to the rescue. With lies of false imputation, she ruined Naboth's honor, engineered his death, and obtained the vineyard (material gain) for the king. Not only did the king obtain what he wanted, but the acquisition of the vineyard augmented his honor as well.

SHEER CONCEALMENT

Unrelenting community curiosity stimulated by secrecy in Mediterranean culture generates yet another kind of deception prompted by the unknown and feared power of the nosey community. The strategy of deception is honed and practiced and soon becomes part of each individual's daily life "just for the fun of it," because one never knows what others might do with the truth.

Concealing one's whereabouts is one example of this kind of deception. In John's Gospel (7:1-10), Jesus did not wish to visit Judea "because the Judeans" were looking for an opportunity to kill him (v. 1). His relatives knew this but urged him to go to Judea so that his works might enhance his honor-rating (vv. 3-5; or perhaps they figured that death would finally rid the family of this disgrace to family honor). Jesus flatly announced, "I am not going to this festival" and remained in Galilee. But after his relatives departed, he also went, "not publicly but as it were in secret."

The possibility of enhancing honor exerts a strong pull on Mediterranean folk. Jesus was no exception, but he employed a deception regarding his travel plans because he wanted to minimize the certain risk to his life (see v. 1). The sheer desire for concealment on the part of Jesus is more clearly evident in Mark 7:24.

LIES OF PURE MISCHIEF

While excellence in deception gives an expert deceiver a claim to honor in the Mediterranean world, the targets of this deception have to work all the harder not be taken in by it. At stake is nothing less than *their* honor! In this culture, honor and not money is the greatest form of wealth.

The comments of the pastor in 2 Timothy 3:1-17, which conclude with the classic New Testament verse on the inspiration of Scripture, take on fresh meaning when read in the context of deception and lying as normal events in Mediterranean culture. The pastor describes "the last days" and warns that there will be slanderers, people of corrupt mind and counterfeit faith who oppose the truth, but their folly will be clear to everyone. "Wicked people and impostors will go from bad to worse, deceiving others and being deceived" (3:13).

How can a believer avoid confusion and deception? "Continue in what you have learned and firmly believed . . . . All Scripture is inspired by God," who is not a liar or a deceiver (3:14-17) to his friends. God's enemies, however, are fair game for God's deception (see 1 Kgs 22:23).

ON BEHALF OF FRIEND, GUEST, OR KIN

Honor being primarily a group-centered quality, it is clear that deception is a useful strategy in protecting the honor of a group. The familiar story of Rahab and Joshua's spies demonstrates this (Josh 2).

Hospitality in the Middle East is extended primarily to *strangers*. (The same gestures extended to kinfolk are not identified as hospitality but rather as *hesed*, that is, steadfast loving-kindness.) The purpose of hospitality is to provide a stranger with safe passage through a region where he is suspected of being up to no good simply because he is not kin to anyone or known by anyone.

Joshua's spies were shrewd in selecting Rahab's household as their lodging rather than that of the strongman in the community, who was culturally bound to provide such hospitality. The prostitute's lodging provided the spies with a deception to confuse the king, which would not have been the case if they had lodged with the village strongman. Rahab then engaged in her deception to protect her guests (vv. 4-7). But there was also another reason for her lie. She hoped to obtain favors from Joshua in return for her lie. Her lie was also a lie for gain.

Presumably the spies left Rahab as friends rather than as strangers, and the deceptions utilized in this story achieved their respective goals.

CONCLUSION

Western readers will have to set aside their own cultural convictions about secrecy, deception, and lying in order to appreciate the distinctive role that these strategies play in Mediterranean culture. The key to appreciating the importance of secrecy, deception, and lies in Mediterranean culture is a solid understanding of honor as the core value of this culture. Cultures are value-driven systems, and honor, the public claim and public acknowledgment of worth, governs all behavior in the Mediterranean world. When analyzing biblical narratives, a reader must always keep in mind the public judgment and response to what is being reported. This public, after all, is the final judge of whether honor is to be granted or denied.

FURTHER READING

Boulay, Juliette du. "Lies, Mockery and Family Integrity." *Mediterranean Family Structures*, ed. J. G. Peristiany, 389–406. Cambridge: University Press, 1976.

Gilsenan, Michael. "Lying, Honor, and Contradiction." *Transaction and Meaning: Directions in the Anthropology of Exchange and Symbolic Behavior*, ed. Bruce Kapferer, 191–219. Philadelphia: Institute for the Study of Human Issues, 1976.

Léon-Dufour, Xavier. "Lie." *Dictionary of the New Testament*, 267–268. San Francisco: Harper & Row, 1980.

Pilch, John J. "Lying and Deceit in the Letters to the Seven Churches: Perspectives from Cultural Anthropology." *Biblical Theology Bulletin* 22 (1992) 126–134.

Robert, J.J.M. "Does God Lie? Divine Deceit as a Theological Problem in Israelite Prophetic Literature." *Congress Volume: Jerusalem, 1986*, ed. J. A. Emerton, 211–220. Leiden: Brill, 1988.

DRINKING AND EATING

What were the basic necessities of life in ancient Palestine? Sirach offers two answers. At the very least, "Life's prime needs are water, bread, and clothing; a house, too, for decent privacy" (29:21). In another place he lists ten necessities of life: "Chief of all needs for human life are water and fire, iron and salt, the heart of the wheat, milk and honey, the blood of the grape, and oil, and cloth" (39:26). In this chapter we focus on things to drink and to eat.

THINGS TO DRINK

Most people would agree with Sirach that water is a necessity of life. Many would go along with milk, but probably all Westerners would wonder about the blood of the grape, that is, wine.

Water. Not only is water a basic drink for humans and animals, but it is also needed to make plants grow. Ancient Palestine was relatively poor in water. It had few perennial streams, so it had to depend on two other water sources: one beneath the earth (fountains or springs and wells) and another above the earth (rain, which falls only about six or seven months of the year).

Ancient people settled near springs or fountains (Deut 8:7) and wells (Gen 26:19). A "true" well is fed by water from an underground spring and is literally called "a well of living water" (Gen 26:19; John 4:11). The word *Beer* in the names of ancient villages, like Beer-sheba, is the Hebrew word for "well" and indicates the chief water supply for the residents.

Most towns in ancient Israel did not have a good fountain, so they constructed an artificial pool to gather rain, or water that was channeled from a more distant source, or water from a dammed-up small stream. Such pools were found in Hebron (2 Sam 4:12) and Gibeon (2 Sam 2:13). Two highlighted in the New Testament are the Pool of Siloam (John 9:7) and the Pool of Beth-zatha near the Sheep Gate (John 5:2).

With the discovery of a method for plastering, and thereby waterproofing, huge, underground limestone cisterns around 1550

B.C.E., the ancient Israelites were able to store a larger volume of water for year-round use. Joseph's brothers placed him in such a cistern (Gen 37:24), and visitors to Israel can see and enter the huge cistern atop the fortress Masada. Even so, the value of cisterns only underscores the scarcity of water.

Milk. A more available and plentiful fluid was milk. Unless otherwise specified, every mention of milk in the Bible refers to goat's milk (Prov 27:27). Goats can go for as long as two weeks without drinking water and replenish it quickly. They also graze on marginal land that cannot sustain sheep and cattle. Until very recent times, goats were the principal suppliers of milk in the Middle East, for goat's milk is easier to digest than cow's milk. Goat's milk is available for seven to eight months a year.

Though the Bible mentions milch cows (1 Sam 6:7), they are used primarily for pulling objects such as carts. Getting milk from cows is particularly difficult in unimproved breeds, and ancient literature reports amusing strategies for obtaining milk from the cow. Even so, only children in antiquity did not get sick from cow's milk. Contemporary nutritional science confirms that only children, European Alpine and circum-Baltic adults do not get ill from cow's milk.

Camels were another source of milk in the ancient Middle East (Gen 32:15), particularly among the Bedouins. Since camels lactate for twelve months of the year, Bedouins have a reliable source of nutritional fluid even in the dry season, which extends approximately from April to October.

Sheep provide only about half the quantity of milk that goats do, and for only three or four months a year, from about February or March onward. Though sheep usually outnumber goats in Middle Eastern flocks of past and present, the Bible's two references to sheep's milk (Deut 32:14; 1 Cor 9:7) are so ambiguous that they can also be interpreted as references to goat's milk.

In any case, because milk does not keep well without refrigeration, the ancients drank sour milk (which was kept in skins: Judg 4:19; 5:25) and more often than not partook of milk in the form of yogurt (a stage in the formation of cheese) and cheese, usually in the form of curds (Gen 18:8; Deut 32:14; Isa 7:15; Prov 30:33).

While the combination might be revolting to a modern Western stomach, a mixture of milk and wine was a favorite drink among the ancients (Song 5:1; Isa 55:1), particularly since the milk turned rapidly sour anyway.

Honey. "Milk and honey" is a phrase commonly used in the Bible to describe the Promised Land (Exod 3:8, 17; Lev 20:24; Num

13:27; Deut 6:3; Jer 11:5; and many other places). The Hebrew language has a few words that unmistakably describe true bee honey (see Prov 16:24; Ps 19:10), which is quite viscous.

The Hebrew word in the phrase "milk and honey" is different. It is a generic term describing any sweet liquid like a syrup made from dates, grapes, or other fruits. Such syrups were very abundant and were a major export (Ezek 27:17). Large supplies were also stored (Jer 41:8).

Jacob instructed his sons to take some of this syrup on their return trip to Egypt (Gen 43:11). Jeroboam sent some of this free-pouring syrup to the prophet Ahija (1 Kgs 14:3). While it was used to sweeten food (Ezek 16:13), it was also used as food itself (Ezek 16:13). In spite of its abundance and its status as a necessity of life, sages advised against eating too much of it (Prov 25:27), perhaps to avoid gluttony and its consequences (see Prov 23:19-21).

Wine. As Moses' spies discovered (Num 13:23), the soil of Palestine was favorable for cultivating grapes. Eaten as such or as raisins, grapes were also crushed to make syrup and wine. Of all the fluids mentioned, wine was the most plentiful and the most readily available anytime during the year. Given the scarcity of water, the tendency of milk to turn sour without refrigeration, and the excessive

Sun-ripened grapes in a Jerusalem arbor.

sweetness of syrup, it is no wonder that Sirach includes the plentiful "blood of the grape," or wine, as one of the necessities of life.

Wine was apparently of good enough quality to rank as an important commercial crop. The royal house was deeply engaged in its production and trade. Solomon paid for the timber and artisans he received from Hiram of Tyre with provisions of grain, wine, and oil (1 Kgs 5:7-12; 2 Chr 2:10, 15).

Wine was drunk at the common meal (Gen 27:25; Luke 7:33) and at banquets (Dan 1:5; 5:1; Est 1:1-9; John 2:1-10). The Hebrew word for "feast" is derived from the word "to drink." Wine was taken on a journey (Judg 19:19) and considered a basic provision for a garrison at a fortress (2 Chr 11:11).

In Hellenistic times, wine was routinely mixed with water (2 Macc 15:39). Isaiah's comment about water diluting wine (1:22) suggests that this was not a practice in earlier periods. "Mingled" or "mixed" wine was not diluted but rather enhanced with herbs and spices (Prov 23:30; Isa 5:22; Song 8:2). On the other hand, peasants often had to settle for sour wine or wine vinegar (Ruth 2:9, 14).

The Hebrew Bible also speaks of a "strong drink," a general term for any kind of alcoholic beverage (Deut 29:6). Prophets cautioned against drinking this to excess (Isa 28:7). Strong drink included ciders made from dates or other fruits and may have also included beer, which was well known in ancient Mesopotamia and Egypt.

Yet when Moses led the Israelites out of Egypt, they complained about missing "the fleshpots" and "bread" (Exod 16:3) and the fish, "the cucumbers, the melons, the leeks, the onions, and the garlic" (Num 11:4-6). They thirsted for water (Exod 17:2-3) and were pleased to discover that the Promised Land flowed with "milk and honey" (Num 14:8). But there is no explicit mention of missing Egypt's beer!

It is plausible that the relative scarcity of water for basic needs like irrigation and watering animals and humans, combined with the abundance of other potable liquids like wine and milk, discouraged the "waste" of precious water to mix with relatively scarce grains in order to make beer.

Oil. While oil is a fluid, the ancients didn't drink it like wine or milk. The oil mentioned in the Bible is almost always olive oil. The cultivation of the olive tree, the Mediterranean fruit par excellence, extends back at least to the fourth millennium. A mature tree can produce about half a ton of fruit annually. The fruit ripens in September, and its color is reddish-purple to black. The olive has a bitter taste.

The ancients seem to have used the olive predominantly for its oil, which was a basic ingredient of foods (Num 11:8; Ezek 16:13). It was also a major export (Rev 18:13). Olive oil served many other purposes as well: as fuel in lamps (Exod 27:20; Matt 25:3, 8); as an anointing oil (1 Sam 10:1; 2 Kgs 9:3; Isa 61:1); as a salve for wounds (Isa 1:6; Luke 10:34) or other healing purposes (Mark 6:13; Jas 5:14); and as a base for perfumed ointment (Amos 6:6; Pss 23:5; 45:8; etc.).

Summary. We began this review of Sirach's necessities of life from the perspective of things to drink (water, milk, honey or syrup, and wine) but have discovered that many of these items met other basic needs as well. The ability to trade superfluous quantities of oil and wine, for instance, provided Israel with other necessities not available locally. Other fluids, like milk, proved to be more important in its solid form as yogurt, curds, and cheese.

Ancient olive press found near Capernaum, Israel. Crushing olives (to release the valuable oil) has been common for centuries in the Mediterranean region.

THINGS TO EAT

Among solid foods on his list of necessities, Sirach names literally "the fat of the wheat." This common phrase (see Deut 32:14; Pss 81:17; 147:14) describes the best quality of wheat or the choicest wheat meal. It is plausible to conclude that Sirach intended to embrace in this phrase the three grains other than wheat mentioned in the Bible.

1. Wheat was certainly the most important cereal grain in Israel. It was eaten as parched grain (particularly by travelers: see 1 Sam 17:17; 25:18) and in the form of bread. Its stems served as fodder, bedding for the animals, mulch, compost, and fertilizer. Stems were also woven into hats, baskets, chair seats, and beehives.

2. Barley was the next most common grain. It survives heat and water shortages better than wheat and ripens in less time. (Passover coincided with the barley harvest; Pentecost coincided with the wheat harvest seven weeks later.)

Since barley could be raised on soil of poorer quality, it was less expensive (Rev 6:6). Barley bread was the ordinary food of the peasant classes (2 Kgs 4:42; John 6:9), but the grain was most often mixed with other grains, such as millet, spelt, or pea meal (Ezek 4:9). It was also used as fodder (1 Kgs 4:28). The Talmud (Pes 3:1) seems to refer to beer brewed from barley that was prohibited at the feast of Passover.

    3. Spelt, or emmer, is a variety of coarse wheat or coarse corn resembling wheat; it was raised both in Egypt (Exod 9:32) and in Palestine (Isa 28:25). It was used in bread (Ezek 4:9), as fodder and

A Palestinian farmer winnows the grain of a bountiful harvest.

porridge, and sometimes it was even eaten fresh after plucking (Matt 12:1).

4. Millet, or sorghum, mentioned in the Bible only in Ezekiel 4:9, is one of the ingredients for making bread in time of famine. Its more common use was as fodder or in porridge.

WHAT'S MISSING?

Notice that fish and meat are not mentioned in Sirach's list of necessities. The Israelites' access to the sea was quite limited during the biblical period, so fish would have to be purchased (Neh 13:16). The Sea of Galilee and the Jordan, the alternative source for fish, supplied only limited amounts, and then very likely only for the local markets.

Similarly, meat was not a common item in the average diet. As noted above, female animals provided mainly milk curds and cheeses. Since few males were needed to serve the females, they constituted the majority of sacrificial victims.

The slaughter of an animal was a very special event. When the slaughter was for a sacrifice, the meat was eaten as a sacral meal. Other special occasions for slaughtering an animal were the need to extend hospitality (Gen 18:7), to host a feast (for the entire village, of course) on the occasion of a wedding (Matt 22:2-10), or to celebrate the return of a wayward son (see Luke 15:23). Since Sirach was concerned to list necessities, it is clear why fish and meat were excluded.

CONCLUSION

Modern scholars estimate that in Roman Palestine cereals provided about 50 percent of the required caloric intake. Wine, olive oil, legumes (beans, lentils), and fruit (figs, dates, apricots) provided the rest. This tallies well with Sirach's list, except for salt. We shall consider the function of salt in the next chapter.

FOR FURTHER READING

Avner, Uzi. "Ancient Agricultural Settlement and Religion in the Uvda Valley in Southern Israel." *Biblical Archaeologist* 53 (1990) 125–141.

Broshi, Magen. "The Diet of Palestine in the Roman Period: Introductory Notes." *The Israel Museum Journal* 5 (1986) 41–56.

Douglas, Mary, ed. *Food in the Social Order: Studies of Food and Festivities in Three American Communities.* New York: Russell Sage Foundation, 1984.

Jenks, Alan W. "Eating and Drinking in the Old Testament." *Anchor Bible Dictionary* 2:250–254.

Limet, Henri. "The Cuisine of Ancient Sumer." *Biblical Archaeologist* 50 (1987) 132–147.

FORGIVENESS

Matthew's Jesus gives two explicit, seemingly contradictory instructions on forgiveness within the community of believers. To the disciples he recommends a policy of "three strikes and you're out!" (Matt 18:15-20). To Peter he recommends limitless forgiveness (Matt 18:21-22), presumably counterbalancing Lamech's boast of culturally approved, limitless blood vengeance (Gen 4:23). Commentators in general do not seem to recognize this contradiction. For them, the first case illustrates the need to correct and direct the sinner to conversion; the second case concerns forgiveness. How are the two pieces of advice related?

SIN = SHAMING A FELLOW BELIEVER

Modern believers often forget that they are heirs to theologically sophisticated notions that developed through twenty centuries of reflection, argumentation, and consensus-building. The Greek word for "sin" in Matthew 18:15, 21 should not be interpreted in the refined modern understanding. Sin here describes a situation in which a person has missed the mark, that is, has failed to meet cultural expectations in relationship with another person. In each of Matthew's examples, the other person is human, a fellow believer, not divine. While this Greek word for "sin" does not necessarily include the idea of a deliberate, intentional transgression, the result in the Mediterranean cultural world is the same whether intentional or not: shame! One person has shamed another.

In this Mediterranean world, every person is honorable. Culture expects each person to maintain and safeguard the honor that derives from birth into a specific family that for generations has accumulated a praiseworthy reputation. To fail is to bring shame to the family name. Outsiders, that is, other families and particularly their males, will attack the reputation of this family in order to shame them. Successfully shaming others increases one's reputation, one's honor.

SHAMING STRATEGIES

A common strategy for shaming others is to ask a question. Relatively few if any questions in the Middle East are honest requests for information. The hope is that the one of whom the question is asked will not know the answer. To trick another into admitting or displaying ignorance is to shame that person. A common defense is to lie, to offer any answer, even if incorrect. Not to answer is an admission of ignorance or an admission that any answer will only result in defeat and shame. Mark's Jesus asked his opponents whether it was permissible to heal the man with the withered hand on the Sabbath, but recognizing the trap Jesus posed to them, they did not respond (3:1-4). In Matthew's version of this same event, the Pharisees asked Jesus a question, but his masterful and indisputable answer shamed them instead (12:9-12).

Jesus' customary defense when asked a question was to reply with a counter question, an insult, or both. When the Pharisees asked Jesus why his disciples did not observe the ritual washing of hands before eating, Jesus countered by asking why they subverted the commandments of God in favor of their traditions (Matt 15:1-20). Then he called them hypocrites (actors), an insult used many times in Matthew's Gospel only by Jesus and only in reference to the Pharisees.

Keeping in mind that publicity is a key element in honor and shame, that is, an audience is always present to witness the event and determine the winner and loser—the one who is shamed and the one whose reputation is enhanced—it is not difficult to appreciate the potential consequences of losing too many such skirmishes. The cumulative effect of Jesus' relentless insults against his opponents could only lead to disaster for him.

VENGEANCE: THE RESPONSE TO BEING SHAMED

At the ordinary level of everyday life, the game of challenge and riposte, or push and shove over matters of honor, results in an increased reputation for the winner and a minor loss for the loser. The loser lives to fight another day. There can be other opportunities to shame the winner and redress the score of the ongoing game.

At a slightly higher level, where the stakes are greater because they involve a threat to, or loss of, life or property, the "loser" or the one perceived to be shamed ought to take revenge. The Israelites assigned this task to the next of kin *(goʾel)* or the avenger, that is, the male in a given family (father, son, brother) whose function it was to remove the stain of shame from the family's reputation. The psalmist compares dutiful sons to arrows in the hands of a warrior. The man who has a quiver full of them will not be put to shame in hostile exchanges with enemies at the gate (Ps 127:4-5). Sirach reminds a father that the result of raising a son successfully is to leave behind after his death an avenger against family enemies and one who would repay the kindness of friends (30:6). So serious was this obligation that provision was made for cities to serve as a refuge from the avenger who might act too hastily against anyone who murdered someone unintentionally (Exod 21:12-14, 23-25; Num 35:9-28).

Recalling that everything human beings know and say about God is rooted in human experience that itself is culturally conditioned, it is no surprise that the biblical God is sensitive to the divine reputation and reacts in typical Mediterranean fashion when that honor is offended. In the moving poem about the relationship between God and Israel penned by Ezekiel, the Lord is angered by Israel's infidelities, takes out his vengeance against her, and is satisfied (Ezek 16:42-43). Leviticus 26 presents an incredible list of vengeful actions toward Israel that God will take if she elects to ignore the Lord and disobey the commandments. Conversely, Israel frequently resorts to tugging at God's sense of honor when she is suffering at the hands of enemies (e.g., Pss 44; 94).

ALTERNATIVES TO REVENGE

In matters of honor and shame, the customary give-and-take can evolve into a feud, which in turn can move on to violence. If blood is shed, a blood feud emerges and can continue for generations. Actually, no one in the Middle East ever wants matters to reach this level. A key person in such an agonistic culture, therefore, is the mediator or peacemaker (see Matt 5:9). Ideally, such a person is at least five links removed in relationship from the feuding parties and acceptable to both. The role of peacemaker or mediator is ordinarily very honorable, unless circumstances render it otherwise (see Luke 12:13-14).

A second strategy for avoiding bloodshed is for the family to declare the guilty member crazy. The life of such a transgressor against another's honor will be spared, but it will be a life hardly worth living. Such a person must remain secluded, cannot have relationships with people outside the family, and must remain under the watchful eye of the family. For group-centered Mediterraneans, such a life is equivalent to a death sentence. The transgressor might as well be dead. According to Mark, in a very short time after Jesus initiated his ministry, he shamed his opponents so strongly that they determined to seek vengeance by killing him. Not long afterward, the family of

Jesus publicly declared he was crazy, perhaps in an effort to avert his death (Mark 3:6, 21).

A third strategy for dealing with shame is to forgo vengeance for some other good reason. The father of the two less-than-respectful sons in Luke 15:11-32 is publicly shamed by his offspring but doesn't harm either as the culture would permit. Indeed, his acceptance of the returning youngster manifests paternal concern to protect him from the ire of the villagers, who wouldn't hesitate to mete out the punishment the father has neglected to do. If "sons are guns," killing these two weakens the father's position against enemies. It also deprives him of social security in his later years. And if these are the only two sons he has, to destroy them is equal to suicide.

Matthew presents a similar example (13:24-30). The man who sowed good seed in his field learns that an enemy has sown weeds among the wheat. In the Middle East, a person inherits not only the family's honor but the family's enemies as well. It would not be difficult for this man to identify the culprits and seek revenge. To everyone's surprise, he doesn't, and the villagers take their daily pleasure from watching the weeds grow with the wheat because of this man's refusal to redress his honor. In the long run, the owner of the field has the last laugh and public revenge against his enemies when he harvests nourishment (wheat) and fuel (weeds) for the winter months. The shaming tactic backfired and shamed the enemy instead.

FORGIVENESS

Just as sin in Matthew 18 is best understood against the backdrop of honor and shame as missing the mark or failing to meet cultural expectations in relationships with another person, forgiveness should be similarly interpreted. The person who forgives forgoes vengeance and freely offers to restore the mutual relationship to its appropriate state. In Matthew, the people involved are fellow believers, insiders to the group. For Matthew's Jesus, Samaritans and non-Judeans (Gentiles) are outsiders and do not fall under consideration here (see 10:5-6 and the consistent reference throughout the Gospel to "brothers" = insiders, fellow believers).

The two different pieces of advice here may reflect different statuses among the insiders. It would seem that equals are considered in verses 15-20 (disciples and other disciples; brother and another brother), while superior and subjects are considered in verses 21-22 (Peter and a brother). The parable (vv. 23-35) appears to confirm this view.

Equals determine the rules of the honor game among themselves. On the one hand, insults, lies, and other behaviors are normal parts of everyday life between equals in this agonistic culture. Each can give as good as he or she gets; the ongoing game is generally a "tie," with a relatively equal number of wins and losses on each side. At a certain point, one party crosses the line and transgresses honor in a way that cannot be easily remedied. This scenario becomes complicated when the transgressing party refuses to continue to play the game or to play "fair" by apologizing to allow the game to continue. This would seem to be the context for "three strikes and you're out."

The situation is quite different between superiors and subjects. A subject cannot challenge a superior, for they are not equals. By the same token, a superior is entitled to ignore a subject (or inferior), as Jesus paid no heed to the Canaanite woman (Matt 15:21-28). But it is often advantageous to a superior, especially a patron (a person of means), to be gracious to a subject. A client may become indebted many times over to a patron and may require repeated release from indebtedness. What the patron may lose temporarily in material wealth will be more than compensated for in honorable reputation. The beneficiary will enhance that reputation on an ongoing basis by repeated public praise of the benefactor. This scenario is not possible among equals.

Thus, if Jesus raised Peter's status among the brothers or disciples (Matt 16:16-19), then it behooved this superior to be gracious and to forgive or forgo vengeance many times over (Matt 18:21-22), perhaps even where there is obstinate refusal to "play the game according to the rules" (Matt 18:15-20).

CONCLUSION

Cultural insights help a modern Western reader to understand what these specific texts about forgiveness might have plausibly meant to Mediterranean audiences, whether the texts are contradictory or accurately reflect Mediterranean society, and why a Mediterranean teacher might have taken such a position. Scholars are agreed that one distinctive aspect of Jesus' teaching is an insistence of forgiveness or the forgoing of vengeance. Matthew's Jesus appears to limit forgiveness to insiders, while Luke's Jesus extends it to outsiders as well. The parable (Matt 18:23-35) raises further questions that are beyond the limits of this present article. Thus, if the king represents God, why does this person play "one strike and you're out!" with the servant? At the very least, the parable suggests that forgiveness poses a difficult challenge for humans and takes time and patience to develop into a habit.

FOR FURTHER READING

Malina, Bruce J., and Richard L. Rohrbaugh. "Forgiveness of Sins." *Social Science Commentary on the Synoptic Gospels*. Minneapolis: Fortress, 1992, p. 63.

———. "Conflict Resolution," ibid., pp. 118ff.

HAIR

The well-known artistic representation of the "Laughing Jesus" is a highly implausible image. His head is cocked back, he is laughing, his open mouth showing a perfect set of teeth. His skin is tanned; his long, blond hair flows in the breeze. He sports a closely trimmed beard. Among the relatively few people who reached the "ripe old age" of thirty in the ancient world, none would have had such a perfect set of teeth. Suetonius (792) says of Emperor Augustus: "His teeth were wide apart, small, and ill-kept." Peasants fared worse. Paleopathologists have not yet found any surviving healthy, adult teeth. Tooth decay, damage, and loss was the rule.

Gleaming eyes would also have been rare, since few escaped the problems caused by trachoma, a virus common in the ancient Middle East that scarred the cornea and distorted vision. Perhaps the most anachronistic feature of this picture is Jesus' long, flowing hair. Scholars believe that Ezekiel's report (44:20) likely reflects common practice in ancient Israel: "They shall not shave their heads or let their locks grow long; they shall only trim the hair of their heads." Early in the Common Era, Paul would remind the Corinthians that "nature" teaches that "for a man to wear long hair is degrading to him [that is, shameful], but if a woman has long hair, it is her pride" [that is, honor: 1 Cor 11:14-15].

Experts note that human hair, like all body symbols, is multivocal, that is, it has an unlimited number of potential meanings. Insofar as hair is part of the local symbol system, much of its significance is local. Paul's comment about long hair needs to be understood in the cultural context of the Hellenistic world in which he lived. Yet, at another level of analysis, there is also a range of crosscultural meanings. The recent insight of Anthony Synnott seems to be a key to discovering the significance at this level. His research indicates that public body symbols such as hair work by way of oppositions (e.g., long-short) to signify that certain types of people are different from others. In Paul's world, length of hair (shoulder length or short) distinguished men from women. Differing hairstyles

65

(braided or free-flowing) distinguished between certain kinds of women (married/virtuous and "loose"). A closer look at hair in the Bible from cultural perspectives helps a reader gain fresh appreciation for familiar passages.

LONG AND SHORT HAIR

Art historians, among others, point out that in Greece, short hair for men began to predominate from the fourth century B.C.E. In the Athens National Museum, one can observe the change in hairstyles from long to short hair on the statues of the *kouroi* (young boys). This piece of archaeological and historical data helps to understand Paul's use of the word "nature" in 1 Corinthians 11:14-15. Clearly by this word he means custom, culturally determined and approved. Moreover, custom means something observed with regularity "as long as people can remember." In Paul's Hellenistic world, this usually referred to three generations at most. Thus Paul says that for as long as anyone can remember (three generations at most), men have worn their hair short.

As the noted archaeologist and biblical scholar Fr. Jerome Murphy-O'Connor demonstrated nearly twenty years ago, hair length itself was less an issue for Paul and others than the styling of long hair on males. Pseudo-Phocylides, a contemporary of Paul, instructed parents: "If a child is a boy, do not let locks grow on his head. Braid not his crown nor make cross-knots on the top of his head. Long hair is not fit for men, but for voluptuous women. Guard the youthful beauty of a comely boy, because many rage for intercourse with a man" (*Sentences*, vv. 210-214).

Philo raged: "Such people deserve that one should burn with zeal to spill their blood in obedience to the Torah, which commands that one should kill with impunity the pervert who falsified the stamp of nature, not permitting him to live a day or even an hour, since he is a disgrace to himself, to his family, to his country, and to the whole human race" (*Special Laws*, 3:38).

The statements of Paul, Pseudo-Phocylides, and Philo clearly link long, stylized hair on a man with homosexuality. Their main concern is that long hair blurs the distinction between the sexes. The ancient Mediterranean world was rigidly divided along gender lines. To blur the lines was to introduce confusion and chaos into society and the order God placed there at creation.

In the ancient Mediterranean world, where boys were raised exclusively by the women until the age of puberty, with little to no contact with males, gender ambiguity was common. Upon entry into the men's world, pubescent boys were subjected to vigorous physical discipline, which they were expected to bear stoically, without crying or complaining (see Prov 13:24; 19:18; etc.). Men spent their adult lives proving and demonstrating manliness. Jesus' desire to "mother hen" the inhabitants of Jerusalem (Matt 23:37) or Paul's claim to be in "birth pains" until Christ is formed in the Galatians (4:19) might plausibly be interpreted as vestiges of gender ambiguity. By deliberately choosing to wear long, stylized hair, a man would be yielding to this ambiguity, presumably embracing homosexuality, and thereby jeopardizing divinely willed order in society.

NAZIRITES

Some scholars think that the reference to Paul's cutting his hair at Cenchreae (Acts 18:18) indicates that he had made a temporary Nazirite vow. By this vow to abstain from all products of the grapevine and from cutting or shaving one's hair, a person was especially set aside as sacred to God (see Num 6:1-21). The dedication could be lifelong, as with Samson (Judg 13:5, 7), Samuel (1 Sam 1:11), and John the Baptist (Luke 1:15), or for a short while, as with Paul (Acts 18:18) and others (see Acts 21:24; compare 1 Macc 3:49).

During the time of his temporary vow, Paul's hair could not have grown to any noticeably significant length. During a lifelong vow, however, the hair would grow quite long. Paul was certainly aware of this and with the stories of long-haired holy men in the Bible. Since there is no evidence that these holy men groomed or styled their long hair, Paul probably would not have disapproved of the length or style of their hair.

Scholars speculate that renouncing every form of the fruit of the vine was a symbolic rejection of Canaanite culture that preceded and co-existed with Israelite life. But what did long hair symbolize? Or in the case of the Nazirite, was the symbolism located in not cutting the hair?

THE SYMBOLISM OF HAIR

Jeannette Marie Mageo, an anthropologist who recently investigated the symbolism of hair, concluded that culturally shared fantasies about social events played out on one's own body or that of others can be the "symbolic body." This body has several features that differ from the physical body. For one, it has replaceable parts. Shaving the hair can symbolize castration, but castration is irreversible, while shaved hair will grow back again. Symbolic castration through the hair, however, always allows that the person can choose at some time to resume normal sexual activity, since the genitals have not been directly affected. Medieval scholars suggest that the tonsure of clerics carried such a symbolic meaning. In the Bible, as in many cultures, women's long hair is considered sexually attractive (Song 4:1; 6:5); hence shaving it can be a symbolic sacrifice of sexuality, which can always be resumed.

Secondly, the symbolic body allows multiple representation for parts, or "repeated parts." Thus head hairs are hairs, but in some cultures they also represent sex organs. After raising Lazarus from the dead, Jesus dined with him in Bethany (John 12:1-8). Remember that in the ancient Mediterranean family, women and men did not eat in the same place at the same time. The fact that Martha served could indicate that she was a widow. Such a status could also explain why she lived with her brother; perhaps her father had already died.

At the same time, her sister Mary's behavior was very inappropriate even for a widow. Not only did she intrude into male space (as in Luke 10:39), but using her hair to wipe Jesus' feet, which she had just anointed with nard, could plausibly convey sexual innuendo. In the Hebrew Bible, feet are often a euphemism or symbol for the male sexual organs (see Isa 7:20). John's Jesus, however, interprets her symbolic actions as relating to his imminent death. (Jesus also seems to reinterpret the potential sexual symbolism in Luke 7:36-50 along similar lines.)

Thirdly, repeated parts of the symbolic body imply an attribution of male and female genitals to all bodies. In each culture, Mageo observes, males and females possess this hermaphroditic body in fantasy. This suggests a second possible interpretation for two texts mentioned above. Paul's description of experiencing the pains of childbirth while Jesus Messiah is being formed in the Galatian believers (4:19) may be more than evidence of typical gender ambiguity among males. According to Mageo's insight, in his fantasy about his ministry among the Galatians, Paul can legitimately speak of birth pains. Perhaps Jesus' desire to "mother hen" the residents of Jerusalem (Matt 23:37) is a similar fantasy.

NAZIRITE HAIR

What was the symbolism of hair for the Nazirite? Hair continues to grow after a person's death and symbolizes life in many cultures. The Nazirite refused to cut his hair as a sign of the total dedication of his life to God. There was no interest in trimming the hair in order to make oneself attractive to other humans or to abide by cultural, and hence temporal and unpredictable, custom.

Mageo observed a connection between hair and spirits. In Samoa, where she conducted her fieldwork, female spirits were predominant possessors and were jealous of the long hair of females. To dismiss the spirit, the healer cut the girl's hair. Such an insight prompts a reader to notice how often in the Samson saga the hero is possessed by the spirit of the Lord (Judg 13:25; 14:6, 19; 15:14), who provides him with extraordinary strength to perform super-manly deeds. Since this strength leaves him when his hair is cut (Judg 16:19-20), it is plausible to conclude that in the case of this Nazirite, uncut hair symbolized abiding and undiminished strength deriving from the spirit of the Lord (Judg 16:22).

The distinctive vesture and hair style identifies this father and son as ultra-orthodox Jews. The flowing hair and beards reflect a literal interpretation of Leviticus 19:27.

THE BEARD

It would seem that the custom of wearing a beard or being clean shaven underwent the same cyclical changes in the biblical world as other styles, for instance, men wearing their hair long or short. Anthropologists have noted systematic cycles of changes in hairstyles in various cultures, and the changes were frequently related to changes in female dress.

Leviticus (19:27) prohibits trimming the beard, and the psalmist (133:2) describes the anointing oil running down the beard. Thus, wearing a beard was definitely a custom at certain periods in history, and perhaps was present, if not prevalent, throughout history in the Mediterranean world. In general, the beard symbolizes vigor, wisdom, energy, and sexual potency. The Cynics believed that it was as essential an ornament for men as the mane was for a horse or lion. Perhaps the closely trimmed beard on the picture of the "Laughing Jesus" is the only plausible feature.

Shaving the beard had many meanings. In some cases it symbolized anger and shame (Ezra 9:3); in many cases it was a part of the mourning process (Jer 41:5; Ezek 5:1). Like hair on the head, the beard, too, symbolized male sexuality. Hanun intended to shame David by shaving half the beard of each of David's emissaries and cutting their garments at the hip so as to expose their genitals (2 Sam 10:4). The paired symbols (hair and garments) reinforce their common meaning. Once again, the meaning of the beard as symbol derives as much from what one does to the hair as from its length or style.

CONCLUSION

A colleague relishes reminding his classes that according to Genesis, God created human beings in the divine image and likeness. These creatures have been returning the favor to the Deity ever since. Christians insist that Jesus was like us in all things except sin, hence the popularity of the "laughing Jesus" picture. A more realistic view would suggest a very different picture.

FOR FURTHER READING

Delaney, Carol. "Untangling the Meanings of Hair in Turkish Society." *Anthropological Quarterly* 67 (1994) 159–172.

Derret, J. Duncan M. "Religious Hair." *Man*, n.s., 8 (1973) 100–103.

Edwards, Douglas R. "Dress and Ornamentation." *Anchor Bible Dictionary* 2:232–238.

Glowczewski, Barbara. "Death, Woman and 'Value Production': The Circulation of Hair Strings Among the Walpiri of the Central Australian Desert." *Ethnology* 22 (1983) 225–239.

Klaniczay, Gabor. "Fashionable Beards and Heretic Rags." Chap. 4 in *The Uses of Supernatural Power: The Transformation of Popular Religion in Medieval and Early-Modern Europe*. Trans. Susan Singerman. Ed. Karen Margolis. Princeton, N.J.: Princeton University Press, 1990.

Mageo, Jeannette Marie. "Hairdos and Don'ts: Hair Symbolism and Sexual History in Samoa." *Man*, n.s., 29 (1994) 407–432.

Murphy-O'Connor, Jerome. "Sex and Logic in 1 Corinthians 11:2-16." *Catholic Biblical Quarterly* 42 (1980) 482–500.

Synnott, Anthony. "Hair." Chap. 4 in *The Body Social: Symbolism, Self and Society*. London and New York: Routledge, 1993.

Thompson, Cynthia L. "Hairstyles, Head-coverings and St. Paul: Portraits from Roman Corinth." *Biblical Archaeologist* 51 (1988) 99–115.

HEALING

Sickness is a common and universal human experience, but cultures differ from one another as well as within themselves in what they identify as sickness, how they experience it, and the remedy they seek for it. Modern readers of the New Testament stories of sickness and healing need to put aside modern understandings and search out what the biblical author intended. Here are a few notions proper to the biblical situation that will help today's believer to be a respectful and considerate reader.

1. The New Testament stories about sick people (lepers, blind, lame, mute, etc.) report episodes of illness, misfortunes with serious social consequences. Not having a microscope, biblical people could not know of germs, viruses, and diseases.

2. For biblical people, every misfortune was caused by a "who" (God, evil spirit) and not a "what" (germs, viruses, genes, hormones). The problem, therefore, could only be helped by a "who" rather than a "what" (injection, pill, ointment). Even when Jesus used spittle or mud, he was the one who healed.

3. Modern readers look for cures or a pill or technique that will kill the germ, remove the cancer, or provide a new limb. Biblical people above all looked for meaning in their experience of sickness. In modern technical terms, we call this healing. In other words, healing takes place always for all people in all cultures; all people ultimately come up with some meaning in life, no matter what their condition and no matter what happens.

4. Sick people in the Bible are those who have fallen from an appropriate human state or condition of human integrity or wholeness. Health as reflected in the New Testament, therefore, can be defined as "a state of complete well-being and not merely the absence of disease or infirmity." Such a definition fits with the Mediterranean emphasis on the value of simply living or being rather than on achieving or doing. The modern Italian proverb says "It's sweet to do nothing."

The cultural system of the United States prefers the value of achieving much more than simply being. This culture has difficulty enjoying simple existence; it needs to be ever active about things. Hence a definition of health suitable to the United States is "the ability to perform those functions that allow the organism to maintain itself in the range of activity open to most other members of the species."

In the New Testament, then, Jesus heals people by restoring them to a proper state: lepers are made clean, the blind see, the mute can speak. In the United States, the expectation is that a sick person be restored to function, to doing, in order to go back to work and be a productive member of society once more.

These four basic understandings proper to the Mediterranean world can help a modern believer read the New Testament with respect and without seeking from a foreign culture "all the direct answers for living" in the United States or any other culture.

SICKNESS AND HEALING IN LUKE–ACTS

Luke's report of Jesus' sermon in the Capernaum synagogue (4:14-30) presents the main guideline for grasping Luke's interpretation of Jesus' healing ministry. Here is the structure of the text from Isaiah that Jesus read (Isa 61:1-2):

> A Preach good news to the POOR
> B proclaim release to CAPTIVES
> C SIGHT TO THE BLIND
> B' liberty for the OPPRESSED
> A' proclaim acceptable YEAR OF THE LORD

The "C" line casts into bold relief Jesus' chief healing activity according to Luke: sight for the blind. The "B" lines highlight a second focus: freedom for captives and oppressed. The "A" lines point to a third focus: good news for the poor. It is possible to cluster all Jesus' healing activities reported by Luke into these three categories. If read with the above guidelines in mind, these sickness and healing stories can be appreciated in their cultural context so as to be better probed or translated for contemporary interests.

BLINDNESS

A modern reader who searches for passages discussing physical blindness in Luke–Acts is surprised to find but a handful. Jesus tells a parable illustrated by physically blind men (6:39-42), discusses the "eye biology" of his day (11:33-36), and heals an apparently physically blind man (18:35-43). While Luke assures us that Jesus bestowed sight "on many that were blind" (7:21-22), he relates only one such healing story! Yet Luke appears to emphasize that blindness truly does occupy a central place in Jesus' ministry (Luke 4:18; 7:21).

By focusing too narrowly on physical blindness (understandable, since in Western culture this is a serious loss and a subject for specialized healers called ophthalmologists), a reader will miss the majority of Luke's "blindness" passages. It is never a good practice to read any single passage, like the healing of the blind man in Luke 18, outside its total context in Luke's complete work, which includes not only the Third Gospel but also the Acts of the Apostles. The skilled interpreter keeps in mind the entire writing of the author.

From this perspective, the conclusion of Luke's two-volume work, Acts 28:23-31, takes on special importance. After spending an entire day with the leaders of the Jews in an attempt to convince them about Jesus, Paul is disappointed to see them depart in disagreement among themselves. He comments by citing Isaiah 6:9-10, a text that highlights people who see but never perceive, and hear but never understand. Among our biblical ancestors, the heart and eyes together were involved in seeing and understanding and interpreting.

By concentrating the reader's attention on blindness (Luke 4:18) and the refusal to see and understand (Acts 28:23-31), the beginning and end of Luke's two volumes not only confirm that blindness and restoration to sight is central to Luke's report but also invite the reader to look beyond physical blindness to other types, especially social and cultural blindness, namely, a refusal to believe and accept Jesus' true identity.

In this light, many other "blindness/seeing" passages stand out. The parable that begins with an illustration of physical blindness then talks about people whose vision is skewed or impaired (6:39-42). The parable about the sower and the seed (8:4-15) is "illuminated" by the image of a lamp whose light must be seen. Jesus' thanksgiving prayer to God for his revelation to "babes" upon the return of the seventy-two disciples concludes with this beatitude: "Blessed are the eyes which see what you see!" (10:21-24).

The evil generation seeks a sign but refuses to heed it (11:29-32). Jesus advises that people get an "eye checkup!" (11:33-36). If their eyes are not working well, how else will they be able to see and interpret what they see (12:54-56)? People who want to see revelation of the Son of Man may actually miss it (17:22-37)! Poor Herod hoped so desperately to see Jesus in hopes of witnessing a "sign" that he missed the opportunity his encounter did offer (23:8). On the other hand, when the crowds saw Jesus die and everything that had taken place, they returned home beating their breasts (23:48).

In the broader context created by these texts, it becomes clear that for Luke blindness refers especially to refusal to see and understand even as it includes physical blindness. The healing activities of Jesus in this Gospel and of his disciples in Acts are directed to facilitating and improving understanding that should accompany seeing.

Some scholars say that the blind man's address of Jesus as "Son of David" (in Luke 18:38, a first-time occurrence in that Gospel) is borrowed from Mark with no special significance. Perhaps its significance is similar to the point Mark makes by sandwiching Jesus' three predictions of his passion between two stories of healed blind men (8:22-26 and 10:46-52). It is easier for physically blind people to regain sight than it is for sighted people to truly understand Jesus. In Luke, the physically blind man knows Jesus' true identity, while sighted people repeatedly refuse to listen and understand. The healed man immediately follows Jesus and glorifies God.

One pastoral conclusion to be drawn from this analysis of texts is that modern Bible readers, whether blessed with good vision or suffering impaired vision, should frequently pray for insight and continued growth in the knowledge and awareness of Jesus' true identity. The Second Vatican Council urged believers to search diligently for the "honest truth about Jesus" (*Dei Verbum* no. 19) that the evangelists present. Moreover, the Pontifical Biblical Commission cautioned about adding "imaginative details which are not consonant with the truth" (*The Historical Truth of the Gospels,* no. XIII).

PRISONERS AND OPPRESSED

The New Testament reports no instances in which Jesus literally visited prisons or freed prisoners. But people assaulted or possessed by unclean or evil spirits or demons can properly be described as oppressed or possessed. This, in fact, appears to be how Luke intended Jesus' sermon text to be understood. The man in the Capernaum synagogue was thrown to the ground by his demon and thus oppressed (4:31-37), while the boy who was convulsed is described as "seized" or possessed (9:37-43). In this last-mentioned episode, notice that literal translations refrain from describing this individual with a modern term ("epileptic") but use instead the ancient understanding ("possessed") reflected in the phrase "a spirit seizes him."

To properly understand and interpret passages describing the influence of evil or unclean spirits, demons, or Satan upon human beings, the modern reader must keep the following principles in mind.

1. In the Bible, God's people believe that God is and should be in charge of every dimension of existence. Often God exercises this

dominion through the spirit. This is life as it should be lived. This would be another way in which biblical people would define and understand good health: a state of being in which one lives faithfully and obediently under the influence of God's spirit.

In Luke, the Spirit is especially prominent. Jesus is conceived by the power of the Holy Spirit (1:35), and he received the Spirit at his baptism (3:21). Still under the impulse of this Spirit, Jesus went into the desert to do battle with a malicious spirit, the devil (4:1-3). Then, returning in the power of the Spirit, Jesus taught in synagogues and in one sermon says, "The spirit of the Lord is upon me," and he continues his ministry.

2. Some people are overcome or possessed by an evil or unclean spirit, a demon, Satan. This is sickness, for it is not an appropriate state of life. Such people can be considered prisoners of, and oppressed by, evil spirits. A summary statement of Jesus' ministry in Luke 4:40-41 suggests that many people suffered from this illness: Jesus healed people sick with a variety of illnesses, and "demons also came out of many."

In the synagogue at Capernaum, the spirit of an unclean demon threw a man down without harming him (4:31-37). In the land of the Gerasenes, a possessed man lived in bizarre fashion among tombs (8:26-39). A lad possessed by a demon was convulsed by him and made to foam at the mouth (9:37-43a). Sometimes the demon could make a person mute (11:14), and at other times many demons might rule a single person (11:24-26).

All these people were considered ill. Their lack of good health consisted in the fact that they were not under the dominion of God but were rather dominated by unclean spirits.

3. Jesus proved himself to be more powerful than the evil and impure spirits. "By the finger of God," Jesus drove these demons out of those whom they had made prisoners or taken possession of. He freed a man from the unclean spirit that possessed him (4:31-37) and freed Simon's mother-in-law from the demon named "Fever" that had possessed her (4:38-39). There is even a summary statement similar to the one about his healing of the blind: Jesus healed people sick with a variety of diseases, and "demons also came out of many" (4:40-41). Only in Luke does Jesus identify himself as an exorcist: "Behold, I cast out demons and perform cures today and tomorrow" (13:32).

Disciples can do the same in Jesus' name: the seventy-two rejoice at their success (Luke 10:17); the deacon Philip casts out unclean spirits (Acts 8:7); Paul's power against evil spirits is exerted through handkerchiefs and cloths (Acts 19:12). Even "unofficial" disciples are powerful in Jesus' name! (Luke 9:49).

Mainstream American culture does not believe in spirits, though some believers do literally accept spirit intrusions into human life just as reported in the Bible. To the spirits mentioned there, they add the demons of alcoholism, spouse and child abuse, substance abuse, and many other illnesses. Other modern believers prefer to interpret stories of spirit possession as instances of a lack or loss of good mental health.

Both groups of believers fail to grasp the meaning that the biblical author intended to express and actually expressed in these stories. Luke's main point is that God ought properly to be in charge of existence. Where that dominion has been usurped, believers should implore Jesus to restore it. God's dominion is as important in modern health concerns as it was in antiquity.

THE POOR

Since economics is the major social institution of United States citizens, there is a tendency to interpret the word "poor" economically. Among our ancestors in the faith, however, kinship was one of the two major social institutions. In this context, poor people were those who had temporarily lost or were lacking their appropriate social status, inherited or acquired. They had in some sense become disconnected from kin. This understanding offers a fresh perspective for interpreting the remaining healing stories in Luke–Acts.

1. Illness removes a person from status and disturbs kinship patterns, both actual and fictive. Being dead or near dead (the centurion's servant: Luke 7:1-10; the widow's son: Luke 7:11-16; Jairus' daughter: Luke 8:40-42a, 49-56) obviously removes a person from the human family as well as one's own family. The dead have no status whatever.

People who suffer from the skin problem called "leprosy" are excluded from the worshiping community. This human experience was much more depressing than the skin lesions. Some individuals lost the capability of purposeful activity (the paralytic: Luke 5:17-26; the man with a withered hand: Luke 6:6-11; the crippled woman: Luke 13:10-17; women experiencing difficulty conceiving: Luke 1:24, 35; or women experiencing menstrual irregularity: Luke 8:42b-48). Others lost the capacity for self-expressive speech and hearing (Zechariah: Luke 1:20, 64; the mute man: Luke 11:14-23; the man in the garden whose ear was cut off: Luke 22:47-54a). All these people could be viewed as poor in that they did not possess the status proper to the human condition, their sex, position, or group membership.

2. Jesus' healing activity in each instance restored individuals to their proper status, to a desirable state of being, to life as God intended

it to be lived. Lepers could join the worshiping community, women could resume their duties, etc.

Bible readers in the United States will likely experience great difficulty appreciating this interpretation of these illness stories. Our emphasis on activity and achievement tends to interpret many of these illnesses as an inability to perform tasks rather than as an undesirable state of existence. Did not Jesus himself say: "Why do you call me 'Lord, Lord' but do not *do* what I command?" (Luke 6:46). Yet the sterling example of Jesus "doing" the Father's will is his prayer of resignation in the garden (Luke 22:42), submissively accepting his entire passion with all its suffering. Our ancestors perceived, not something Jesus did (suffer), but a state he exemplified (obedience).

Contemporary American believers should recognize and embrace and bless their cultural emphasis on activity, on the ability to perform, and all related values. At the same time, they must refrain from imposing this value upon these healing stories about our biblical ancestors, who cherished the proper state of being and human integrity much more than doing. The paralytic who lay at the pool thirty-eight years was to be pitied, not because of his physical condition, but because he had no one to put him into the water when it moved. Totally bereft of kin, he failed to make friends, a cultural necessity for "economic" survival. Jesus' healing involved becoming his first friend.

In modern American culture, as in many cultures, value preferences often change at different stages or conditions of life. Our overwhelming emphasis on performance in the workaday world stops quite suddenly at retirement or debilitating illness. Then one needs to learn the pleasure of living, the sheer enjoyment of existence while others "do."

This cluster of healing stories shows Jesus helping individuals to measure up to acceptable cultural expectations. He truly restored meaning and joy to the lives of those individuals. Contemporary believers can take comfort in that lesson and feel encouraged to remain faithful to their cultural emphasis on "doing" by asking Jesus to help them personally or through others, to convince their culture that "the disabled are able" and that "they also serve who only stand and wait" (John Milton, "On His Blindness").

FOR FURTHER READING

Pilch, John J. "Sickness and Healing in Luke–Acts." In *The Social World of Luke–Acts: A Handbook of Models for Interpretation.* Ed. Jerome H. Neyrey, S.J., 181–209. Peabody, Mass.: Hendrickson, 1991.

_____. *Healing in the New Testament: Insights from Medical and Mediterranean Anthropology.* Minneapolis: Fortress Press, forthcoming (1999).

HOLY MAN

How did Jesus know there were fish to be caught after Peter and his partners spent a futile night fishing on that same sea (Luke 5:1-11)? Did Jesus and Peter really walk on the Sea of Galilee (Matt 14:22-33)? Modern Western Bible readers ask these questions because so-called "laws of nature" say it can't be done. Interpreters suggest that the evangelist added certain astonishing dimensions to each event or perhaps even created the story to create a specific impression.

For our ancestors in the faith, every event had to have a personal cause. They did not know or recognize impersonal ("laws of nature") or secondary causes (viruses; germs). In other words, their understanding of persons was much richer than the modern notion. A key person in their world was the Holy Man, someone who had relatively easy access to God and who could obtain and do many favors for fellow human beings. In Hebrew, this person was called a *hasid* or *saddiq*. Jesus and other prophets were considered Holy Men. Other examples would include Pythagoras, Hanina ben Dosa, and Honi. Understanding two characteristics of ancient Holy Men and their culture gives us a better appreciation of some biblical passages. One is the special relationship of Holy Men with animals and plants. Another is their ability to adopt alternate views of reality.

HOLY MEN AND ANIMALS

For about thirty or more years, a special branch of anthropology that specializes in animal communication has been developing. One pioneer and expert in this area is Thomas Sebeok. He and his colleagues have investigated the ways in which animals communicate with one another and ways in which animals and humans communicate. Their discoveries are fascinating. One general mode of animal communication, technically called "biological acoustics" or "bio-acoustics," is by means of sound. This can be through the air, as with birds, the most vocal of animals, or under water, as with fish and aquatic insects. Some fish generate electric fields that may also be used for signaling. These are similar to the song displays of birds and may have a territorial function.

Could it be that the Holy Man Jesus, like other Holy Men in antiquity, was particularly sensitive to animal communication? Did he hear or sense the fish communicating with one another or with other species in the sea so as to know when to give his apostles a precise command to lower the nets for a catch at just the right time? In such a scenario, Jesus' skill would hardly be out of the ordinary for Holy Men in his culture.

The situation is similar in the matter of communicating with animals. Iamblichus (fourth century C.E.), one of three famous biographers of the ancient Greek Holy Man Pythagoras (sixth century B.C.E.), described how the Holy Man communicated with an ox.

> At Taras he [Pythagoras] saw an ox, in a field of mixed fodder, munching on ripe beans as well. He went over to the oxherd and advised him to tell the ox to abstain from beans. The oxherd made fun of his suggestion. "I don't speak Ox," he said, "and if you do you're wasting your advice on me; you should warn the ox." So Pythagoras went up and spent a long time whispering in the bull's ear. The bull promptly stopped eating the bean plant, of his own accord, and they say he never ate beans again. He lived to a very great age at Taras, growing old in the temple of Hera. Everyone called him "Pythagoras' holy bull" and he ate a human diet, offered him by people who met him (*On the Pythagorean Life*, 61).

Historians of medicine note that some Pythagoreans had a lethal allergy to beans. Pythagoras thus offered life-saving advice to the bull.

Should it be surprising, then, to hear Job challenge his accusers by saying: "Ask the beasts, and they will teach you; the birds of the air, and they will tell you; or the plants of the earth, and they will teach you; and the fish of the sea will declare to you" (Job 12:7-8)? All creation knows and will tell anyone who asks that God is in charge of everything, the personal agent responsible for all that happens.

Matthew (4:1-11) and Luke (4:1-13) rely on "Q" (the source of material common to Matthew and Luke, mostly sayings of Jesus, that is not from Mark) for their interpretation of the "temptation of Jesus" to report that Jesus wins a Scripture-quoting contest with a spirit and thereby demonstrates unswerving fidelity to the Father, confirming the Father's judgment at the baptism. Mark's version of this same event (1:12-13) makes no mention of specific tests but reports that Jesus "was with the wild beasts." Some commentators relate Mark's account to the Genesis 2 report that the first earthling lived in harmony with the wild beasts prior to the fall. Others suggest that Jesus fits the description of the righteous person (or Holy

Man) in Psalm 91:11-13, who is protected by ministering spirits from dangerous animals. Perhaps in line with Job, Mark's Jesus-as-Holy Man was exploring and learning his identity and destiny in conversation with the wild beasts and then testing his insight in a contest with a spirit, as detailed in Matthew and Luke.

HOLY MEN AND PLANTS

Job also advised asking the plants of the earth for instruction about God. Modern research seems first now to be understanding something the ancients knew very well: humans and the plant world can communicate with each other. In the Greek Magical Papyri, there is a spell for picking a plant:

> Use it before sunrise. The spell to be spoken: "I am picking you, such and such a plant, with my five-fingered hand, I, N.N., and I am bringing you home so that you may work for me for a certain purpose. I adjure you by the undefiled name of the god: if you pay no heed to me, the earth which produced you will no longer be watered as far as you are concerned—ever in life again; if I fail in this operation, MOUTHABAR NACH BARNACHOCHA BRAEO MENDA LAUBRAASSE PHASPHA BENDEO (these are magical words); fulfill for me the perfect charm" (*Papyri Graecae Magicae*, 4:286-295).

Recall when the Holy Man Jesus, during a journey from Bethany to Jerusalem, sought figs to allay his hunger but found only leaves, "for it was not the season for figs" (Mark 11:12-14). He cursed the fig tree, saying, "May no one ever eat fruit from you again." When they next passed the tree in the morning, it had withered away to its roots. Peter was astonished, but Jesus replied with an exhortation to fidelity and loyalty (Mark 11:20-25). One element that cannot be omitted from any interpretation of this scene is the ancient world's belief that a plant could hear and understand human speech. And just as the well-known pan-Mediterranean custom of casting the evil eye could bring injury, illness, and even death to another human being, a curse could work similar deleterious effects against plants, especially when uttered by a Holy Man.

ALTERNATE REALITY

Cultural anthropologists have discovered that approximately 90 percent of the cultures on the face of this planet have and enjoy the ability to enter into trance, ecstasy, or a similar altered state of consciousness with ease. The percentage is highest among Native Americans, but still high among circum-Mediterranean cultures. The experience is rare and suspect in the modern West. Contemporary psychiatrists explain that Western cultures since the Enlightenment have become so fond of objectivity and the ability to stand apart from the self to observe the self that they have extinguished this pan-human capability.

Studies of this phenomenon indicate that it follows a pattern. The content of the experience is often vacuous; one's culture provides the information needed to interpret the experience. The people one sees are not recognized at first. Then, after an assurance from that person ("Do not be afraid") and a revelation of identity ("It is I, N.N."), the one experiencing the vision or trance can dialogue with the person seen. In general, experiences in altered states of consciousness provide the person with new information or, more commonly, solutions to troubling problems (this includes healing, as in the visions experienced at Asclepian healing shrines).

JESUS WALKS ON THE SEA OF GALILEE

When modern Western scholars explore the Gospel story of Jesus walking on the Sea of Galilee (Matt 14:22-33), they tend to do so from the perspective of "the laws of nature." Human beings cannot walk on the surface of water in the way a fly or insect can. Such an action is contrary to the "laws of nature." Therefore this event must be a miracle, that is, something contrary to the laws of nature. This familiar discussion was, of course, foreign to the ancient mind. The ancients had no concept equivalent to the contemporary understanding of "laws of nature." When Paul, for instance, argues that "nature" tells us it is improper for men to wear their hair long, he is describing cultural custom, not "human" or any other "nature."

In the ancient world, whatever happens, happens; it is real. A person is responsible for what happens—if not God, then some spirit (e.g., "by the finger of Beelzebul"). If no human being can walk on the surface of the sea but one human being is seen doing it, then some other person (God or other spirit) must have enabled him or her to do it. This is one way in which the ancient reader would hear this story.

But there is another, perhaps culturally more plausible way to interpret the story. Matthew may be recounting an experience the disciples had of Jesus in an altered state of consciousness. According to Matthew, Jesus went up into the hills "alone" (very rare in Middle Eastern culture) to pray. His friends were in a boat on the sea. Late in the night, Jesus came to them, walking on the sea. The fact that the disciples were at first alarmed and then misidentified the person they saw ("a ghost") strongly suggests that this was an experience in alternate reality, a trance. True to the nature of this experience, the person seen allays their fear and identifies himself: "Take heart, it is I [Jesus]; have no fear" (Matt 14:27).

But Peter was still skeptical; he could not believe his eyes. "If it is you, Lord, bid me come to you on the water" (Matt 14:28). The hypothetical question is revealing. Who else but Jesus could walk on water? Why, any other Holy Man, of course. Indeed, anyone enabled by a more powerful person (good or evil spirit) could do this. Would a stranger be responsive to Peter's request? Was Peter peeking in on someone else's experience? Assured by the person in the vision, Peter ventured out, only to sink shortly thereafter. The trance was shattered, but it achieved its effect. The disciples learned new information. They were urged not to allow their loyalty to Jesus flag. And they recognized Jesus as divinely favored, a son of God (Matt 14:32).

A little while later, in another experience of alternate consciousness, the disciples would witness Jesus experiencing the Father in an alternate state of consciousness. Tradition has called this vision (Matt 17:9) the "transfiguration" of Jesus. Antiquity records at least

Detail of a mosaic of the transfiguration in the Basilica of the Transfiguration, Mount Tabor, Israel. The church was built in the 1920s.

one other experience like this, when a mother sees the healing god Asclepius minister to her sleeping son, who simultaneously sees this same god answering his prayer for help. Upon awaking, the son tells the mother even before she can tell him what she saw. The result was that the disciples again learned new, even more precise information about Jesus: "This is my beloved Son, with whom I am well pleased; listen to him" (Matt 17:1-8).

CONCLUSION

Jesus' experiences fit the pattern of experiences shared by many Holy Men in antiquity. They were able to communicate with plants and animals. They and their admirers (or disciples) enjoyed experiences in alternate states of consciousness. For Jesus, his baptism and the transfiguration were such experiences with the Father. Bystanders, for example John the Baptist at the baptism, would have been aware that such an event was taking place even if the bystanders did not participate in it. Bystanders could also interpret such an event differently (e.g., "a voice from heaven," "thunder," "an angel spoke to him": see John 12:28-29).

Jesus' followers shared his experience of altered consciousness in the event we know as the transfiguration. But the most significant experience for the followers was their communication with the Risen Jesus, the raised Holy Man, in events tradition calls the resurrection appearances. Culturally, these may have been experiences of Jesus in altered states of consciousness. We Westerners would do well to regain this lost, pan-human potential our ancestors enjoyed.

FOR FURTHER READING

Goodman, Felicitas. *Where the Spirits Ride the Wind: Trance Journeys and Other Ecstatic Experiences*. Bloomington and Indianapolis, Ind.: Indiana University Press, 1990.

Pilch, John J. "Altered States of Consciousness: A 'Kitbashed' Model." *Biblical Theology Bulletin* 26 (1996) 133-138.

_____. "Appearances of the Risen Jesus in Cultural Context: Experiences of Alternate Reality." *Biblical Theology Bulletin* 28 (1998) 52-60.

_____. "The Transfiguration of Jesus: An Experience of Alternate Reality." In *Modelling Early Christianity: Social Scientific Studies of the New Testament in Its Context*. Ed. Philip F. Esler, 47-64. London and New York: Routledge, 1995.

HOUSE

What kind of houses did our biblical ancestors have? Were there many rooms or only one room? Did the children have a room of their own? Did they have pets? What image did Jesus have in mind when he said: "In my Father's house there are many rooms or dwelling places" (John 14:2)? By itself, the Bible doesn't provide enough information to answer such questions. We turn for help to other sciences such as archaeology, cultural geography, and cultural anthropology.

IN THE BEGINNING

Primitive people had two ready-made shelters: trees and caves. When these were not available or proved inadequate, people invented substitutes. The tent replaced the tree; the built house, usually stone, replaced the cave. In countries like Greece, which has an abundance of trees, or Egypt, whose rains are moderate and light, the tent gradually evolved into booths or wooden huts, and ultimately pillared architecture. In Palestine, which experiences torrential rains, the limestone rock is pockmarked with caves, and the rock is easily quarried for the construction of houses. Stone houses seem to have been known in Palestine from earliest times.

Tents. Jabal is honored as the founder of the nomadic lifestyle, the ancestor of "those who live in tents and have livestock" (Gen 4:20). The patriarchs lived this form of life (Gen 18:1; 24:67; 31:25). The ark of the covenant was sheltered for a long time in a tent (2 Sam 7:2). Tents were erected for a newly married couple, and contemporary Jewish couples are married under a canopy reflective of a tent.

The contemporary Bedouin tent gives us a glimpse into the ancient world. The material of the tent is black haircloth, spun and woven from goat's hair (Song 1:5; 4:1). The tent is rectangular in shape, supported on nine poles, approximately six to seven feet high. The poles are arranged in rows of three, the middle row being slightly higher than the other two. A curtain of this same material is stretched across the width of the tent to separate the women's section from the more public one. Strangers never enter the women's part, and valuables are usually kept there. It is the women's task to pitch and strike the tents, and then to take them down and pack them for travel. Even today tents like these dot the hillside along the road from Bethlehem toward Hebron.

Bedouin and camels.

Caves. The oldest cave dwellings in Israel have been discovered on Mount Carmel. They date from about 8000 B.C.E. Cave archaeology is notoriously difficult, but specialists are convinced that the practice of living in caves was never widespread in Palestine. Caves were a refuge during times of crisis (Gen 19:30; Judg 6:2; 1 Sam 13:6) but served more frequently as storage places for grain or livestock, hiding places for bandits and their booty, and burials.

Some famous caves in Palestine are Machpelah, the burial place of Abraham's family (Gen 23:19); the caves at Qumran, in some which the now famous scrolls were found; and the cave at Bethlehem, where tradition holds that Jesus was born.

It is not the Gospels but Justin the Martyr and the Protoevangelium of James (both from the second century) that record this information. The archaeologist Fr. Jerome Murphy-O'Connor explains that houses in this area are still built in front of caves, and it is possible that this was the context of Jesus' birth. The manger, or feeding trough for animals, is often cut out of rock at the sides of a cave where the animals are stabled.

STONE HOUSES

The Bible makes various references to specific parts of houses such as roofs (2 Sam 11:2; Mark 2:4), upper rooms (Mark 14:15; Acts 1:13), doors (John 20:26), courtyards (Matt 26:58, 69), and the like, but offers no full description of a typical house. Here again archaeology assists. Though archaeologists have little more than foundations and partial walls of ancient buildings with which to work, they have reconstructed some typical homes of antiquity.

Bronze Age. House styles varied in each historical period and in each geographical location, even within Palestine itself. During the Bronze Age (3500 to 1200 B.C.E.), a one-room, rectangular house with its entrance on the longer side seemed to dominate. It served mainly for sleeping and eating. Larger homes with several rooms were built around an open courtyard that frequently contained a bake-oven and a well.

Iron Age. In the Iron Age (1200 to about 537 B.C.E.) two major types of stone houses emerged and dominated in Palestine: the "four-room" and the "three-room." These are called "Israelite houses." Generally speaking, they had an entrance through a front wall, leading into a central space. Pillars at the edges of this space made "aisles" at either side. Toward the rear of this central space, the pillars turned into walls and formed small rooms. A rectangular room stretched along the back of the house. The courtyard disappeared, but it did remain in house-complexes.

Purpose. What purpose did the various rooms serve? This is a difficult question to answer from the Bible itself. Fortunately other sciences fill in the gaps in our biblical texts. Archaeology proposes that the one-room house was mainly for sleeping and eating, while the three- and four-room house provided additional space for stabling and storage.

Mediterranean anthropology, a subdiscipline of cultural anthropology, provides another basic, guiding idea as we pursue this question further. The traditional Mediterranean world is deeply and rigidly divided by gender into two spheres, male and female. There are male places, like the fields, and female places, like the common oven or the kitchen. This gender-based division of reality generates two core cultural values: honor, associated with the male, and shame, associated with the female. Shame in the positive sense means sensitivity to maintaining honor, as in "Have you no shame?" In the negative sense, shame is a loss of honor or lack of concern for maintaining honor.

Since women are the point at which a man's honor is most vulnerable to attack, the house is necessary to protect the women and safeguard the family's honor. Within the house there is a special place for the women, the women's quarters, just as the Bedouin tent is divided into men's and women's sections. The Jerusalem Temple replicated this division of space in the Israelite house and designated a special court reserved exclusively for the women.

These anthropological insights help us understand Sirach's statement that a house is necessary "to cover shame" (29:21, literal translation, preferable to that of the New Revised Standard Version: "to assure privacy"). The house protects the women from attacks against family honor. Privacy, which was a rarity and almost entirely absent in the very public, nosey, traditional Mediterranean world, is not the point here. Children freely roamed everyone's houses and women's quarters at will to be sure no secrets were being kept.

The rooms. Now we can discuss the purpose served by the various rooms. People ate (Luke 22:11), slept (Luke 11:7), and gathered (Acts 1:13) in the various rooms. And since the house space was divided into male and female quarters, we know that the use of the rooms was governed by gender. For example, women and children ate together, usually before the men but separate from them. Men ate afterward, and one woman served them (Mark 1:29-31).

As for specific uses of the rooms, ethnology and ethnoarchaeology offer additional information. These sciences study contemporary primitive communities living in conditions very similar to those of the biblical period, especially at the same stage of development (e.g., Iron Age) and with the same environmental restraints. Research in Iraq, Iran, and Turkey has proved particularly helpful.

About half the total room space was used for storing agricultural produce, tools, supplies, and even cows, bullocks, and donkeys. In some houses there was folding space for about twenty-one sheep and goats. Room use changed with the seasons and needs.

Of particular interest in contemporary houses is the dung storage room, a revolting concept to the modern reader. While dung was important as fertilizer, it was even more valuable as fuel. Since it is the women's task to gather and look after the fuel supply in this culture, young girls are taught from an early age how to form the (camel and ass) dung into patties, salt and dry them in the sun, and then store them for use as needed.

Salt is the catalyst that makes such dung fires burn. The dung patty is placed upon a plate of salt that forms the base of the oven. After a while the salt loses its ability to keep the fire going. Then, as Luke's Jesus observes, such salt is no good for the oven nor to prepare fuel for the oven (14:35). People just throw it away. Jesus' challenge to his disciples is to be catalytic, like salt for the hearth (Matt 5:13).

From such a cultural perspective, "salt" in Sirach's list of the necessities of life ("water and fire, and iron and salt") is connected more plausibly with fire than with food. Iron is tempered in fire. The grains that Sirach lists do not require seasoning or preservation but are sometimes roasted or baked in bread (39:26).

Was there a kitchen in the ancient home? Syro-Palestinian archaeologists have found very few cooking hearths or cooking pits in the remains of ancient homes. Ovens are more common, but they are located in sheltered exterior places and only sometimes in the central place of a home. As fuel preparation and cooking in this culture are generally women's tasks, so the common (village) oven is generally women's space. Given the comparatively long rainy season (about seven months), storing dung fuel indoors to keep it dry and usable is as essential to life as storing grain in a sheltered place.

The roof. The roof of these stone houses was flat. Beams and lintels were lined across the walls, and over these poles, reeds, slats, or other such material was placed and then covered with mud and chaff plaster. This was then compacted by foot or with a round stone. Mark records how people dug through this roof to let the paralytic down close to Jesus (Mark 2:4).

The roof was an important area of domestic activity, and thus predominantly the women's domain. Here women socialized, dried clothes, food, or other agricultural products (Josh 2:6-8), or stored dried fodder, brush, wood, and wooden equipment. In villages that were more densely settled or at a large family compound like Peter's house, women used the rooftops as thoroughfares between households. In the dry season, people slept on the rooftops (2 Sam 11:2).

Houses with stronger walls were able to sustain a second story, hence the "upper room." In this arrangement, the lower level served storage and folding purposes, the upper level served living purposes.

House sizes varied. Ethnoarchaeologists calculate that on average a person needed about one hundred square feet of roofed living space, more like two hundred if one includes stabling, storage, and other activity space. Syro-Palestinian archaeologists calculate that the Israelite house averaged about 227 square feet of roofed space (about a fifteen-by-fifteen-foot room), and that about four or five people lived in this space. Of course, housing complexes allowed for more space. Housing styles began to change in the Hellenistic age, but we have less information about these houses than we do about the "Israelite houses."

PETER'S HOUSE

Peter's house was found in 1968 during the first of eighteen campaigns by the Franciscans led by Fr. Virgilio Corbo. The house had already been built by the Hellenistic period. It was a large complex with three courtyards surrounded by numerous living rooms. Cross-cultural studies strongly suggest that a nuclear family (mother, father, dependent children, servants, and slaves) occupied its own living room. The clustering around these courtyards reflects the patrilocal residence pattern usually called "the house of the father" in the Bible. Peter and Andrew had their "living room" in the house complex of his father, Jonah. Jesus lived part of his adult life in Capernaum, and he may well have had a "living room" in Peter's house complex (Mark 2:1). This house complex is also the plausible image behind Jesus' reference to the many rooms in his father's house in John 14:2.

The entrance to Peter's house was off the cardo, the main north-south street of Capernaum, into the north court. On the south side of this court were two rooms. Herodian lamps found in the floor date the rooms to the first century. Crushed limestone floors instead of the black dirt found in the other rooms, and plastered and decorated walls with graffiti naming and honoring Peter, confirmed the identity of the place as his home, subsequently turned into a church.

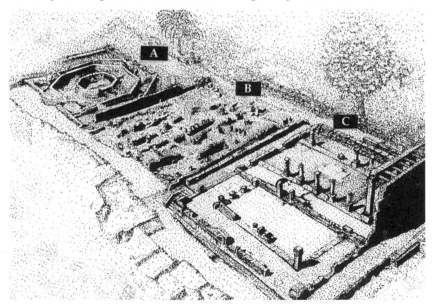

Capernaum synagogue complex, near the Sea of Galilee. (A): St. Peter's house and a fifth-century octagonal church; (B): residential area; (C): the remains of a fourth-century synagogue.

CONCLUSION

Sunday morning television programs in many cities feature video tours of select homes for sale. A foreigner visiting America could learn much about home styles, home design, interior decorating, types of furniture, and many other features of home life that we take for granted. Modern foreigners visiting the homes of their biblical ancestors in modern Israel find only ruins. The Bible records precious few details about houses. Thanks to sciences like archaeology and ethnoarchaeology, cultural geography, and varieties of anthropology, we now have the next best thing to a video.

FOR FURTHER READING

Holladay, John S. "House, Israelite." *Anchor Bible Dictionary* 3:308–318.

Loffreda, Stanislao. *A Visit to Capharnaum*. Jerusalem: Franciscan Printing Press, 1982.

White, L. Michael. *Building God's House in the Roman World: Architectural Adaptation Among Pagans, Jews, and Christians*. ASOR Library of Biblical and Near Eastern Archaeology. Baltimore and London: Johns Hopkins University Press, 1990.

Yegül, Fikret. *Baths and Bathing in Classical Antiquity*. New York and Cambridge, Mass.: The Architectural History Foundation and the MIT Press, 1992.

HUMOR

A picture popularly known as "The Laughing Jesus" represents him with head cocked back and mouth wide open, laughing heartily and sporting a perfect set of teeth. Judging by ancient skulls they examined, paleopathologists doubt that any adult in that culture had such a beautiful set of teeth after a lifetime of poor nutrition and no dental care. Well, did Jesus laugh even with a less than perfect set of teeth? Did anyone in the Bible laugh? Are there any jokes in the Bible?

LAUGHTER

Abraham and Sarah provide some clues to understanding humor in the Bible. When God promised the aged Abraham a son through Sarah (Gen 17:16), Abraham "fell on his face and laughed." The first part of the sentence doesn't describe a kind of laughter but rather Abraham's respect to God while Abraham proposes a counter-offer: Accept Ishmael! God refuses and wittily instructs Abraham to call the new son "laughing boy" (*yiṣhaq* = Isaac = "he laughs"). God has the last laugh. Thus a basic form of humor in the Bible is the pun, the play on words.

In another version of the above story, when strangers predict to Abraham the birth and gender of a child for his eavesdropping wife, Sarah "laughed to herself" (Gen 18:12). The phrase "to herself" suggests that the Middle Eastern laugh is not usually loud and raucous like the Western laugh. A sudden smile may give way to a "heh, heh" but hardly ever a "hearty, har, har." Nevertheless, the visitors heard her. Gentleness is thus a second aspect of laughter among biblical characters.

When the boy was born, Abraham named him Isaac, as God had instructed. Recalling her own skeptical laughter, Sarah reflected on the boy's name and observed, "God has given me good reason to laugh; everyone who hears this tale will laugh with me" (Gen 21:6).

On the day Isaac was weaned, Sarah was disturbed when she saw Ishmael "playing" (a form of the Hebrew verb "to laugh": Gen

21:9). Or was she disturbed because Ishmael was "Isaac-ing," that is, laughing, rejoicing, or possibly ridiculing, mocking, making sport of, or laughing at Isaac? (See Gen 39:14, 17 for laughter as mockery.) Only the punster knows.

Finally, Abimelech, the Philistine king, looked out the window and saw Isaac "Isaac-ing" Rebekah, the wife he passed off to the king as his sister (Gen 26:9). Translators usually render the laugh-word here as "fondling" or "caressing." This translation makes good sense if one can imagine the king at a vantage point that allowed him to see into the private domain of Isaac and Rebekah. Such behavior in public is indiscreet and shameful.

This brief reflection on the various meanings of the Hebrew word for "laugh" suggests some further considerations: puns and wordplay, rip-roaring laughter, and "locker-room" humor. To Westerners, the Bible's humor may seem strange, morbid, and not funny at all.

PUNS AND WORDPLAY

On one occasion, when the Philistine lords who had imprisoned Samson were drunk, they summoned him to amuse or make them laugh (Judg 16:25). Samson was no stand-up comic but rather a master of language. This skill, along with his legendary strength, was Samson's chief claim to honor.

With his legendary strength, Samson slew a thousand men. He punned about it in a play on the Hebrew word *hamor*, meaning both "ass" and "heaps": "With the jawbone of an ass, heaps upon heaps [repeating the Hebrew word three times]." Then he explained: "with the jawbone of an ass have I slain a thousand men" (Judg 15:16).

With his legendary strength, Samson slew a lion barehanded (Judg 14:5-9). With his impressive wit, Samson composed a riddle based on what he alone knew happened to the lion's carcass:

> Out of the eater came something to eat
> Out of the strong came something sweet (Judg 14:14).

No English translation reflects Samson's language skill adequately. In Hebrew, Samson's riddle consists of two lines, each neatly divided into three sections with two *m*'s (the Hebrew letter mem) carefully arranged in each line.

> *mᵉhaʾokel*   *yaṣaʾ*   *maʾakal*
> (from the eater came something to eat)
>
> *umᵉʿaz*   *yaṣaʾ*   *matoq*
> (and from the strong came something sweet)

It would be impossible to guess that Samson was describing the bees and honey he saw in the decayed carcass of the lion he slew. No one else saw this. To beat Samson in the game of honor, it was necessary to solve his riddle with another riddle—a contest of wits equal to hand-to-hand combat.

Having pressed Samson's wife to extract the riddle's reference from him, the townsfolk had little difficulty casting their answer into a superior riddle. It had five *m*'s and answered his two lines (AB) in reverse order (B'A')

> *mah   mmatoq   midbaš*
> (what is sweeter than honey?)
>
> *umeh   ʿaz   meʾari?*
> (and what is stronger than a lion?)

The obvious answer to this riddle is love—a fitting theme for a wedding feast. Samson scolded the cheats with another rhyming couplet. He had brain *and* brawn.

JESUS AND WORDPLAY

Jesus exhibited mastery of language by quoting from tradition (citing Scripture) on the spot, creatively, to answer a question or pose a challenge (e.g., Luke 6:1-5). He also seems to have been adept at wordplay. In Matthew's Sermon on the Mount (7:6), Jesus' advice "Do not give (a) dogs what is (b) holy; and do not throw your (b') pearls before (a') swine" does not sound clever or witty. The statement is composed in parallelism, but holy things and pearls (b and b') are not as well related as dogs and swine (unclean animals, a and a'). In the Aramaic language that Jesus likely spoke, the root word behind holy things is *qdš*, which can be read as (1) *qudšayyaʾ* = holy things; or preferably in this case (2) *qadašayyaʾ* = gold rings, earrings, nose rings, bracelets. Any of these latter words form a perfect parallel to pearls. The original Aramaic pun might look something like this: "Do not give to *kalbayyaʾ* (dogs) your *qadašayyaʾ* (bracelets or holy things) and do not cast your *harozayyaʾ* (string of pearls) before *hᵃzirayyaʾ* (swine)." Observe the similar sounds. The pun would evince a smile to accompany the warning the Christians should be careful not to allow unworthy, actively anti-Christians to come into contact with Christian values and behavior patterns they cannot appreciate. (*Didache* 9:5 refers this verse to the closed table of the Eucharist.)

Fisherman though he was, Jesus' pun was probably not lost on Peter when Jesus promised: "You are *petros* (Aramaic: *kepha,ʾ* "rock") and on this *petra* (Aramaic: *kepha,ʾ* "rock") I will build my church" (Matt 16:18). The pun is better in Aramaic than in Greek, and "Rocky" *(Kepha)* was likely Peter's nickname even before this incident. Nicknames are inescapable in the Middle East, and they are determined by the community. There likely was a basis for the nickname in Peter's personality.

In another well-known play on words, Jesus and Nicodemus each use one and the same Greek word *(anothēn)* with two different meanings: "from above" (Jesus) and "again" (Nicodemus). Because there is no known Aramaic or Hebrew equivalent to this pun, it may be original to the evangelist rather than to Jesus.

All these puns evoke a very gentle humor. Wordplay will produce a smile but hardly a guffaw or a belly laugh. Did the ancients ever laugh hard?

RIP-ROARING HUMOR

Some scholars have proposed that the Book of Esther is the Bible's joke book. The opening scene of King Ahasuerus (Xerxes I, 485–44 B.C.E.) hosting a banquet for the elites that lasted approximately 180 days followed by a seven-day banquet for the residents of his capital city is the opening joke. A six-month banquet?

After dismissing his disobedient wife, Ahasuerus sought a replacement. Each prospective wife prepared for twelve months: six months with oil of myrrh and six months with spices and ointments for a chance to please the king in a one-night encounter. Esther won. Sexist to modern ears, the fiction demonstrates laughable stupidity to the ancients.

Haman proposed to the king a reward he thought the king wanted to bestow on him. The king ordered Haman to personally give that honor to Mordecai, Haman's hated enemy. Haman led Mordecai, regally robed astride a steed, around town for all to admire and broadcast Mordecai's honor while doing so. If Judeans were laughing at Haman, the event was not funny to Haman, his family, and friends.

When Esther revealed Haman's nefarious plot to kill all Judeans, Ahasuerus stormed out of the room in a rage, only to return and find Haman begging mercy from Queen Esther but perceived by the king as attempting to seduce Esther. This humorous scene ends with Haman's execution on the gallows he prepared for Mordecai and his fellow nationals. The book is a parade example of gallows humor, and humor at another's expense.

In the Gospels, Jesus exhibits traces of what modern readers might identify as material worthy of a stand-up comedian. Imagine what Seinfeld could do with the beam and splinter in the eye (Matt 7:1-5).

George: Jerry, I hate to be the one to tell you, but you got a splinter in your eye.

Jerry: Me, A splinter? Are you serious?

George (smiling smugly): Yup! A splinter.

Jerry: I can't imagine how you can see my splinter.

George: 20-20 vision, that's how.

Jerry: George, your 20-20 vision is blocked by a beam. You have a beam in your eye. How can you see anything?

George: A beam? Oh, no. This is it; this is the end. My reputation is ruined!

Some scholars have proposed that in this episode Jesus may be speaking from his experience as an artisan who worked with wood. He would have been familiar with splinters, beams, and occupational hazards. One can imagine similar scenarios for his other exaggerations: a camel and the eye of a needle (Mark 10:25); straining out a gnat but swallowing a camel (Matt 23:24); and washing the outside of a cup but leaving the inside dirty (Matt 23:25).

"LOCKER-ROOM" HUMOR

It is anachronistic to apply the phrase "locker-room" humor to biblical times and passages, yet it describes a type of humor that does appear in the Bible and could easily elicit belly laughs. Some call it scatological (obscene or bordering on the obscene) humor.

In the days of Israel's judges, the people of Israel suffered defeat and occupation by Eglon, the king of Moab. His name derives from a Hebrew word whose semantic field includes the meanings "round," "rotund," and "bovine." Lest the reader miss the point, the storyteller is explicit: "Now Eglon was a very fat man" (Judg 3:17). In itself, obesity is no laughing matter. It's what happens next in the story that can stir raucous laughter.

The Lord raised up Ehud, a left-handed man, to save Israel from Eglon. Ehud made a two-edged (literally "two-mouthed") sword one cubit long and strapped it to his right thigh under his clothes. Then he brought a tribute to Eglon and said, "I have a secret message for you, O king." Understanding the high value placed on secrecy in this culture, one can appreciate the king's eagerness to hear the secret. He dismissed everybody.

Ehud came close and said, "I have a word [or thing] from God for you," and with that, his left hand thrust the sword into Eglon's belly. The hilt followed after the blade, the fat closed over the blade, and "dirt" (feces) oozed out. Realizing he was dying, Eglon went into the roof chamber and locked himself in. Ehud escaped.

When Eglon's servants returned, saw the doors locked, and smelled the odor, they thought, "He is only relieving himself in the closet of the cool chamber." After a long while, they opened the doors and found him dead.

Apart from the humorous way in which this hated enemy died, a left-handed assassin increases the humor. In the Middle East, the left hand is used exclusively for toilet functions. In the Aja language of Benin, West Africa, the word for "left hand" literally means "push-the-excrement-away hand." The left-handed Ehud was the perfect savior from a man considered "dirt."

Jesus' parable of the barren fig tree (Luke 13:6b-9) is not advice for growing trees but a political comment on failed community leaders. Imagine his audience's reaction when the caretaker pleads with the owner to give the trees one more chance by dumping manure on them. That's exactly what the peasants would love to have done to these #!?*%$ leaders! Jesus has an earthy sense of humor.

CONCLUSION

On his radio show Garrison Keillor once observed: "Actually, God writes a lot of good comedy. Trouble is he's stuck with so many bad actors who don't know how to play funny." The best way to understand the Bible's humor is to realize it is funny in Middle Eastern rather than American terms.

FOR FURTHER READING

Bremmer, Jan, and Herman Roodenburg, eds. *A Cultural History of Humour from Antiquity to the Present Day*. Cambridge: Polity Press, 1997.

Culpepper, R. Alan. "Humor and Wit (NT)." *Anchor Bible Dictionary* 3:333.

Fisher, Eugene J. "The Divine Comedy: Humor in the Bible." *Religious Education* 72 (1977) 571–579.

Greenstein, Edward L. "Humor and Wit (OT)." *Anchor Bible Dictionary* 3:325–333.

_____. "Wordplay, Hebrew." *Anchor Bible Dictionary* 6:968–971.

JEWS AND CHRISTIANS

On Pentecost Sunday, 1995, in the Cathedral of Mary Our Queen, Baltimore, the preacher read the assigned gospel (John 20:19-23), which reports that after the death of Jesus, the disciples gathered behind locked doors "for fear of the Jews." In his homily the preacher explained: "The use of the term 'the Jews' is not meant to apply to the Jewish people as such but to the people who sought Jesus' death."

A Jewish woman in the congregation that day to witness her granddaughter's first Holy Communion took offense and registered complaints with the Archbishop and the local chapter of the American Jewish Committee. The preacher replied in writing with an apology and an explanation that he had weighed his words carefully because he was quite aware of the Church's official repudiation of blaming the Jews as a people for the death of Jesus.

The American Jewish Committee and Christian groups resolved to sponsor preaching colloquiums prior to Advent and Easter in the future in order to counter "anti-Judaic bias" in Christian sermons during the period of the year.

A PERENNIAL PROBLEM

This episode reflects a perennial problem that appears to have emerged with greater intensity in recent years. The problem is especially acute when the Gospel of John is read, for John uses the Greek word translated as "the Jews" seventy-one times, more frequently than any other book of the New Testament! In thirty-seven instances, the term describes authoritative groups that "other Jews" fear (the preacher's point above in John 20:19).

Johannine scholar U. C. van Wahlde studied these occurrences thoroughly and distinguished a variety of meanings in John's Gospel. He concluded that sometimes the word *ioudaios* describes the region Judea (3:22) or its inhabitants (1:19; 3:25; 11:19, 31, 33, 36, 45, 54). At other times it has a national or religious sense (2:6, 13; 6:4; 7:2; 11:55; 19:40, 42). [This meaning, however, is debatable because

the concept of "nation" is a relatively recent one, and "religion" in the ancient world was a social institution embedded in politics and not free-standing as in the modern West.] Finally, at still other times the Greek word carries an overtone of hostility when, for instance, it describes the Pharisees (9:13) as *ioudaioi* (9:18), whom other *ioudaioi* feared (9:22). Van Wahlde's purpose was to use these shifts of meaning, ideology, and theology to identify and sort out the different traditions that the Johannine redactor compiled into the final edition of this Gospel. Would an article like this be useful for those who want to read the Bible respectfully yet critically?

A FRESH INSIGHT

Increasing numbers of contemporary biblical scholars observe that the problems raised by the term "the Jews" in the Bible is specious. The various tortuous solutions are generally unsuccessful and indeed unnecessary. The real problem lies with translators and interpreters who share the ethnocentric tendencies and lack of historical sense of contemporary Western culture.

The Hebrew word *yehudîm* and the Greek word *ioudaioi* should be properly translated "Judean." The contemporary English word "Jew" is traced linguistically to the Middle English period (ca. 1200 C.E.), deriving from the Old French *Giu, Juiu,* and ultimately back to the Latin, Greek, and Hebrew, but it is not an appropriate translation of the Greek and Hebrew words.

All language derives its meaning, not from dictionaries or etymologies, but rather from the social system. Westerners living in the twentieth-century world do indeed know Jews and Jewish beliefs and practices. Yet Jewish scholars like Shaye Cohen and Jacob Neusner remind us that contemporary Jewish beliefs and practices are rooted in the formation of the Talmud of the sixth century C.E., a process that began with the compilation of the Mishna perhaps late in the first century, around 90 C.E. Some of these practices, like the bar and especially the bat mitzvah, have no root in the Hebrew Bible or in biblical times.

Similarly, it was also late in the first century of the Common Era that rabbis, as we know and understand them, and the synagogue as a place of worship began to develop. The title "Rabbi" given to John the Baptist (John 3:26), Jesus (Matt 26:25, 49), and others (Matt 23:7) was nothing more than a respectful way of addressing important teachers. It derives from the Hebrew word *rab,* meaning "lord," "master."

As for the synagogue, Heather McKay has demonstrated that in Jesus' day and until the year 200, it was like a community center

where men gathered to read and listen to Torah, dispute and argue with others (Luke 4:16-30 and par.). They did not gather for services because none existed at this time. Sabbath was a day of rest. It became a day of worship in reaction to the practice of the Messianic group (usually called Christians) in Palestinian Yahwism, who assembled to celebrate the Lord's Supper on the seventh day.

It is equally anachronistic to speak of "Christians" in the biblical period, since that term, as it is understood today, emerged only from the Christological debates of the fourth century, particularly from the question: How did Jesus of Nazareth relate to Yahweh, the God of Israel? It is clear from Acts 11:26 that the name was given to the group by outsiders, and in Acts 26:28 the outsider, Agrippa, uses it in a mocking sense. In 1 Peter 4:16-17, it appears again with a plainly pejorative meaning best translated as "christ-lackeys." Thus in biblical times and texts there existed neither "Jews" nor "Christians" as these terms are understood and used today. First-century Yahwism included a variety of groups: Pharisaic, Messianic (usually called Christian), Sadducean, Essene, and others.

THE PAST

How, then, are we to speak of the past: the time of Jesus? the time of the Old Testament? Contemporary scholars propose three terms to accord with a major, threefold division of Jewish history.

1. Israelites: The Period of the First Temple (950 B.C.E. to 586 B.C.E.) is the period of First Temple religion. It extends from the completion of the First Temple under Solomon to the time of that Temple's destruction by invading Babylonian armies. In this period, the country is known as Israel. The people of this period are described as Israelites (literally "sons of Israel" in the Hebrew Bible). Their religious beliefs and practices are properly called Israelite religion. Political religion has the Temple as its focal point, along with Temple sacrifices, Pilgrimage festivals, and similar practices (see Leviticus). Domestic religion centers on ancestrism rooted in burial in the family grave (Gen 49:29-33).

2. Judeans: The Period of the Second Temple (520 B.C.E. to 70 C.E.) marks the period of Second Temple religion. It extends from the completion of the Second Temple under Ezra and Nehemiah to the destruction of the Temple by the Roman armies led by Titus. The country is called Judea, and its inhabitants are called Judeans. The religion is properly called Judean or Judaic religion.

3. Jews: The Period of Rabbinic Judaism (sixth-century C.E. Babylonian Talmud, beginning perhaps as early as 90 C.E.–the date of the reputed gathering of the so-called Council of Jamnia–and

continuing to the present day). The religion of this period is currently termed "normative Judaism," deriving from Pharisaic scribalism, which is the foundation of contemporary Jewish belief and practice. It is this form of Judaism and these Jews who are familiar to the contemporary world. In the modern day, the terms "Jewish religion," "Jewish beliefs," etc., are most appropriate but cannot and should not be retrojected into the Bible, which belongs to the previous two periods. Such anachronism, however, is unfortunately too common.

Insiders and Outsiders. When analyzing societies and cultures, anthropologists observe how people distinguish between ingroups and outgroups, insiders and outsiders. This distinction is very useful in understanding the terminology "Judean" proposed for the second period of history.

Insiders, particularly those who embraced and practiced Second Temple religion, generally referred to themselves as "the people of Israel" (e.g., Ezra 2:1; 3:1; etc.) or as members of "the house of Israel" (Matt 10:6). Israel was thus an ingroup name (see John 1:47). Fellow ethnics who mocked Jesus called him "King of Israel" (Matt 27:42). Insiders or ingroup members were usually very kind and very loyal to one another, especially when in need (Luke 11:5-9). Such behavior was rarely extended to outsiders. The whole house of Israel was one big ingroup, even though its boundaries were fluid and always shifting.

Model of the Jerusalem Temple, built by Herod the Great, as it would have appeared in A.D. 66.

The first-century "house of Israel" ingroup recognized three geographical divisions: Judea, Perea (the land east of or across the Jordan), and Galilee. The people living in these areas also represented three ingroups within the overall ingroup of the house of Israel: Judeans, Pereans, and Galileans. What they had in common was birth into one people known as the "house of Israel" and allegiance to the Jerusalem Temple. The parable of the Good Samaritan (Luke 10:29-37) tries to address a common question: Who belongs

in Israel? From this ingroup perspective, Jesus the Galilean was put to death by outsiders (Romans) at the instigation of some Judeans.

It is important to note that the ingroup name also applied to émigrés living in various colonies outside the country as well as members of the house of Israel born outside the country. Paul of Tarsus commonly identified himself as a Hebrew or Israelite (2 Cor 11:22; Phil 3:5; Rom 11:1).

Jesus was not a Judean, yet the title placed upon his cross read: "Jesus of Nazareth, King of the Judeans" (Matt 27:37; Mark 15:26; Luke 23:38; John 19:19). Notice the objection that Jesus' opponents make in John's Gospel. They know full well that he is a Galilean, but they do not ask Pilate to change the wording "King of Judeans" to "King of Galileans." Instead, they ask only to indicate that Jesus made such a claim.

Jesus' opponents accept the outgroup or outsider identification. Outsiders, like the Romans, called the entire land "Judea" and all its inhabitants "Judeans." Paul also accepted this outsider usage (Acts 22:3; Gal 2:15) and identified himself accordingly. Outsiders justified this global term for the entire country and all its inhabitants, as well as those with ethnic roots here but living elsewhere, because they all affirmed allegiance to the God of Israel, whose Temple was in Jerusalem in Judea. Ingroup members accepted the designation "Judean" precisely because their Temple, the focal point of their beliefs and practices, was located in that country.

Members of the ingroup known as the house of Israel similarly lumped all outsiders into a large group called "non-Israel" or "the nations" (Hebrew *goyîm*; Greek *ethnoi*; English "gentiles"), ignoring all distinctions. The same is true of the various Hellenic people lumped together as "Greeks" or "Hellenes" and their typical behavior described as "Hellenism." Such stereotyping is normal for group-centered cultures, such as those reflected in the Bible, and is part and parcel of the insider-outsider perspective. More than 90 percent of the world's contemporary cultures are group-centered or collectivistic in perspective.

IDENTIFYING PEOPLE IN ANTIQUITY

The ingroup/outgroup terminology proposed above is intelligible from the ancient point of view because, generally speaking, ancient Mediterranean people tended to identify and label persons and animate beings primarily in terms of their geographic place of origin. Simon of Cyrene helped Jesus carry his cross (Matt 27:32). Jesus was called the Nazarean, or man from Nazareth (Matt 21:11; Mark 1:24;

10:47; Luke 24:19; etc.). He was also called a Galilean (Matt 26:69). Outsiders (the Romans) called him (and everyone in that country or those for whom this was their country of ethnic origin) a Judean (Matt 27:29, 37).

Another way of identifying people was by their family. "Is this not Joseph's son?" (Luke 4:22), or "Is this not the carpenter's son? Is not his mother called Mary? And are not his brothers James and Joseph and Simon and Judas? And are not all his sisters with us?" (Matt 13:55-56). We also recognize Simon bar Jonah (Matt 16:17), James and John the sons of Zebedee (Mark 10:35), and the blind Bar-Timaeus, known only by his father's name and not by his own (Mark 10:46).

Yet a third way of identifying people was by their occupation. "Is not this the carpenter . . . ?" (Mark 6:3). Similar group designations include: a lawyer (Luke 10:25), a Levite (Luke 10:32), a Pharisee (Luke 11:37), a tax collector (Luke 18:10), a leper (Matt 26:6), and so on. Paul sometimes identified himself by his group: a Pharisee (Phil 3:5; Acts 23:6; see also Acts 22:3), but as Paul's usage indicates, geography is always primary.

CONTEMPORARY BIBLICAL SCHOLARSHIP

There is a steadily growing consensus among scholars that from a historical point of view, there were no Jews or Christians in the first century of the Common Era. Richard Horsley, in *Studying the Historical Jesus* (p. 398), affirms that insofar as Judaism in the New Testament bears and reflects rabbinic concerns and expressions, it is anachronistic. Judaism did not yet exist in this form. Contemporary Jewish scholars who choose to use the word for this second historical period, insist on the plural, "Judaisms," to highlight the historical fact that there was no monolithically uniform system of beliefs embraced by all who considered themselves members of the house of Israel. In that period, there was no single, standard expectation of "the messiah" or a "prophet of the end-time."

Helmut Koester, in *Studying the Historical Jesus* (pp. 541–542), goes further and suggests that because of this diversity in the first century, the term "Judaism" should be entirely removed from discussions of the historical Jesus. It is the ambiguous and imprecise understanding of this term that permits Jesus to be described as a precursor of the rabbis, a Hellenized Galilean Cynic, an apocalyptic Essene, or a messianic zealot. Instead, he suggests that we speak of Israel understood as the "sum total of the highly diversified phenomenon of various groups who were committed to the interpretation of the religious and cultural heritage of Israel." This historically accurate picture is already evident in recent books (see "For Further Reading" below: Ord and Coote; Malina; Malina and Rorhbaugh; and Pilch).

CONCLUSION

Westerners in general and Americans in particular have a very poor sense of history. Teachers recognize that for their students history begins with their birth date, and all the past is fused into one amorphous mass of irrelevant information. Instilling a historical sense in students is a worthy task and a major accomplishment. Truly fortunate is the teacher who achieves that.

In the meantime, our inaccurate translations cause the kind of unnecessary problem described at the beginning of this article. It would seem a very prudent and responsible thing to do, at least when studying and reading the New Testament, to replace the erroneous word "Jew" in all instances with the more appropriate "Judean." This is already occurring in many books, so why wait for revised translations? In this matter, the time to act is now.

FOR FURTHER READING

Horsley, Richard A. "The Death of Jesus." In *Studying the Historical Jesus*. Ed. Bruce Chilton and Craig A. Evans, 395–422. Leiden: Brill, 1994.

Koester, Helmut. "The Historical Jesus and the Historical Situation of the Quest: An Epilogue." In *Studying the Historical Jesus*. Ed. Bruce Chilton and Craig A. Evans, 535–546. Leiden: Brill, 1994.

McKay, Heather A. "From Evidence to Edifice: Four Fallacies about the Sabbath." In *Text as Pretext: Essays in Honour of Robert Davidson*. Ed. Robert P. Carroll, 179–199. Sheffield: JSOT Press, 1992.

Malina, Bruce J. *Windows on the World of Jesus: Time Travel to Ancient Judea*. Louisville: Westminster John Knox, 1993.

Malina, Bruce J., and Richard L. Rohrbaugh. *Social Science Commentary on the Synoptic Gospels*. Minneapolis: Fortress, 1992.

Ord, David Robert, and Robert B. Coote. *Is the Bible True? Understanding the Bible Today*. Maryknoll, N.Y.: Orbis, 1994.

Pilch, John J. "Jews or Judeans: A Translation Challenge." *Modern Liturgy* 20, no. 3 (April 1993) 19.

_____. *The Cultural World of Jesus Sunday by Sunday: Cycle A, B, and C.* 3 vols. Collegeville, Minn.: The Liturgical Press, 1995–1997.

von Wahlde, U. C. "The Johannine 'Jews': A Critical Survey." *New Testament Studies* 28 (1981–1982) 33–60.

MILITARY

A centurion asked Jesus to heal a sick loved one (Matt 8:5). In Luke's version this centurion is proposed as deserving because he loves the people and built a synagogue for them (7:3-5). A soldier who stood watch at the crucifixion of Jesus pierced his side to ascertain whether Jesus had died yet (John 19:34). A centurion impressed by Jesus' manly comportment as he died professed admiration for him (Mark 15:39). These and other references to the military in the Gospels challenge the modern reader to consider what it might have meant or how it might have felt to live under domination by a foreign power and under military occupation of its forces.

THE ROMAN ARMY

In general, the army in the Roman Empire took this shape. A legion consisted of about 5,000 men. A legion was made up of ten cohorts, each of which included about 480 men. Each cohort contained six centuries (about 80 men, not the 100 implied by the name), and each century was led by a centurion. A legion had 60 centurions.

Centurions were the real professionals of the legion. The majority were seasoned military men promoted from the ranks. While the period of service for most of the military eventually became fixed at twenty-five years, there was no limit for a centurion. He could serve until he died. As for his pay, the centurion received sixteen times that of the basic legionary salary! Clearly, the centurion possessed enormous military and social status and significant wealth.

THE AUXILIARIES

Rather than learn new ways of fighting when they faced a new enemy, the Romans preferred to hire mercenaries. This was not difficult, for the pay, food, clothing (provided by the Romans but paid for by the soldier by a deduction from his salary), and the general improvement of living conditions (including the ready availability of a regimental bath building) made military service more appealing than life as a disgruntled subject in a newly formed Roman province.

The promise of eventual citizenship sweetened the pot. In wartime these soldiers were considered equals of their Roman counterparts; in peacetime they served as police and patrolmen.

HEROD'S ARMY

Herod the Great was familiar with the Roman army's two keys to success: fearless leadership from accomplished "native" (= Roman) warriors and unwavering loyalty from accomplished "mercenary" warriors. When he was appointed by Rome as client-king of Judea, Herod realized it was an empty title. Parthians had earlier driven him out of Judea, and on his return he had to dispose of a Hasmonean rival, Antigonus. To accomplish this, he formed an army by gathering fellow countrymen (Idumeans) and recruits from his settlements (e.g., Samaria, renamed Sebaste in honor of Emperor Augustus, where he relocated six thousand loyal subjects, mostly veterans) or from elsewhere. Loyal warriors give better assurance of success.

JESUS AND THE CENTURION

In Capernaum a centurion approached Jesus and asked him to heal a sick servant at home. Who was this centurion? Scholars do not believe that there were any Roman troops in this region at this time. The eighty soldiers he commanded were probably mercenaries, foreigners, or if Judeans, they would likely have been considered compromisers or traitors. The centurion himself was probably Roman or some other non-Judean (see Matt 8:10).

Luke's note that this centurion loved the people and built a men's community center (synagogue) for them is culturally plausible. Centurions had both the wealth and the connections to perform such a favor. And whether authentic or feigned, "love for the people" would make life easier for a leader of the occupying military forces.

Be that as it may, Jesus was impressed by the centurion's "faith," the likes of which he has not found in Israel (Matt 8:10//Luke 7:9). The Greek word usually translated as "faith" is better translated as "loyalty." In this culture the concept included standing by someone, no matter what. Jesus had not found such loyalty among fellow countrymen, but he recognized and admired it in this centurion. Like all his compatriots, Jesus knew that unflinching loyalty explained the success of the Roman military and the spread of the Roman Empire. The prophetic testimony suggests that such loyalty remained ever elusive in Israel.

The interpretation of John's version of this event (4:46-54) benefits from this insight as well. Jesus, the master of insult, may well have intended to be offensive in verse 48. In the Middle East, no question or petition is innocent. Every question is considered potentially shaming, because someone may not know the answer. Hence it is customary to answer with an insult. This was not lost on the petitioner in John's Gospel. As soon as Jesus replied harshly, the petitioner came right back with his request. This was loyalty, sticking with someone (Jesus), no matter what (see vv. 50, 53). The result of such stick-to-it-iveness (otherwise known as loyalty or faith) was to obtain the favor requested.

THE ANTONIA FORTRESS

In general, ancient cities were densely populated and protected by a wall, sometimes twenty-five feet thick, with a single city gate (except for large cities like Jerusalem) often flanked by two towers. Within the city, the chief public building constituted a strong fortress or citadel. In Herodian Jerusalem, this was the Antonia, which bordered the western end of the northern wall of the Temple. Such a structure is first mentioned in Nehemiah (2:8; 7:2: fortress, castle). According to Josephus (*Antiquities,* 15.11.4, par. 403), the Tower of the Hundred in Nehemiah's wall (3:1) was the structure on which the Antonia eventually arose. This tower was repaired by Hyrcanus I (135–105

Detail of the Fortress Antonia as depicted in a scale model at the Holyland Hotel, Jerusalem.

B.C.E.) and further renovated and expanded by Herod the Great (37–35 B.C.E.). He named it after his patron, Mark Antony, to whom he owed his position as client-king in Judea.

Under the rule of Roman procurators (6–41 C.E.), soldiers were garrisoned at the Antonia to keep watch over activity in the city and the Temple area and to scotch disturbances before they got out of hand, particularly during the major festivals. Imagine making a pilgrimage to the Temple in the Holy City now under scrutiny by foreign troops. In this context, the imagery of Psalm 122 takes on a new meaning. In its original setting, the pilgrim expresses joy and satisfaction with the visit and confidence on returning home that the Holy City will have peace within its walls and security within the towers (v. 7). In the Herodian period, the pilgrim suspects that treachery is probably being plotted within the palace and knows that foreign troops are spying on pilgrims from the towers of Antonia.

The degree of hostility that occupying forces could arouse is evident in a particular insult reported by Josephus (*War*, 2.12.1 [223–227]). On the feast of Passover during the prefecture of Cumanus (48–52 C.E.), a soldier atop a portico "turned his back to the Judeans, bent forward, raised his skirt in an indecent manner and broke wind noisily while keeping his posture." The people became livid with anger and began to hurl stones at the soldiers. Cumanus sent soldiers into the area to control the crowd, but Josephus reports, no doubt with considerable hyperbole, that more than thirty thousand people were trampled to death in the ensuing panic.

JESUS AND THE ANTONIA

During his ministry, Jesus encountered friendly or sympathetic military personnel. In his last days, he fell into the hands of military who did their job with customary roughness: retaining a prisoner, preparing him for death, and carrying it out. Hostile fellow nationals played a role in arranging the arrest and subsequent execution of Jesus. In times of threat from outside, some people will resist and engage in protest or guerrilla tactics (e.g., the Maccabees); others might flee and wait for better times (the Essenes), while still others will decide to collaborate with the conquerors as means to a better life (e.g., those who bid for the privilege to serve as high priest when that became a possibility).

Contemporary travelers to Jerusalem visit the convent of the Sisters of Sion to see the flagstone pavement where Jesus was flogged and get the general impression that this was the site of the Antonia. Archaeologists, however, have been unable to locate the fortress precisely. It was destroyed by Titus in the year 70 C.E. While Herod lived here for a while before his palace was built, it is questionable whether governors like Pilate resided here or whether the Tower of Antonia served as the praetorium. The more likely place where Jesus met with Pilate was Herod's palace.

FORTRESSES

Herod the Great was quite aware that his subjects distrusted him and would turn hostile at any opportunity. His military forces were one means to keep them under control, as they did in Jerusalem. To keep an eye on these subjects elsewhere in his kingdom, Herod established major fortresses throughout. In the region east and south of Jerusalem, there is Cyprus overlooking Jericho, the Herodium, Hyrcania, Alexandrium, and Masada. Elsewhere there were strongholds at Caesarea, Gaba (Galilee), Heshbon-Esbonitis (Perea), and Sebaste-Samaria.

The Herodium was built by Herod the Great (about 23 B.C.E.) on a site approximately seven miles south of Jerusalem and three and a half miles southeast of Bethlehem. It is a steep, cone-shaped, artificial mountain that encloses a building. The palace-fortress served a number of functions, but mainly it was the summer residence of Herod and his family. His winter palace was at Jericho. Herod chose the Herodium to be his burial place, but his tomb has not yet been found. If the slaughter of infant boys in Bethlehem after the birth of Jesus was historical (Matt 2:16), the troops responsible might have been dispatched from the Herodium. Scholars are not agreed about the significance of this range of palatial fortresses, but it seems safe to conclude that they testify to Herod's siege mentality, shaped by his justified fears of the populace.

MILITARY IMPACT ON LIFE

The concept of the legion as a large group (4,800 men) is reflected in the story of the man possessed by multiple spirits (Luke 8:30) and in Jesus' assertion that if need be, his Father could send more than twelve legions of angels to rescue him (Matt 26:53). In this latter instance, the listeners would have been struck by the size of a potential defensive force, which would equal one-fourth of the regular Roman army. The information does not appear to have frightened them, for they proceeded with the arrest.

In the East, Roman military camps are difficult to locate. It seems that troops were stationed in towns or in a quarter of a city, or they were lodged in local households. Of course, this was hardly a pleasant experience. Ancient documents report many examples of undisciplined behavior and even obnoxious demands by the soldiers. The Sermon on the Mount appears to reflect one such practice, namely, forcing a citizen to carry the soldier's equipment for a mile. Matthew's Jesus exhorts followers not to resist one who is evil (that is, not take him to court to protect one's rights) but to go the extra mile (5:41).

CONCLUSION

I was inspired to research and write this article by a recent trip to Europe. For a Westerner who has never experienced conquest by a foreign power or military occupation by a conqueror's forces, a visit to Eastern Europe proved to be an eye-opener. Though recently liberated from foreign domination and military occupation, citizens of the Czech Republic still live with the consequences of that experience. There are daily reminders in the architectural styles of buildings and monuments from that era. There are also traces in the diverse opinions, personal lifestyles, and future hopes among the now liberated people. A week later, the archaeological remains of a Roman frontier outpost at Carnuntum, outside Vienna, prompted the visitor to think of another region dominated and occupied by that same world power at that same time: ancient Judea in the time of Jesus. The author of the Letter to the Hebrews reminds us: "In your struggle against sin you have not yet resisted to the point of shedding your blood" (12:4). As always, a fresh perspective on the Gospels gives them new vibrancy and enhances their challenge.

FOR FURTHER READING

Gracey, M. H. "Herodian Army." *Anchor Bible Dictionary* 3:173–174.
Hobbs, T. R. *A Time for War: A Study of Warfare in the Old Testament.* Wilmington, Del.: Michael Glazier, 1989.
Jobst, Werner, ed. *Carnuntum.* Museum Catalogue. Carnuntum, Austria: Carnuntum Archaeological Park, 1992.
Kennedy, David. "Roman Army." *Anchor Bible Dictionary* 5:789–798.
Reid, T. R. "The Power and the Glory of the Roman Empire." *National Geographic* 192 (July 1997) 2–41.

MUSIC

Prior to conducting the Baltimore Symphony Orchestra and Chorus in a performance of Mozart's *Mass in C Minor*, the famed choral conductor Robert Shaw recalled the comments of a Frenchman after Shaw had conducted a Bach Mass in a French cathedral.

"When the angels sing to please God," the Frenchman observed, "they sing Bach." Shaw listened attentively as the Frenchman paused. "And when the angels sing for their personal enjoyment," the Frenchman continued, "they sing Mozart." Shaw smiled. "But when the angels sing Mozart," the Frenchman concluded with a wink, "God listens at the keyhole."

The story echoes rabbinic traditions. The Midrash on Lamentations (III.23) says that God loves singing so much that "every day the Holy One . . . creates a band of new angels who sing a new song before him and then pass away." According to the Midrash on the Song of Songs (VIII.13), "whenever God hears Israel's song, He calls the Heavenly host to listen." Yet another rabbinic tradition says that God sings too. Clearly, God enjoys vocal music.

What kinds of songs are these? Do angels' songs differ from those of humans? Are there other kinds of songs in the universe? What kinds of songs are mentioned in the Bible? Is it possible for us to imagine or reconstruct the sounds of these songs from a time before musical notes or electronic recorders were invented?

SINGING IN ANTIQUITY

Singing is a form of communication. In its primitive form, singing consisted of accented speech delivered in a melodic pattern. It seems that most songs consisted of a single verse, which was repeated over and over. Miriam's refrain repeated by the women who danced to the sound of tambourines after Pharaoh's forces drowned in the Reed Sea is a good example:

> Sing to the LORD, for he has risen up in triumph;
> the horse and his rider he has hurled into the sea (Exod 15:21, NEB).

111

Other refrains include the song the women sang to greet Saul: "Saul made havoc among thousands, but David among tens of thousands" (1 Sam 18:7; 21:12, NEB), and the taunting chants exchanged by children at play in the marketplace: "*We* piped for you, and *you* would not dance; *we* wept and wailed, and *you* did not mourn" (Matt 11:17, NEB).

Lamech's longer song (Gen 4:23-24) is one of the earliest recorded in the Bible. The translation in the New English Bible reflects the accented Hebrew verses rather well:

> Adah and Zillah, listen to me;
> wives of Lamech, mark what I say:
> I kill a man for wounding me,
> a young man for a blow.
> Cain may be avenged seven times,
> but Lamech seventy-seven.

Western music is characterized by melody, harmony, and rhythm. Ancient Middle Eastern music is characterized by melody and rhythm; it lacks harmony (see 2 Chr 5:13). The passages above manifest steady rhythms, and we can imagine that they had very simple melodies.

SONGS OF ANGELS

In a trance, Isaiah (6:3) sees the seraphim standing above the throne of the Lord and singing antiphonally: "Holy, holy, holy is the LORD of hosts; the whole earth is full of his glory." Adam, in a testament bearing his name (second century C.E.), says he used to hear the sound of these seraphim beating their wings in rhythm to their triple song of praise, but after he sinned he no longer heard the sound. They sang during the fourth hour of the night, while the songs of human beings praising God would pass through the gates of heaven at the tenth hour of the night. This beautiful concert of praise filled the entire night and day.

An angel of the Lord announced to shepherds the birth of Jesus (Luke 2:10-12). This angel was then joined by a multitude of angels praising God and singing, "Glory to God in the highest, and on earth peace among mortals with whom he is pleased."

The Book of Revelation reports many cosmic songs. Seven appear between chapters 4 and 7. The four living creatures sing unceasingly: "Holy, Holy, Holy, is the Lord God Almighty, who was and is and is to come" (4:8). The twenty-four elders sing: "Worthy are you, our Lord and God, to receive glory and honor and power, for you created all things, and by your will they existed and were created" (4:11). A third song hymns the Lamb's cosmic preeminence (5:9), which is echoed by God's entourage (fourth song, 5:12) and repeated by all created beings (fifth song, 5:13). A limited number of Israelites (144,000) and a limitless number of others acknowledge their rescue by singing to God and the Lamb (sixth song, 7:6). God's entourage responds with a seventh song (7:12). Many other such songs are spread throughout the book.

ANGELIC MELODIES

What did the angelic songs sound like? The ancients believed that music fills the cosmos, but the ears of human beings are unable to hear it, just as human eyes cannot look into the sun. The few humans blessed with the experience found it impossible to report what they had heard or seen (see 2 Cor 12:1-4). Nevertheless, the ancients believed that this cosmic musical concert was going on since creation.

All the ancients knew about the "harmony of the spheres." The seven planets (five plus the sun and moon) in passing through the zodiac were believed to produce the seven tones of the basic musical scale. Some thought that this movement produced the sounds of the lyre, which constituted a harmony because of the intervals. Cicero believed that learned men who could imitate that harmony on the lyre or in singing could thereby gain return to this region; so too could those who pursued divine pursuits intellectually. But hearing this music deafens one to the sound. Human ears simply cannot handle it. Thus there is no way of telling what melodies Isaiah, Paul, or John the Revealer heard.

HUMAN MELODIES

Musicologists recognize that the foundation of all ancient Middle Eastern music is the *maḳammat*, that is, a basic, stereotyped musical pattern or melodic formula (called melodicles) consisting sometimes of only a few notes. These "tunes" have been preserved in the Arabic-Persian cultural sphere. Each tune or *maḳam* is an invariable, independent melodic unit. To Western ears this feature is boring and even hypnotic or mantric. To the Middle Eastern ear, it is a challenge. The musician or singer strives to embellish the *maḳam* with ever-changing variations, especially by gliding through musical intervals in one continuous sound like the sound of a siren. (The technical term is "portamento" or "glissando.") In Middle Eastern music, interpretation is more important than the original musical idea.

This insight suggests that the instruction "according to . . . " in the "titles" of the psalms probably identifies familiar melodic kernels that the singers would be challenged to embellish. Thus, "muth labben" (Ps 9), "the hind of dawn" (Ps 22), "lilies" (Pss 45; 69; 80), "virgins" (Ps 46), "mahalath" (Ps 53) would identify the basic, simple melody that the singer would develop in impressive and exciting variations.

Zither player from Canaan.

What did these melodies sound like? About ten years ago, Ann Draffkorn-Kilmer, R. I. Crocker, and R. P. Brown published their re-creation of a Hurrian cult song from Ugarit and Old Babylonian tuning techniques in *Sounds from Silence: Recent Discoveries in Ancient Near Eastern Music* (Berkeley: Bit Enki Publications, n.d.) along with a cassette. If this source is not readily available, readers with a piano at hand can get some idea of ancient melodic patterns by playing all the white keys from E just above middle C to E an octave below. This is the Dorian mode, the oldest and central musical mode of the Greeks from which all the other modes developed.

If this mode sounds strange or even unpleasant to modern ears, the modern believer will have taken an enormous step toward appreciating how very different from our songs were the songs sung by our Middle Eastern ancestors in the faith. No sweet harmonies, multi-voice choruses, "easy-listening" music, but rather homophonic melodies modified by singers who hoped that their variation was better than that of other singers. Following these insights, try to imagine the sound of the hymn sung by Jesus and his disciples at the end of the supper before they proceeded to the Garden of Gethsemane (Mark 14:26).

MOOD MUSIC

The repetitive nature of stereotyped melodies *(makammat)* sung without harmony had the ability to induce altered states of consciousness. The prophets whom Saul encountered processing down from the high place to the accompaniment of harp, tambourine, flute, and lyre were prophesying, quite likely entranced by one of the stereotype tunes. This entire experience appeared to put Saul into a trance that enabled him to join in the prophesying also (1 Sam 10:5-6). Elisha employed a musician for the same purpose (2 Kgs 3:15: "the power of the LORD came upon him").

HALLELUJAH

Paul urged the Ephesians to forgo inebriation with spirits in favor of being filled with the Spirit, who would facilitate the singing of psalms, hymns, spiritual songs, "singing and making melody to the Lord with all your heart" (5:18-19). One gets the impression of an unrestrained expression of emotion (see also Col 3:16). Such free expression appears to have continued and evolved until the time of Augustine, who urged a return to singing hymns and psalms "according to the Oriental custom" (*Confessions,* IX.7). He was especially concerned about the Alleluia (see Commentary on Psalm 106:1). The Hebrew word *hallelujah* means "Praise the LORD." Psalms 146–150 are framed by a *hallelu yah,* forming the closing words of praise to the entire Book of Psalms.

What was the earlier Oriental custom? The power of the psalm melodies was very strong. These repetitive melodies led singers into a state of ecstasy, causing them to drop the consonants and sing only the vowels. Soon both singers and listeners considered the words as superfluous. Songs became wordless. The Alleluia became the most popular wordless hymn. Leaving out the consonants, the singer pronounced only the vowels: A E U I A. By Augustine's time, these Hebrew vowels were replaced by those of the Latin doxology "saeculorum Amen" (= forever Amen): E U O U A E, which was another wordless ecstatic song. Such songs were called in Latin "jubilus," which Jerome characterized as a song that cannot be expressed in words or syllables or letters or in any utterance other than these vowels.

It is quite plausible that the bel cantostyle of singing that developed in Italy in the seventeenth and eighteenth centuries may have had its roots in these wordless songs of the Church. Bel canto singing highlights the beauty of the vowel produced by the energy of the airflow shaped into words ever so subtly with gently pronounced consonants. The resulting mellifluous melody can easily enchant the listener and produce alternate levels of consciousness.

CONCLUSION

Bible readers are very familiar with the lyrics of the Bible's songs: psalms, hymns, the Song of Songs, and the others. Is there any way to imagine how these songs might have sounded? A discussion among scholars about this topic on the Internet last year frequently mentioned Ali Jihad Racy, an ethnomusicologist at the University of California, as someone whose (recorded) performances of traditional Arab music, based on careful research and fieldwork, seem to bring a listener very close to plausible melodies of antiquity. Life has changed very little in the Arabic-Persian culture sphere over the past four thousand years.

To all that has already been said about rhythm and melody, Racy adds and highlights the importance of audience participation. The delighted cries and exclamatory gestures of the listeners become part of a dialogue with performers. Without such dialogue, Racy notes, the performer loses heart and the performance loses its soul. One can gain a fresh experience of biblical texts by adopting these melodies and audience participation provisionally as a plausible "listening" scenario for imagining the setting of many of the Bible's songs. (A listening scenario is a correlative to a reading scenario. Scenarios are the means by which human beings make sense out of their experiences.) Racy's and other ethnic recordings from around the world are available from Audio-Forum, 96 Broad Street, Guilford, CT 06437 (800-243-1234; E-mail: 74537.550@Compuserve.Com).

FOR FURTHER READING

Haïk-Vantoura, Suzanne. *The Music of the Bible Revealed*. Trans. Dennis Weber. Ed. John Wheeler. Berkeley, Calif.: BIBAL Press, 1991.

Jones, Ivor. "Musical Instruments [in the Bible]." *Anchor Bible Dictionary* 4:934–939.

Matthew, Victor H. "Music in the Bible." *Anchor Bible Dictionary* 4:930–934.

Sendrey, Alfred. *Music in Ancient Israel*. New York: Philosophical Library, 1969.

Stainer, John. *The Music of the Bible, with Some Account of the Development of Modern Musical Instruments from Ancient Types*. Rev. ed. Reprint of the 1914 ed., New York: Da Capo Press, 1970.

Werner, Eric. "Two Types of Ritual and Their Music." In *Salo Wittmayer Baron Jubilee Volume on the Occasion of His Eightieth Birthday*. English Section: Vol. 2, pp. 975–1008. Jerusalem: American Academy for Jewish Research, 1974. Distributed by Columbia University Press.

Wilson-Dickson, Andrew. *The Story of Christian Music*. Minneapolis: Fortress Press, 1996.

NONVERBAL COMMUNICATION

A popular American adage observes: "Who you are is shouting so loudly I can't hear a word you're saying." This reflects the truth that human beings use more than words, whether spoken or written, to communicate. To appreciate the importance of nonverbal communication, consider John the Baptist. His verbal and vocal message (words and sounds) is "Repent, for the kingdom of heaven is at hand" (Matt 3:2). Did he speak loudly or softly? fast or slow? breathlessly or in measured tones? Was his voice pleasant or grating? Was he shouting or speaking in smooth cadences? This nonverbal but vocal aspect of John's sentence added something to the message. The vocal aspect was evident and significant to his listeners but lost for the most part to modern Western readers. We can only surmise whether the vocal aspect of John's verbal message frightened people or made them laugh, resounded with authority or faded into inaudible endings.

As written in the Bible, John's sentence is verbal but nonvocal. A reader who understands Greek or Hebrew can grasp the power of the specific words but can only make an educated guess about how to pronounce them correctly. Moreover, since written words make no sounds, the reader cannot know the pitch, intensity, or timbre of John's voice. Was it high or low? shrill or resonant? squeaky or robust? Each characteristic would make a different impact on the listeners.

John's nonverbal and nonvocal communication is clearly reported in the text. He wore a garment of camel skin cinched around his waist by a leather girdle (Matt 3:4). Commentators correctly indicate that this garb aligns John with Elijah the prophet (see 2 Kgs 1:8) and suggests that he is a new Elijah (Matt 11:7-15; 17:10-13). If this was John's intent in wearing such garb, his listeners who knew him well would be shocked to see the son of a country priest dressing like a prophet. Prophets were generally critical of priests in the Hebrew tradition. Furthermore, in Middle Eastern cultures the son is expected to take up the profession or occupation of his father. Would Zechariah be proud of his son John?

The nonverbal and nonvocal message of John's baptism was ritual purity. He does not seem to have used a formula while baptizing those who came forward. This action intensified the significance of John's peculiar diet: locusts and honey. This nonverbal and nonvocal act of communication is best understood as signifying a desire for ritual purity rather than asceticism. Taken in all of its verbal, vocal, nonverbal, and nonvocal dimensions, the message of John was pointed, unmistakable, and powerful. No wonder his audience was stirred to repentance or driven to vengeful anger.

Nonverbal communication includes all human behaviors, other than the voice, that convey a message. Body shape, size, posture, clothing, hairstyle, gestures, facial expressions, use of space, touching behaviors, cultural custom, and many more elements fall into this category. A fresh look at familiar passages helps a reader to appreciate this aspect of communication embedded in the text of the Bible.

CULTURAL CUE FOR A YOUNG MAN

Thanks to Sirach, we have an explicit statement of a cultural cue that is hidden from modern readers in many biblical passages but familiar to Middle Eastern natives: "Young man, speak only when necessary, when they have asked you more than once" (32:7). Asked by God to be a prophet (Jer 1:5), Jeremiah declined and reminded the Deity: "I am only a youth" (1:6). God follows the cultural rule and invites the lad a second time (1:7-8). After his initiatory visions (1:9-19), Jeremiah took up his task with determination (2:4ff.) The apparent lack of such a cultural cue in Isaiah's call-vision (6:8-9) suggests that Isaiah was not a young man when he began his ministry.

Perhaps like many other young men in this culture, the brash Elihu couldn't wait to be asked even once. "Listen to me; let me also declare my opinion" (Job 32:6-10). The rich young man who sought eternal life also apparently did not wait to be invited by Jesus to speak. He asked his question directly (Matt 19:16-22), only to recognize with sadness—very likely immediately evident on his face—that he was unwilling to act upon the answer Jesus gave him.

Such a penchant for a double invitation permeates this culture's behavior even more deeply. Double invitations to banquets were common (see Luke 14:16-17). During the time between the first and second invitation, those invited "checked" out the reputation of the host, the rest of the guest list, and sought other information needed to determine whether to attend or to decline when the time came.

After hearing these ideas explained in class one day, a student from Greece said he now understood what he considered to be very rude behavior from fellow students at the university. When they invited him to join them for a movie or other social event, he always declined, fully expecting to be asked again. But they never asked him a second time! Through disappointing experience he learned that in the United States he had better say what he meant the first time. There will be no second invitation.

WATCH THOSE HANDS!

In his Sermon on the Mount, Jesus instructed his disciples how to respond to (presumably) unprovoked violence, a challenge to one's honor: "If anyone strikes you on the right cheek, turn to him the other also" (Matt 5:39). When two people face each other, the only way for one to strike the other on the right cheek is to do it with the back of the right hand. A slap with the back of the hand is insulting indeed but awkward to deliver, especially in view of the fact that people in the Middle East stand much closer to each other than the sixteen inches that usually separate Westerners standing face to face. It isn't easy in such close quarters to draw one's right hand across one's chest in order to slap an opponent on the right cheek.

It is much easier—in fact, probably necessary—to use the left hand to slap the right cheek with full force. This nonverbal and nonvocal statement was doubly insulting in the ancient Middle East. The left hand was used exclusively for toilet functions. One never pointed with it, gave a gift with it, or touched another with it. Matthew's Jesus described a positively revolting scenario that cried out for retaliation ("an eye for an eye, a tooth for a tooth"), yet Jesus advised restraint instead. Imagine how the audience would have responded to this advice. Did their eyes widen, their jaws drop, their tongues click from shock? Did his disciples flick their chin with their fingertips and vocally object: "Get real, cobber (= brother)!"? What does your newly developing Middle Eastern imagination suggest?

WATCH THOSE EYES!

Matthew's Jesus tells a parable about the behaviors of the owner of a vineyard and day-laborers he hired for the harvest (20:1-15). With parables, a speaker says one thing but means another. This is not a story about employer-employee relations, fair wages, or the need for collective bargaining. It is about God. The point of the story is that God is free to interact with people on God's own terms: with some by strict contract, and with others by favoritism (called patronage in the Middle East). One hopes for favoritism but is wise to fulfill the contract for safety's sake.

When the first hired in the story realize that the last hired are being treated with favoritism, they cast an evil eye on the owner of the vineyard. This is serious, a matter of life and death. Jesus' audience would be horrified to hear him include it in the parable.

What does it mean to have or cast an evil eye? In the ancient Middle Eastern view, the eye was connected to the heart, in which God had planted two drives: one toward good and another toward evil. Evil intents came from the heart through the eyes and worked an effect in the world (see Mark 7:21-23; Rom 7:15-20).

Since people in this culture judged others by externals (see 1 Sam 16:7), body characteristics were extremely important. People with joined eyebrows or a "lazy" eye or some other eye irregularity were considered capable of inflicting harm upon people or things simply by looking or glaring at them. In the modern Middle East, this is called "the fierce look." It is dangerous.

Middle Eastern people protect themselves (and their possessions) against the evil eye with a combination of talismans and colors. Blue (sometimes red) is especially powerful. Eye-shaped amulets worn outside and inside one's clothes are also powerful.

One can imagine the listeners' reaction at this point of the parable. Mere mention of the evil eye set danger in motion. The listeners and Jesus the storyteller immediately clutched tightly the tassels on their cloaks. These tassels (Hebrew *ṣiṣit*) were bound with a twined cord of blue (Num 15:37-41; Deut 22:12) to protect against the evil eye. Perhaps they also showed "horizontal horns" by thrusting their left hand forward, extending pinky and forefinger while withdrawing the middle two fingers into the palm, a common hand symbol in the Middle East to ward off the evil eye.

Still others may have begun to spit ritually, perhaps three times after biting the knuckle of the middle finger on the right hand as is customary in contemporary Mediterranean countries at the mere suspicion that the evil eye has been cast. (There seems to be an indication of this in Galatians 4:14, where "despise" literally means "spit." A tradition says that Paul had joined eyebrows and may have been suspected by some of having the ability to cast the evil eye. People would spit to protect themselves. The Galatians apparently did not fear this from Paul.)

Since this story is about God and not about an employer, the listeners are horrified that some people would give God's judgment and generosity an evil eye, a wish for destruction. Such people are perverse, perhaps insane. It is not difficult to imagine that Jesus' story quite likely provoked among the listeners heated discussions, denials supported by oaths, furious anger that human beings would "evil eye" God. Jesus the master storyteller knew how to use symbols and cultural beliefs to enormous effect.

Of course, none of this is written in the texts, but a savvy Middle Eastern reader instinctively knows and supplies to the text what the author or speaker presumed they would supply, namely, the non-verbal and nonvocal signs that are essential to deflecting threats of evil.

SIGNS ARE IRREVOCABLE

Specialists point out that all human communication is dynamic and irreversible; it is constantly in motion and changing. Nothing one says or does can ever be completely retracted. Apologies cannot erase scars (think of Judas' betrayal or Peter's denial of Jesus), nor can subsequent disappointing experiences eradicate an initial, intensely pleasurable one (think of the love relationship between Yahweh and Israel described in Ezekiel's allegorical folk tale [16:1-63]).

The major prophets incorporated the irreversible nature of non-verbal and nonvocal communication into their ministry, especially in their symbolic deeds. Jeremiah's behavior with the loincloth (13:1-11) or his breaking a flask (19:1-2, 10-11) was more than an imaginative and clever illustration of his message. Once performed, the deed cannot be canceled. The deed sets irrevocably in motion the message it symbolizes. Theologians observe that Jesus' actions with the bread and wine at the Last Supper are best interpreted in this same category of communication. While the modern conclusion drawn from this aspect of human communication is "Think twice before you say or do anything," or "Better to be careful than to be sorry," the ancients could go ballistic to realize that symbolic deeds performed by God's prophets set God's will irreversibly in motion.

CONCLUSION

Anyone who has traveled abroad knows how careful a visitor must be with regard to sign language. While the "horizontal horns" hand signal in the Middle East is a protection against evil spirits and the evil eye, in some African countries a variation on this gesture (pointing the index and third fingers toward someone) puts the evil eye on that person. In 1985 the Parker Pen Company compiled and published a guide for international travelers entitled *Do's and Taboos Around the World* and included an "International Gesture Dictionary" to help avoid embarrassing miscommunication. This article sketches the beginnings of a similar handbook for Bible readers.

FOR FURTHER READING

Barakat, Robert A. "Arabic Gestures." *Journal of Popular Culture* 6 (1973) 749–792.

Elliott, John H. "The Evil Eye in the First Testament: The Ecology and Culture of a Pervasive Belief." In *The Bible and the Politics of Exegesis*, ed. David Jobling et al., 147–159. Cleveland: Pilgrim Press, 1991.

Gruber, Mayer I. *Aspects of Nonverbal Communication in the Ancient Near East*. Studia Pohl 12. 2 vols. Rome: Biblical Institute Press, 1980.

Pilch, John J. "Gestures." *The Eerdmans Dictionary of the Bible*. Grand Rapids, Mich.: Eerdmans (forthcoming).

Poyatos, Fernando, ed. *Advances in Nonverbal Communication: Sociocultural, Clinical, Esthetic and Literary Perspectives*. Amsterdam and Philadelphia: John Benjamins Publishing Co., 1992.

PRAYER

Nearly all commentators on Luke's Gospel observe that prayer is one of the salient motifs of its twenty-four chapters. Yet few define prayer, and discussions of prayer in the commentaries seem to follow simply the concordance listing of occurrences of the Greek words for prayer. In a companion piece to this entry that first appeared in *The Bible Today* (July 1980), Bruce Malina presented a rather comprehensive, social-scientific definition of prayer and listed seven purposes. I applied that model to Luke's Gospel, with richer results than one will find in many commentaries, even the more recent ones, which still seem oblivious of our published joint efforts.

PRAYER–ALWAYS TO PERSONS

Malina defined prayer as "a socially meaningful symbolic act of communication, bearing directly upon persons perceived as somehow supporting, maintaining, and controlling the order of existence of the one praying, and performed with the purpose of getting results from or in the interaction of communication." Thus, not all prayer is religious prayer. In the various healing stories in Luke's Gospel, for example, those who approached Jesus with a request for healing were engaged in a prayer (a petition from a subordinate to a superior) in a very broad sense. Recall Luke 4:38; 5:12-14; 17:11, or notably 7:1-10, where the centurion sent two sets of intermediaries to present his requests to Jesus, much as we would hire a lawyer to deal with a judge in court. However, from the perspective of the Gospel writer and of today's believer, these petitions were indeed religious prayer.

Religious prayer is directed to a person who is perceived as controlling the general order of existence. In the biblical tradition, this is God. Jesus reminds the Gerasene to "go and report all that God has done for you," and he, recognizing that God was working in Jesus, went and reported all that "Jesus had done for him."

Probe this notion further: How is God perceived in the Gospel? He controls fertility (Luke 1:13-15); he shows great kindness (1:58). He is kind to the ungrateful and the wicked (6:35) and does not engage in a human sort of tit-for-tat. He looks after nature (12:24-26). Since all theology is analogy, which means that everything human beings know and understand about God is rooted in human experience (which itself is culturally shaped), we see that perceptions of God are based on human qualities purged of their human flaws. The full context of "Be merciful as your Father is merciful" (6:27-40) lists such human-like divine characteristics, or if you prefer, God-like human qualities.

After grasping the Lucan perceptions of God, a reader must assess the perceptions of God held by her or his culture. Who is the "god" in "God bless America"? Or the "god" in "one nation, under God, indivisible. . ."? Is it the God of Abraham, Isaac, and Jacob? The Father of Jesus? The deist god? The god of civil religion? What impact will this have on the way people pray? What can one do to sharpen personal understanding as well as the understanding of others about God?

COMMUNICATION–WHAT PRAYER IS ALL ABOUT

Prayer is the purposeful transfer of messages from source to receiver. In religious prayer the receiver is God. (Consider the contemporary prayers that seem to be composed more for the edification of the listeners than for affecting God.) Consider the Pharisee and the tax collector (Luke 18:9-14). Two individuals send messages to God for a purpose. The Pharisee's message is self-righteousness and complacency. By his body language (standing at an antiseptic distance from the tax collector) he projects his righteousness. His mental prayer evidences his conviction of being virtuous and despising others. The tax collector, by contrast, beats his breast (a gesture) and pleads, "God, have mercy on me a sinner."

One kind of gesture in prayer that does not appear in the New Testament but is found in the Hebrew Scriptures is dancing. There are eleven Hebrew verb roots related to dancing. See, for instance, *ḥul* ("to whirl," "to dance," "to writhe") in Psalm 87:7 or the verb *kārar*, which occurs only in 2 Samuel 6:14, 16. This varied vocabulary suggests to scholars that an advanced stage of choreography existed among the Israelites. The Talmud gives impressive testimony to the place of dance in prayerful observance of the festival of Sukkoth: "Whoever has not witnessed the joy of the festival of water-drawing has seen no joy in life. Pious men and men of affairs danced with torches in their hands, singing songs of joy and of praise, and the Levites made music with lyre and harp and cymbals and trumpets and countless other instruments" (Sukkoth, 51b). The only dancing mentioned in the New Testament (apart from the children's games in Matthew 11:17 and Luke 7:32) is that of Herodias's daughter (Matt 14:6; Mark 6:22), which was a form of communication in that it obtained from Herod a desired favor: the head of John the Baptizer. (See pp. 32–38 above). In recent years, dancing has been revived as a legitimate liturgical prayer form (see Gloria Weyman, *Dancing for God* [Cincinnati: World Library, 1969]).

GETTING RESULTS–THE PURPOSE OF PRAYER

Malina identified seven types of prayer based on the kinds of results desired. Reading the Gospel of Luke with these seven categories in mind highlights the following illustrations.

1) Instrumental prayers ("I/we want . . .") are prayers of petition. Zechariah prayed for a child (1:13). Jesus urged his disciples to ask for more laborers for the harvest (10:2). The Lord's Prayer (11:1-4) contains model petitions. Jesus didn't say "Repeat these formulas" but rather "Pray like this." Jesus urged his listeners to pray for strength to escape impending calamity (21:36) and not to be put to the definitive test (22:40). He himself asked God to forgive his executioners (23:34). These are genuine "gimme" prayers without the unflattering implications of that word.

2) Regulatory prayers ("Do as I tell you") presume that the one praying is somehow superior to God. Such prayers seek to control God's activity. In truth, there is no example of such prayer in Luke (though many contemporary, popular devotional prayers might fall into this category). Jesus rejected the disciples' suggestion: "Lord, do you want us to bid fire come down from heaven and consume them [inhospitable Samaritans]?" (9:54; this is actually an instrumental prayer). Indeed, Jesus' prayer "Father, if you are willing, remove this cup from me; nevertheless not my will but yours be done" (22:42) is the exact opposite of regulatory prayer. Simon, "who had previously practiced magic" (Acts 8:9), may have had this understanding of prayer in mind when he offered the apostles silver to gain the ability of imparting the Spirit through the laying on of hands (gesture).

3) Interactional prayers ("me and you") seek to maintain emotional ties with God. Practically all the concordance entries about Jesus going off to be alone in prayer (5:16; 6:12; 9:18; 9:28; 11:1) fit this category. So too would 18:1.

4) Self-focused prayers ("Here I come; here I am") identify and express self to God. The parable of the Pharisee and the tax collector (18:9-14) illustrates this type of prayer. So, too, do Mary's prayer (1:46-56) and Simeon's canticle (2:29-32).

With a Torah case in the center of the gathering, Jewish worshipers pray at the Western Wall, Jerusalem.

5) Heuristic prayers ("tell me why") explore the world of God and God's workings with us. This may have been the focus of Jesus' prayer after his baptism (3:21) when the Spirit descended upon him in bodily form. The transfiguration narrative (9:28) might also be an explanation of the prayer and experience of alternate reality by Jesus and his companions on that occasion. The *berakah* pronounced by Jesus upon learning of the success of the mission of the seventy-two disciples illustrates the *fait accompli*: "I thank you, Father, Lord of heaven and earth, that you have hidden these things from the wise and understanding and have revealed them to babes" (10:21). Fi-

nally, the prayer of Luke's Jesus drawn from the psalms as he died, "Into your hands, O Lord, I commend my spirit" (Ps 31:5), is a piece of information (see no. 7 below). But in the tradition prior to the evangelist, the psalms could have been heuristic prayers for exploring the meaning of Jesus' betrayal, suffering, and death.

6) Imaginative prayer ("let's pretend") strives to create an environment of one's own with God (for example, praying in tongues or in languages unknown to the person reading or reciting). Jesus' Aramaic prayer on the cross (Ps 22:2), cited in Matthew 27:46 and Mark 15:34, could be an illustration of this kind of prayer as he adopted the posture of the suffering innocent person.

7) Informative prayer ("I have something to tell you") passes new information to God. Examples are prayers of acknowledgment or thanksgiving for favors. John's long speech-prayers of Jesus fall into this category. For instance, in John 17 Jesus explains (presumably to his Father?) what eternal life is. Similar informative prayers are the praises of God in Luke by beneficiaries (the shepherd in 2:20; the healed leper in 17:18; Anna in 2:38).

Each of these prayer types flows from and blends with the life-situation of the one praying. After mastering the life-situation of New Testament personalities, the Bible reader needs to become equally familiar with the life-settings in her or his culture in order to draw inspiration from corresponding biblical situations or to form suitable biblically based prayers for this different culture.

PRAYERS–ROOTED IN THE CULTURAL GROUP

All prayers are shaped by the religious values and behavior of the group to which the one praying belongs. Thus communal prayer is the basis and the principle of individual prayer in Middle Eastern societies. Recall that Mary's prayer (Luke 1:46-56) borrowed from Anna's prayer (1 Sam 2:1-10) as well as from other Hebrew Scripture. Zechariah's canticle (Luke 1:67-79) is similar to psalms of praise (e.g., Pss 34:6; 67:2) as well as to other psalms. This occurs not because these individuals felt less creative or capable, but because group tradition and continuity are paramount. The challenge to the contemporary community is to make certain that it is always in tune with the Spirit.

CONCLUSION–AND BEGINNING!

Reading the Gospel of Luke from the perspective of the model proposed by Malina reveals that prayer permeates the biblical text much more than the concordance or commentaries suggest. The model, with its definition and seven types of prayer, could well serve

to help understand biblical prayer better and to develop personal prayerfulness along biblical lines.

FOR FURTHER READING

Craghan, John F. *Psalms for All Seasons*. Collegeville, Minn.: The Liturgical Press, 1993.

Malina, Bruce J. "What Is Prayer?" *The Bible Today* 18 (1980) 214–220.

Kodell, Jerome, O.S.B., and Alan Detscher. "Prayer." *The Collegeville Pastoral Dictionary of Biblical Theology*. Ed. Carroll Stuhlmueller, C.P. Collegeville, Minn.: The Liturgical Press, 1996.

SECRECY

In 1901 Wilhelm Wrede published a study that identified and analyzed a "Messianic secret" motif in the Gospels. Jesus seemed determined to keep aspects of his identity and activity a secret. Recall how Jesus responded to Peter's identification of him as Messiah: "He charged them to tell no one about him" (Mark 8:30; see also 9:9 and elsewhere). Modern scholars, however, have noted that there is a "publicity" theme in Mark that is just as pronounced as the "secrecy" theme. Jesus commanded the Gerasene demoniac to go and tell "what the Lord in his mercy has done for you" (5:19ff.). While many scholars followed Wrede in the conviction that secrecy was a motif introduced by Mark, increasing numbers now recognize that secrecy may well be attributable to Jesus himself!

HONOR AND SHAME: MEDITERRANEAN CORE CULTURAL VALUES

The core values of Mediterranean culture are honor and shame. Honor is a claim to worth *and* a public acknowledgment of that claim. Thus, the Baptizer announced "a more powerful one" who was to come after him (Mark 1:7), and the voice from heaven acknowledged and affirmed that claim regarding Jesus: "You are my Son, my beloved one, in whom I am well pleased" (Mark 1:11). That this is not a private experience is clear from the temptation that follows immediately. The demon heard the message. Honor claims always pose a challenge to others and therefore must be tested, disputed, weakened, and even invalidated if possible. Vanquishing the temptation, Jesus emerged with his honor intact.

THE PUBLIC NATURE OF LIFE IN THE MEDITERRANEAN WORLD

Visitors to Mediterranean countries notice that natives spend a lot of time outside. There are outside cafes for eating or just sipping coffee or wine. There are public plazas or squares for people-watching.

There are wide avenues, or *paseos,* for strolling or strutting, especially in the late afternoon and early evening hours. Everyone in this culture minds everybody else's business. Privacy is very difficult if not impossible to achieve.

Recall the difficulty Jesus experienced whenever he wanted to pray alone. "In the morning, while it was still very dark, he got up and went to a deserted place, and there he prayed" (Mark 1:35). But Simon and his friends hunted him down and informed him, "Everyone is searching for you!"

In this society, it is difficult to make a claim to worth that is not self-evident, because everybody knows everybody else's background. In the village of Nazareth, everybody knew everything about Jesus. "Is this not the carpenter, the son of Mary, and brother of James and Joses and Judas and Simon, and are not his sisters here with us?" (Mark 6:3). And the villagers were distressed with him because he had not taken up his father's trade as a dutiful son should but was teaching in the synagogue instead.

HONOR, SHAME, AND SECRECY

The nosy behavior of Jesus' fellow villagers, so typical in the Mediterranean world, demands and encourages secrecy. Otherwise daily life becomes unbearable.

> There is an ideal sphere which lies around every human being. Although differing in size in various directions and differing according to the person with whom one entertains relations, this sphere cannot be penetrated, unless the personality value of the individual is thereby destroyed. A sphere of this sort is placed around man by his "honor." One should not trespass the boundary by questions or other invasions (G. Simmel, 331; see "For Further Reading, p. 129).

Other attempts to invade Jesus' sphere of honor were repeatedly made by his opponents. Jesus routinely responded with a strategy of secrecy or deception. For instance, in Mark 11:27-33, the chief priests, scribes, and elders ask by whose authority Jesus acts. He answers their question with a counterquestion about John's baptism. They recognize in his question a potential no-win situation for themselves, so they say: "We do not know." Jesus responds: "Neither will I tell you about myself." Jesus successfully fends off the challenge to his honor by keeping secret the source of his authority.

Secrecy is thus an important element in gaining and maintaining one's honor. It is a skill that is seriously pursued and arduously practiced until it can be exercised with great success. Jesus was a master at it.

SECRECY IN MEDITERRANEAN CULTURE

Secrecy is a formal, conscious, deliberate, and calculated concealment of information, activities, or relationship that *outsiders* can gain only by espionage (Tefft 14; 320). From another perspective, it is a selective transmission of information. Secrecy divides people into "insiders" and "outsiders." Insiders know the secret; outsiders are kept in the dark. The reason for this division is that secrecy rests on the premise of distrust. It judges that others can't be trusted with certain information mainly from fear of how others might react to the information or what they might do with it.

Mediterranean culture in general tends to distinguish between insiders and outsiders. Insiders are usually one's family and very close associates; everyone else is an outsider. Thus when Jesus traveled to the region of Tyre, "he entered a house and did not want anyone to know he was there. Yet he could not escape notice" (Mark 7:24). He sought to keep his whereabouts a secret because he could not trust how people would respond to him. Would they deluge him with requests for favors as in Mark 1:32, or would they ask him to leave as in Mark 5:17?

CONSEQUENCES OF SECRECY

Secrecy makes it difficult for *outsiders*, whether competitors, rivals, or enemies, to predict the actions of *insiders* and take counteraction against them. When the chief priests, scribes, and elders recognized that Jesus told the parable of the vineyard against them (Mark 12:12), "they wanted to arrest him, but they feared the crowd. So they left him and went away."

The parable was a strategy in the service of secrecy (see Mark 4:10-12). Others in this audience may not have perceived its thrust as clearly as the priests, scribes, and elders did. Or again, they may have perceived it only too clearly ("the large crowd was listening to him with delight": Mark 12:37). In either case, parabolic teaching protected Jesus from the outsiders.

Indeed, his enemy-outsiders had to rely on Judas, an insider, to "leak" the secret of where Jesus would be after the Supper and also to identify which of the characters present in the dark garden was actually Jesus (Mark 14:10-11).

These comments indicate quite clearly that secrecy is both a cause as well as a result of social conflict. Secrecy plays a key role in conflict-group formation. Jesus and the Twelve were a conflict group. Secrecy also plays a role in the dynamics of conflict itself, that is, the process of interaction between conflict groups such as the

Jesus group and the Pharisees, Sadducees, elders, and others. Secrecy furthers social antagonisms and tensions.

THE FASCINATION OF SECRECY

Clearly, having a secret gives a person a position of exception. Since others are excluded from knowing, they assume that the secret must have special value. Specialists point out that the secret is basically independent of the context it guards. What matters is that others know little or nothing about the secret. Mediterranean culture is definitely fascinated with secrecy. One can only wonder to what extent Jesus' penchant for secrecy as reflected in Mark and the other Gospels was driven by this common cultural fascination. Biblical experts point out that the concept of "Messiah" was much too complex and divergently understood in the first-century world to suggest that Jesus engaged in secrecy to keep people from erroneously assigning him a role as "political" Messiah.

THE PROCESS OR PATTERN OF SECRECY

Secrecy is so integral a part of Mediterranean culture that there is a discernible pattern or process to it. The full process seems to have five elements, though secrecy can operate with fewer. One constant characteristic of secrecy is that it separates "insiders" from "outsiders." The process is as follows:

> *Insiders:* secret gives power and security.
> *Outsiders:* must use espionage (surveillance, gossip, etc.) to learn the secret.
> *Insiders:* then devise security methods, including lying or leaking false information, deception, or parables.
> *Outsiders:* now have to evaluate what they have spied out and what has been given to them by the insiders.
> *Insiders:* often engage in post-hoc security in an attempt to weaken the effect of a surprise or unregulated disclosure.

With the aid of this pattern, reflect upon Peter's identification of Jesus as Messiah in Mark 8:27-30.

> *Insider:* Jesus knows his identity (the secret).
> *Outsiders:* make guesses: Is he John the Baptist? Elijah? One of the prophets?
> *Insider:* Peter says: "You are the Messiah!"
> *Outsiders:* the other eleven and everyone else outside are still guessing and evaluating the information they now have: John Baptist? Elijah? Prophet? Messiah?

Insiders: Jesus says: "Still confused? Good! But if like Peter you seem to be on a promising trail, don't tell anybody else." That is, let the confusion continue; keep my identity secret; this secret keeps my enemies off balance.

Again, consider Jesus before Pilate (Mark 15:1-5):

Insider: Jesus knows but conceals his identity.
Outsider: Pilate asks bluntly: "Are you the king of Judeans?" (v. 2).
Insider: Jesus gives an ambiguous answer: "*You* say so" (v. 2).
Outsider: Pilate must now evaluate this answer and the noisy gossip of the crowd. He asks Jesus again: "Have you no reply?" (vv. 3-4).
Insider: Jesus makes no further reply. His secret is safe. And Pilate the outsider is amazed and still in the dark.

MAKING THE SECRET KNOWN

There are at least two ways to make a secret known: to "leak" it to others or to reveal it. Judas has already been presented above as a secret-leaker in his betrayal of Jesus.

Revealing secrets is more common than one might guess. Because secrecy is an element in interpersonal relationships, it cannot be absolute lest the relationship break down. The further development of every relationship is determined by the ratio of persevering and yielding energies contained in that relationship. In other words, the secret is a form that constantly receives and releases content. What was originally manifest becomes secret, and what was once hidden later sheds its concealment.

Mark's Jesus notes: "Is a lamp brought in to be put under a bushel basket, or under a bed, and not on a stand? For there is nothing hid, except to be made manifest; nor is anything secret except to come to light" (4:21-23). The context of this statement is Jesus' teaching in parables, a strategy of secrecy in his teaching ministry.

The passive voice in the verse just cited is probably a "theological passive," which means that God is the unmentioned but understood doer of the action, the revealer. In the long run, God will uncover all secrets, and everyone will know everything. In the life of Jesus, the bottom line then is that at some time, the right time, everything hidden will be made known, every secret will be revealed by God himself. But for now, in Jesus' present moment, secrecy is necessary in order that life may go on.

CONCLUSION

Mark's Jesus was a fully Mediterranean person when it came to using secrecy. He concealed full knowledge of his identity because he wanted to maintain and safeguard his ascribed honor. Relative to his activities, Jesus regularly resorted to sidestepping the question or challenge, or giving interpretation to his disciples privately.

Among the culturally plausible results that Mark's Jesus may well have intended in using secrecy were to enhance his honorable reputation; to frustrate Mediterranean nosiness; to conceal shameful and potentially damaging information about himself (his shameful fate). Confident that he would be ultimately vindicated by his Father, Jesus cited a Mediterranean cultural truism to console his admirers and warn his opponents (see Mark 4:21-23).

FOR FURTHER READING

Pilch, John J. *Introducing the Cultural Context of the New Testament.* New York/Mahwah, N.J.: Paulist Press, 1991. Session Three.

_____. "Secrecy in the Mediterranean World: An Anthropological Perspective." *Biblical Theology Bulletin* 24 (1994) 151–157.

Pitt-Rivers, Julian. *People of the Sierra.* 2d ed. Chicago and London: University of Chicago Press, 1971.

Simmel, Georg. "The Secret and the Secret Society." In *The Sociology of Georg Simmel.* Trans. and ed. Kurt H. Wolff, 305–376. Glencoe, Ill.: The Free Press, 1950.

Tefft, Stanton K., ed. *Secrecy: A Cross-Cultural Perspective.* New York: Human Sciences Press, 1980.

SHEEP AND GOATS

Sheep and goats were some of the earliest animals to be domesticated, and they are still very common in the Middle East. Because they were so plentiful and important in the lives of the ancient Israelites, the Hebrew language is particularly rich in words that distinguish sheep according to sex and age. Moreover, this rich vocabulary flows over into the human domain. For instance, the Hebrew word for the adult female sheep or "ewe" is *rāḥēl* (see Gen 31:38; 32:14), which is also the name of one of Jacob's wives: Rachel. The Aramaic noun for a newborn ewe lamb is *talyāh*, and this word was also used as an endearing term for a little girl. Recall that Jesus called Jairus's little daughter who had just died "Talitha" (Mark 5:41).

The Hebrew word for "ram," *ʿayil*, is often applied figuratively to princes, nobles, mighty leaders (Jer 25:34; Ezek 17:13; 30:13; 31:11). These linguistic tidbits open a window on Mediterranean culture that helps us to understand the literal and symbolic meaning of sheep and goats in the Bible.

HONOR AND SHAME

Honor is a public claim to esteem or value and a public acknowledgment of that claim. Mediterranean men must assert, protect, and if possible augment the family's honor. Women are the most vulnerable point through which a family's honor can be challenged or even taken away (Sir 26:10-12, 22-27). Hence, women are associated with shame in two ways. In a positive sense, a woman must cultivate a sense of shame, a sensitivity to the honor of the family. In a negative sense, when a woman is violated, whether willingly or not, she is the source of shame for the family.

Honor and shame are core values that permeate the entire Mediterranean culture and are also reflected in sheep and goats. Sheep are primarily men's animals; they take care of them. Goats are primarily women's animals; goats often are kept in the house with the women. In the Middle Eastern mind, sheep symbolize honor, while goats symbolize shame. Social scientists agree that human beings use animals to represent the internal differentiation of their society.

MEN AND SHEEP

What struck our ancestors in the faith and contemporaries as well is the fact that sheep do not make noise when they are shorn or even when death is imminent. They suffer in silence. Isaiah knew and attributed these qualities to the faithful servant: "Like a lamb that is led to the slaughter and like a sheep that before its shearers is silent, so he [the Servant] did not open his mouth" (53:7). In his discussion with the Ethiopian eunuch, Philip applied this passage to Jesus (Acts 8:32-35). Mark portrays Jesus' death by crucifixion in precisely this fashion, for Jesus first shrieked after hanging six hours on the cross and only just before he died (15:25-37).

Young Mediterranean boys who are brought up with young Mediterranean girls exclusively by the women suffer from lack of an adequate male role model in their early childhood. When they enter the male world at the age of puberty, they must begin to learn how to be a man. In large measure, this learning entails realizing that silent endurance of suffering, even physical punishment, from all older males is a major way of demonstrating one's manliness. The sheep that suffers and goes to death in silence offers a good example and is easily accepted as a symbol for the honorable male. John, Revelation, and Paul develop the symbol of Jesus as Lamb of God.

MEN AND GOATS

In ancient Greece and Rome, goats were recognized as very lascivious animals. Goats tolerate sexual access of other males to females in their domains. When two male goats fight over a female, the winner will cover her first and then step aside to allow the loser to do the same. With flocks of goats, more than two males often service the same flock.

Mediterranean males projected these same attributes to deceived husbands, that is, males who "permitted" other men to commit adultery with their wives because these males did not watch over and protect their women. Thus the goat was and still is associated with shame and shameful behavior.

In contrast, one ram usually can service a flock of approximately fifty ewes. The shepherd must be very careful as the number of ewes dwindles, for rams will fight one another if one tries to encroach on the ewes of another. Thus, while the goat became the symbol of shame, the ram became the symbol of virility, strength, and fierceness. It is no wonder that the very word "ram" was applied to kings, princes, and other honorable, mighty leaders, as noted above.

Even the deities were linked with each animal in similar fashion. The ram was associated with the honorable gods Zeus, Apollo, and Poseidon, while the goat became associated with nature-like gods such as Pan, Bacchus, and Venus—all known for shameful and unrestrained behavior.

WOMEN AND GOATS

The association of the goddess Venus with goats reveals additional insights about how women were and continue to be perceived in various Middle Eastern cultures. The common assumption is that women are, like goats, lascivious and unprincipled creatures. They are ever on the prowl, untrustworthy, the weakest links in every family. Because women are the most vulnerable to attacks on family honor, they must always be under the watchful eye and care of a male—father, brother, or husband. Recall the list of headaches that a daughter can cause for her father in Sirach 42:9-14.

The goat, perhaps because of traditional association with the nature-like gods mentioned above, also came to be associated with the devil (see Matt 25:33, 41). From this emerged the Mediterranean association of women with both the goat and the devil.

SHEEP, GOATS, AND SUBSISTENCE

Until the invention of the four-for-one plough, which improved agricultural production, sheep and goats were crucial to subsistence. They belong to the category of small livestock that produce milk, cheese, "hair," and wool, and also meat. Yet even here considerations of honor and shame add significant dimensions to basic meanings of nourishment and sustenance.

The hair of Palestinian goats is long and black and looks very much like human hair (Song 4:1; 1 Sam 19:13). It was and is most often spun and woven into a strong, heavy cloth used chiefly for tents like those of the Bedouins (Song 1:5) or the tent over the tabernacle (Exod 26:7; 35:26).

The wool of the sheep provided clothing. It was much more commonly used than linen, though priests' garments were to be made of the latter (Ezek 44:17). And it was fulled to a pure white, which explains the Mediterranean proverbial expression "as white as wool" (see Isa 1:18; Dan 7:9; Rev 1:14; Ps 147:16).

As for the milk and cheese, contemporary cultural descendants of our Mediterranean ancestors in the faith give additional insights into the honor-and-shame dimensions of sheep and goats. Mediterranean men do not normally drink milk; that is for women, children, the weak, and the sick. Rather, men eat cheese, especially goat's cheese (one such Greek product is the familiar feta), and if they drink milk, it will be goat's milk (Prov 27:27).

Beginning a long, hot day, a herd of sheep and goats visit a watering hole in the Sinai Desert.

Moreover, while women tend and milk the goats, the care and milking of sheep is essentially the men's task. Ordinarily a shepherd should wash his hands after sexual intercourse before milking the sheep, but it is generally preferable that unmarried shepherds be assigned to milk the milking ewes.

SHEEP, GOATS, AND RELIGIOUS SIGNIFICANCE

Because sheep and goats are cud-chewing mammals with cloven hoofs, the Hebrew tradition considers them as clean (see Lev 11:1-8) or non-polluting animals. Therefore their meat, milk, and cheese can be eaten.

At the same time, note well their respective use in sacrifice. When the righteous and obedient Abraham wanted to sacrifice an animal to God in place of his son Isaac, he selected a ram (Gen 22), a noble and honorable animal. But sinners who want to appease God must use a shameful animal, a scapegoat (Lev 16:6-10).

The pattern that emerges from these reflections can be schematized thus:

SHEEP	GOATS
honor	shame
men	women
virility	femininity
virile man	deceived man
strong	weak
silence (Isa 53:7; Acts 8:32; Mark 15)	noise (Luke 23:27)
men milk them	women milk them
men do not drink the milk of sheep; they drink goat's milk or eat goat's cheese	women, children, the sick, the weak drink the milk of sheep and goats
outside	inside
pastures	home

The entire Mediterranean world is divided along the lines of the core cultural values: honor and shame, which in turn are replicated in every other dimension of human life, beginning with gender. Let us turn now to one final example.

MATTHEW'S JUDGMENT SCENE (Matt 25:31-46)

The majority of references to sheep and goats among the Synoptics occur in Matthew (7:15; 9:36; 10:6, 16; 12:11, 12; 15:24; 18:12; 25:32, 33; 26:31 citing Zech 13:7).

"Glory" in Matthew 25:31 belongs to the semantic field of "honor." The coming of the Son of Man in glory enthroned on the throne of his glory, and all his angels with him, is clearly a scene in which honor is publicly bestowed (by God, of course) and displayed for all to see. Indeed, "all the nations" (v. 32) will witness the event.

The sheep, men's animals, are on the right, the honorable side. The goats, the women's animals and the source of daily milk and cheese for the family, are on the left, the side associated with shame. Those people assigned to the right side, to the sheep gathering, are those who practiced hospitality, which in the Mediterranean world is extended *mainly* by men and *solely* to complete strangers. (Kindness to relatives is called by another name: steadfast love.) Those assigned to the left side, the goat gathering, are those who failed to practice hospitality, as just explained.

How were people to know of this obligation? It is an essential Mediterranean cultural obligation upon males. Everyone knows it! When the Twelve were sent by Jesus on mission (Matt 10:1), they were told to rely precisely upon such hospitality to strangers (vv. 12-13). Where it was not forthcoming, the Twelve were advised to go elsewhere (v. 14). Then Jesus noted that the final judgment (see Matt 25:31-46) will be far more tolerable for the classic perverters of hospitality in the Old Testament (see Gen 19:1-29) than for those who refuse hospitality to evangelizers (Matt 10:15). Such inhospitable people like the inhospitable residents of Sodom and Gomorrah behave like goats!

CONCLUSION

Because we Westerners read a Bible that originated in Middle Eastern culture, there is always more to what we read than meets the eye. All cultures take many familiar things for granted. What has been said about sheep and goats was understood and taken for granted by our ancestors in the faith. Imposing on these texts our Western understandings of sheep and goats is grossly inconsiderate and inappropriate. Living in an age of increased sensitivity to other cultures, we can be grateful that we can begin to treat our ancestors with greater respect.

FOR FURTHER READING

Blok, Anton. "Rams and Billy-Goats: A Key to the Mediterranean Code of Honour." *Religion, Power and Protest in Local Communities: The Northern Shore of the Mediterranean.* Ed. Eric R. Wolf. Berlin/New York: Mouton, 1984.

Malina, Bruce J. "Hospitality." *Dictionary of Bible Values.* Ed. John J. Pilch and Bruce J. Malina. Peabody, Mass.: Hendrickson, 1992.

_____. "Hospitality." *Harper's Bible Dictionary.* Ed. Paul J. Achtemeier. San Francisco: Harper & Row, 1985.

Pilch, Jean Peters. *Comfort, Comfort My People! (The Corporal Works of Mercy).* Videocassette. New York/Mahwah, N.J.: Paulist Press, 1992.

Pilch, John J. *Introducing the Cultural Context of the Old Testament.* New York/Mahwah, N.J.: Paulist Press, 1991. Session Three: Core Cultural Values.

_____. "'Beat His Ribs While He Is Young' (Sir 30:12): A Window on the Mediterranean World." *Biblical Theology Bulletin* 23 (1993) 101–113.

SICKNESS

If a person could travel back in time to visit the ancient biblical world, what inoculations would be necessary to avoid getting sick? A question like this recently appeared on the Ancient Mediterranean computer discussion group (Internet). A specialist in immunology replied that the contemporary human body very likely contains antibodies against all diseases that existed, disappeared, or were conquered in previous centuries. The more serious concern is the effects of diseases that a modern person would carry backward in time which the immune system of the ancient world would be unequipped to combat.

Interesting as this modern question is, experts agree that the majority of illnesses in the ancient world were related to deficiencies in diet, improper food preparation, and lack of proper sanitation.

TRANSLATION PROBLEMS

Some sicknesses in the Bible seem very obvious. Manasseh, the first husband of Judith, was overcome by the burning heat while he stood in the field supervising the barley harvest. He took to his bed and died, very likely from the effects of sunstroke (Jdt 8:2-3).

Other sicknesses pose a problem. The "leprosy" described in Leviticus 13–14 was definitely not Hansen's disease, that is, what the modern world knows as leprosy. The Hebrew and Greek words should not be translated as "leprosy." The problem discussed in Leviticus affected human skin, clothing, and the walls of houses. It was quite likely some sort of physically harmless but repulsive, scaly condition. Still, the physical problem was a genuine concern in the biblical world and had serious social consequences. Most often these social consequences were a greater concern than the actual physical condition.

UNDERSTANDING ANCIENT SICKNESS

Modern scholars rely upon a variety of tools to investigate, understand, and interpret ancient sickness. The history-of-medicine approach, with rare exceptions, tends to use modern medicine as the measuring stick of information presented in biblical and other ancient texts. These specialists believe that true leprosy was first introduced into the Middle East from India by Alexander's armies.

Paleopathology studies ancient health and disease in humans and animals on the basis of archaeological remains such as bones, fecal matter, dried blood, and the like. Paleopathologists have still not found any evidence of true leprosy or syphilis in human bones from the ancient Middle East that can be dated earlier than the sixth century C.E.!

Medical anthropology views sickness in its cultural setting and seeks to learn the cultural interpretation of a sickness condition. It was an anthropologist who pointed out that biblical personalities interpreted what they called leprosy as a condition to be feared because it was polluting ("dirty") rather than because it was contagious ("catchy").

Insights from these sciences help a reader of the Bible to fill gaps in the biblical text with culturally plausible information. Consider these select examples.

TEETH

A very popular modern portrayal of Jesus depicts him with head tossed back, laughing heartily, and displaying a perfect set of gleaming white teeth. Though very appealing to the modern eye, the picture reflects the artist's imagination more than the cultural reality. To be sure, some ancient people did have good teeth at least for a while in life. The Hebrews prized teeth "whiter than milk" (Gen 49:12). The young man in the Song of Solomon praises his beloved's perfect set of teeth (Song 4:2; 6:6). Even if these sentiments reflect the Middle Eastern preference for the ideal over the real, for appearances over actuality, the appearances do have a foundation in reality, however short-lived.

Tooth problems were very likely the rule. Examination of the mummy of Merneptah, the probable Pharaoh of the Exodus, indicates that he suffered from severe periodontal disease and lost all his upper teeth except for the two front ones. If this was the condition of an elite citizen, imagine the condition of a peasant.

The common tooth problem in antiquity was attrition, that is, the gradual grinding down of teeth. The phrase "grinding or gnashing of teeth," so common in the Bible, should probably be taken literally as describing an actual custom with long-range, harmful consequences (Ps 35:16; 37:12; 112:10; Matt 8:12; 13:42, 50; 22:13; 24:51; 25:30). By old age, few grinders remained (Eccl 12:3).

Archaeological evidence indicates that in earlier times, tooth decay was rather rare. It became more prevalent in the Middle East during the Coptic and Byzantine periods when diets became more refined.

By examining teeth, paleopathologists can determine the age of the individual, the quality of diet, indications of growth disturbance, and sometimes the occupation. For example, the teeth of a weaver are distinguished by grooves caused by pulling fibers from the mouth.

EYES

The history of medicine documents that blindness was very common in the ancient Middle East. Perhaps this explains in part why the blind and the deaf were guaranteed special protection in the Torah (Lev 19:14). Most cases of blindness were due to trachoma, a contagious infection of the inner mucous lining of the eyelids (the conjunctiva) and of the cornea. The disease was transmitted by flies and by poor hygiene.

It was not until the nineteenth century that the Scottish surgeon Joseph Lister succeeded in convincing physicians that washing one's hands was a major step toward preventing the spread of disease. Prior to that, surgeons went directly from dissecting cadavers in the morgue to treating patients in the hospital, causing a high mortality rate. In antiquity, scarcity of water prompted many peasants to omit even required ritual ablutions (possibly the case in Mark 7).

There were other reasons for loss of sight in antiquity. Some persons were congenitally blind (John 9). Sorrow was blamed for some eye problems. Job lamented: "My eye has grown dim with sorrow" (17:7), and the psalmist echoes this belief: "My eye grows dim through sorrow" (Ps 88:9). Old age was also blamed for blindness: "Now Eli was ninety-eight years old and his eyes were set, so that he could not see" (1 Sam 4:15). Still other cases sound to modern ears like cataracts (Tob 6:8).

A widely recognized and accepted cure for blindness in antiquity was gall, a bitter greenish fluid secreted by the liver and stored in the gall bladder. The angel Raphael, whose Hebrew name means "God is my healer," advised Tobias to use the gall of a fish to cure a person with "white films in his eyes" (Tob 6:8). With this remedy, Tobias restored his father's sight (Tob 11:7-15).

One historian of medicine, a physician, believes that blindness was considered the ultimate disaster among biblical people because it caused total dependence on others. This explanation is culturally appropriate for our highly individualistic Western culture, with its emphasis on independence and self-determination. In the Mediterranean world, where people are group-oriented and personalities are other-directed (dyadic), the explanation is culturally irrelevant.

The real bane of blindness in ancient Israel seems to have been the awareness that God who bestows the gift of sight also withholds it or takes it away (Exod 4:11). In some, though not all, instances, loss of sight was associated with displeasing God, that is, sin (Gen 19:11; Deut 28:28; 2 Kgs 6:18; Acts 13:11). Tobit and the man born blind in John 9 illustrate exceptions to this belief.

Yet, despite the pain caused by knowing that for some mysterious reason, God had deprived one of sight, a blind person did not feel cursed. In Genesis (1:3-5), God existed in darkness before creating light. Darkness, therefore, symbolizes the presence of God. To live in darkness, that is, being unable to see, means that one lives in the presence of God. Such intimacy with God compensates the blind person, who can interact with but not see other human beings who are created in the image and likeness of God (Gen 1:26).

This insight provides a fresh context for the Gospel accounts of Jesus' success in healing the blind. Luke makes healing the centerpiece of Jesus' ministry (4:18-19) and reports that "on many that were blind [Jesus] bestowed sight" (7:21). Yet his Gospel describes only one such incident in detail, that concerning the blind beggar at the roadside near Jericho (18:35-43//Mark 10:46-52//Matt 20:17-19).

On the other hand, Luke reports many instances in which sighted people refused or failed to understand the teaching or person of Jesus. Examples of such sociocultural blindness are found in the parable about judging (6:39-42); the parable of the sower (8:9-15); the parable of the lamp (8:16-18); the macarism on seeing (10:21-24); seeking the sign of Jonah (11:29-32); another parable of the lamp (11:33-36); interpreting signs on earth and in the sky (12:54-56); seeing the Son of Man's day (17:22, 30); Herod's hope for a sign but his inability to understand signs he did see (23:8); the crowds moved to beat their breasts by what they see (23:48); the disciples being witnesses to what they saw (24:48).

The ancients were conscious that many were blind physically and culturally. Jesus' ability to restore sight to all categories of sightless people was a welcome restoration of meaning to an otherwise frustrating dimension of normal life in that day.

LONGEVITY

The psalmist's observation that "seventy is the sum of our years, or eighty if we are strong" (Ps 90:10) is familiar to all Bible readers. Presuming that the ancients counted the way we do and used the same calendars that we do, this is an impressive life expectancy. The presumptions, of course, are erroneous.

Study of skeletal remains indicates that life expectancy in the ancient world averaged in the range of thirty to forty-five years, depending on the specific location and time period. In ancient cities, almost 30 percent of the children died before the age of six.

Startling as this may sound, the contemporary experience of successful childbirth and healthy children is very recent. At the turn of the century in the United States, a woman had to bear 6.1 children just to reproduce herself. The early twentieth-century tombstones of five children of the Pabst brewing family of Milwaukee record lifespans of three months, ten days, fourteen months, one day, and thirteen months. Children commonly died of diphtheria and smallpox, diseases now all but eradicated.

In antiquity, another 60 percent died before reaching their mid-teens, 75 percent before their mid-twenties. Only 10 percent might have made it to their mid-forties, and perhaps as few as 3 percent to their sixties.

That Jesus survived birth and lived approximately to the age of thirty places him in a very select 10 percent of the population of his time and place. A large portion of Jesus' audience would have been considerably younger than he was, severely disease-ridden, and facing ten or fewer years of life expectancy. Imagine the impact of Jesus' statement that "this generation will not pass away before all these things take place" on such an audience (Mark 13:30).

Those fortunate enough to live as long as Jesus did would very likely have suffered from dental problems. They would have had worn-down, rotted, or no teeth and halitosis. Other health problems would have included bad eyesight and intestinal parasites.

The death of the twelve-year-old girl whom Jesus restored to life (Mark 5:21-24, 35-43) was, therefore, a very common experience in his day. The Gospel record does not indicate the cause of her death, but we can make at least three plausible suggestions.

She may have died of natural causes, or more likely she may have died of some childhood sickness or disease. But a third cause is conceivable and plausible, namely, a culture-specific syndrome. Perhaps the girl was a victim of the evil eye. (The word "evil eye" appears in the Greek text of Matthew 20:15 and Mark 7:22 but is often translated "envy").

There is a pervasive belief in circum-Mediterranean cultures that some people can cause misfortune (death, crop failure, and other tragedies) by a mere "glance," described in the contemporary Middle East as "the fierce look." Frequently those people have an eye ailment like the modern "lazy eye" or weak muscular control of one eye. Their glance is considered damaging by itself, but it is also considered to be linked with a desire to destroy whatever they behold with "envy." In the Mediterranean world, a person envies a precise object like the young girl, but since it can't be possessed, it must be destroyed. The agents of destruction are invariably any of the capricious and malicious spirits that inhabit the atmosphere and spy on human beings, ever ready to interfere in their lives.

Children, particularly if attractive or gifted, are common targets of the evil eye and malicious spirits. A common preventive measure against the evil eye and its consequences (sickness and death) is to wear something blue or red in color (ribbons, tassels). Special amulets can thwart the evil eye. It is also a custom to spit, sometimes three times. That is how the Galatians reacted to Paul, whom they suspected of having such powers (see Gal 4:14). Others bite the knuckle of the index finger.

Tragedies and deaths believed to be caused by the evil eye are so common and so commonly known in the Middle East that Mark did not even have to mention it. Nor would he have wanted to "risk" the consequences that might result from even saying the words. The unfortunate girl may not have been adequately protected.

Possessing the evil eye was not a sickness in the ancient world. People suspected of having it ordinarily went out of their way to be kind and generous to avoid accusations.

MORE THAN MEETS THE EYE

It is very difficult but necessary to set aside contemporary medical knowledge when reading the Bible. Even though the people in the cultural world of Jesus became sick, improved, or died just as we do, they interpreted their experiences very differently. What mattered above all was the social meaning and consequence of the condition. A superstition from a Western perspective could prove fatal in Middle Eastern perspective.

FOR FURTHER READING

Pilch, John J. "Healing." *The Collegeville Pastoral Dictionary of Biblical Theology.* Ed. Carroll Stuhlmueller, C.P., 413–422. Collegeville, Minn.: The Liturgical Press, 1996.

_____. *Healing in the New Testament: Insights from Medical and Mediterranean Anthropolgy.* Minneapolis: Fortress Press, forthcoming (1999).

SKY

When the heavens opened for Ezekiel, he saw visions of God and heard a voice giving him instruction and direction (Ezek 1–7). When the heavens opened at Jesus' baptism, the Spirit came upon him and a voice declared him to be a beloved and pleasing Son (Mark 1:10-11). After his resurrection, Jesus was lifted up into the heavens and disappeared from the sight of his apostles (Acts 1:11). John the Revealer traveled through an "open door" in the heavens and arrived at the throne of God, where he saw and heard many things (Rev 4:1-11). Where do the heavens open? What is this opening? Why do these and other prophets see and learn new things in the heavens? What did ancient people know about the heavens?

THE "HEAVENS"

A search of a concordance of the Revised Standard Version of the Bible discloses that the word "sky" appears 12 times, but the word "heaven(s)" occurs 750 times. (In the New Revised Standard Version, "sky" appears 27 times, notably in Genesis 1, where it never occurs in the Revised Standard Version; and "heaven" occurs 698 times.) Both English words translate the same Hebrew and Greek words! As the Italian proverb puts it, "Every translator is a traitor" *(traduttore, traditore)*. The English word "heaven" carries so many centuries of theological freight that a reader does well to avoid it and use "sky" unless completely implausible in the context. "Sky" will give us a better understanding of the experiences of Ezekiel, Jesus, and John the Revealer.

The ancients did not have electricity to distract them with movies, television, and computer games. Scholars realize that people in antiquity paid an incredible amount of attention to the earth, with its plants and animals, and to the sky, with its animate beings: stars and constellations. They knew and catalogued all these things quite extensively.

147

HOLE IN THE SKY

The Priests' conception of the world reflected in Genesis 1 is familiar to most readers of the Bible. The earth is a flat saucer resting on pillars and covered by a dome, on the other side of which are waters. There is water and an underworld beneath the saucer too. This Israelite perspective of the fifth century B.C.E. differed considerably from the Hellenistic view of the universe of the fourth century B.C.E. For these Mediterranean neighbors, the earth was a still and stable sphere located at the center of the universe, surrounded by the sun, moon, and five planets, which traveled around the earth in separate orbits. Greek and Roman philosophers, as well as the Fathers of the Church, held this opinion.

Modern Western readers need to continually remind themselves of the impact that Alexander's conquest of the world had as it spread the Greek language and the storehouse of Greek knowledge. It was Washington Irving's novelistic biography of Columbus (1828) that spread the lie that until Columbus's time everyone believed that the world was flat.

The ancients agreed that this universe was a closed system enclosed by a vault or firmament. The high god or gods lived on the other side, and there was an opening that allowed access to the other side. That opening, of course, was located over the place where the deity's temple on earth was located. In the Israelite tradition, this was Jerusalem. Jesus had to ascend to heaven from Jerusalem, since the hole was there and not in Galilee. John the Seer on Patmos and Ezekiel the prophet in Mesopotamia could travel through that opening by means of experiences in altered states of consciousness, an every day pan-human experience among more than 90 percent of the planet's population.

VIEW FROM THE OTHER SIDE

As American school children are familiar with globes of the earth, the ancients from the sixth century B.C.E. forward were similarly familiar with globes of the universe viewed from the "outside." There is a very famous Islamicate globe in the Smithsonian Institutions, but the Farnese sphere from the second century B.C.E. is perhaps better known. These globes are a collection of bands along which each planet, sun, and moon travels, with the earth at the center. They also present the constellations along its band, the zodiac. Pictures of these globes help a Bible reader understand what Ezekiel and John the Seer are reporting. Both prophets traveled

Detail of the ancient zodiac mosaic at the Middle East synagogue of Beth Alfa.

through the hole in the sky to gain a view of this universe from God's perspective.

Their view is from the throne of God (Ezek 1:26; Rev 4:2). Modern readers are apt to imagine this as a seat, but the ancients knew and saw it as a constellation. The Farnese sphere shows a throne near the North Pole over the constellations Leo and Cancer. The Romans identified a constellation as the throne of Caesar. There was also a throne for Cassiopeia. In the Vatican Museum, there is a sculpture from the Villa Albani, dating to the second century C.E., which shows Jupiter, the head of the Roman pantheon, seated on a literal throne in the center of the zodiac supported by Atlas.

The Israelite tradition knew that God's throne was in the sky. "The LORD is in his holy temple, the LORD's throne is in the sky" (Ps 11:4; see also Pss 103:19; 123:1, etc.). Matthew's Jesus knows this too: "He who swears by the sky, swears by the throne of God and by him who sits on it" (23:22; cf. 5:34). Ezekiel (1:26; 10:1) describes the constellation rather well: "Above the firmament over their heads there was the likeness of a throne, in appearance like sapphire." The color of a sapphire is mainly yellow, but often blue, and at times orange. One might begin to imagine the colors of the rainbow (red, orange, yellow, green, blue, and violet, and sometimes indigo, between blue and violet). Ezekiel's description concurs (1:28): "Like the appearance of the bow that is in the cloud on the day of rain, so was the appearance of the brightness round about [the throne]."

FOUR EQUATORIAL CONSTELLATIONS

Just as the earth has an equator, so too the sky has an equator projected from the earth. The sky also has a central point at the north, where the pole and the polar star are located. The yellow color of the sapphire is also the color of the polar star. This is not a fixed spot but rather the central point of control, the center of the vault of the sky and the four equidistant constellations along the equator. The four living creatures that Ezekiel (1:10) saw in his altered state of consciousness suggest the four constellations at four opposite points of the equatorial zodiac. These are Scorpio-man (human face), Leo (face of lion), Taurus (face of ox), and Pegasus (a flying creature, face of eagle). John the Revealer saw the same constellations (Rev 4:6-7): "the first living creature like a lion, the second living creature like an ox, the third living creature with the face of a man, and the fourth living creature like a flying eagle."

The point of the content of Ezekiel's and John's visions is not that the constellations determine fate; rather, since the sky and its planets and constellations were created by God at the beginning of creation, an inspired seer who can read the sky correctly by being privy to God's view of the cosmos can understand and interpret current events as reflecting God's will from all eternity. The difference may be difficult to grasp. Essentially it is God's will rather than the animate constellations that direct life and history. God's will is set at creation when the constellations came into being.

SKY WARS AND SATAN

Luke's Jesus claims that he saw "Satan fall like lightning from the sky. Behold I have given you authority to tread upon serpents and scorpions, and over all the power of the enemy, and nothing shall hurt you" (10:18-19). Hippolytus (*Refutation of All Heresies*, 4.47) cites Aratus to note that there is in the sky "an enormous and prodigious monster, (the) Serpent; and that this is what the devil says in the book of Job to the Deity, when (Satan) uses these words: 'I have traversed earth under heaven, and have gone around (it)'" (Job 1:7). Hippolytus says they suppose the Dragon/Serpent is located near the North Pole, from which vantage point he can see everything.

John the Revealer appears to reflect this perspective when he writes: "Now war arose in the sky, Michael and his angels fighting against the dragon; . . . they were defeated and there was no longer any place for them in the sky. And the great dragon was thrown down, that ancient serpent, who is called the Devil and Satan, the deceiver of the whole world" (Rev 12:7-9). Thus, it is highly plausible that Jesus and John both recount a vision each had in an altered state of consciousness. Reading the sky according to the traditional lore as it has been interpreted by the Israelite tradition, they see an event–a sky war–that took place before humans were created. Jesus may also be referring to constellations when he mentions serpents and scorpions.

According to Israelite tradition, Michael defeated the serpent (starry dragon) and exiled it from the sky to earth, where it later meets the first human beings. In the Israelite tradition, Job 1 reflects the period when Satan was still in the sky. The "J" tradition (Gen 3) reports him to be on the earth before the creation of the first human beings, so the star war took place earlier. The star-war story appears to have been shaped by another ancient star-war story about darkness (Scorpio) causing the sun/light (Orion) to flee. Orion (sun) shamed Artemis (moon), so Scorpio (darkness) came to the rescue, wounded and then slew Orion. Thus the saying that at the rising of Scorpio (darkness) in the east, Orion flees at the western sky.

Traces of this appear in Isaiah: "The stars of the sky and Orion and the whole array of the sky will not give light" (Isa 13:10, Greek version). "In that day, the LORD with his hard and great and strong sword will punish Leviathan the fleeing serpent, Leviathan the twisting serpent, and he will slay the dragon that is in the sea" (Isa 27:1; the Greek version talks about the crooked or dishonest dragon-serpent). Notice that the ancients were not concerned about consistency nor ashamed of inconsistency. Sky knowledge was cumulative. Each culture added and adapted data, and applied its insights to matters or events in need of understanding and interpretation. Above all, the challenge was to discover and understand God's will. The sky offered a ready reference for that task.

CONCLUSION

When the Assyrians gained world dominance in the eighth and seventh centuries B.C.E. and conquered Israel, the Northern Kingdom, pagan worship of the stars became attractive, tempting, and popular. Amos warned that exile would be God's punishment for the house of Israel when it adopted Kaiwan (probably Saturn) as "your star-god" (5:26). In the reign of Hoshea, Israel forsook all the commandments of the Lord and "worshiped all the host of heaven" (= stars). King Josiah attempted to put an end to this idolatry: "He deposed the idolatrous priests . . . those also who burned incense to Baal, to the sun, and the moon, and the constellations, and all the host of the heavens" (2 Kgs 23:5). The effort was in vain.

Modern readers of the Bible have long misunderstood these appropriate condemnations to mean that the Israelites should have had nothing at all to do with the sky and its animate beings (stars, planets, constellations, etc.). A careful and critical reading of the Bible shows that people like Ezekiel, Jesus, and John the Revealer were recognized by their peers as astral prophets. This kind of prophet knows the sky very well and interacts with star-related, celestial personages to learn the will of God. The written narratives in the Bible record the circumstances in which they learned this (in trances or other altered states of consciousness), the interactions themselves (the content of the visions, what is seen and/or heard), and the consequences (the impact or the meanings of the phenomena in the sky). One could learn much about God from reading the sky. Ironically, this enlightening reading can only be done in the dark.

FOR FURTHER READING

Malina, Bruce J. *On the Genre and Message of Revelation: Star Visions and Sky Journeys.* Peabody, Mass.: Hendrickson Publishers, 1995.
Rochberg-Halton, Francesca. "Astrology in the Ancient Near East." *Anchor Bible Dictionary* 1:504–507.

SMELLS AND TASTES

Though Plato and Aristotle assigned first place among the senses to sight, it did not receive cultural prominence until after the sixteenth century. Smell and hearing were the dominant senses upon which people relied first and foremost. When it came time for the aged Isaac to bestow his deathbed blessing upon Esau, he was already blind (Gen 27). Though he felt the hairy animal skin of Jacob's disguise, Isaac trusted his ear instead. He was certain he heard the voice of Jacob. Isaac's "acid" test came just before the blessing: "Come near and kiss me, my son," he said. Isaac trusted that his nose would definitively discern the distinctive body odor of the hairy Esau. He found it indeed on Esau's garments, which were also part of Jacob's clever disguise. "The smell of my son is as the smell of a field which the LORD has blessed!" And he bestowed the special blessing on Jacob, firmly convinced by his nose that it was Esau.

THE HUMAN SENSES

While Westerners understand the human senses to be receptors of information, they don't often reflect upon them as a major form of nonverbal communication. In contrast, the ancients considered the senses primarily as a means of communication rather than passive recipients of data. For example, the eyes emitted rays that touched and mingled with objects of vision. Sighted people emitted light rays; blind people emitted dark rays. People feared the power of blind people. This understanding of vision stands behind the discussion of light and darkness in John's Gospel.

In 1776 Linnaeus listed seven primary smell stimuli: aromatic, fragrant, ambrosial, alliaceous (onion; garlic), hircine (goat-like), foul, and nauseous. According to modern science, the nose can distinguish among four thousand different smells and can detect any given smell in a mix of a hundred or more scents. In the West, however, people consider natural odors such as those of blood and sweat as unpleasant and prefer to mask them with artificial aromas. This denial of odor has reduced the nose's sensitivity.

THE SMELL GOD LIKES

The phrases "pleasing odor" (RSV; NRSV), "pleasing smell" (NJB), "sweet-smelling" oblation (NAB) occur repeatedly in Exodus, Leviticus, and Numbers to describe the kind of burnt food offerings that God likes (e.g., Num 28:2, 6, 13, 14, 19). The Hebrew words literally describe a "quieting, soothing or tranquilizing scent, odor, or breath." Perhaps humans believed that such aromas would tranquilize or "disarm" God, thwart an angry response, or perhaps give the Almighty rest (the root Hebrew word in quieting, soothing, tranquilizing) from burdensome cares over creation.

The Hebrew word for "odor" derives from the word for "breath." In Genesis (2:7), God shaped the first earthling from dust and gave it life by blowing up its nose, breathing into it the breath of life. The Yahwist's story is intriguing. We moderns know that smells are associated with significant emotional experiences in one's personal life. Actually, smells have no names of their own; they are associated with the names of other things. We identify a scent by saying, "It smells like . . ." What did the Yahwist think God's breath smelled like? The first creature knew, and presumably the Yahwist's readers and hearers of this story had a very good idea. By the end of this reflection, we too may have a better notion.

SMELLS HUMANS LIKE

In the West, people are socialized into keeping a distance of about sixteen to eighteen inches between themselves and the person to whom they speak or whom they face. Even so, Westerners depend upon a variety of toothpastes, mouthwashes, and breath-sweeteners in order not to offend others with bad breath.

In the Middle East, the optimal distance between persons speaking to each other is six to eight inches. Arabs routinely breathe into each other's faces when conversing. To avoid communicating in this way is to deny the other person one's breath, a share in one's God-given life force. This is shameful and a serious insult. In ancient Greek mythologies, the soul was associated with breath, and therefore was considered to have a distinct fragrance. Ultimately the soul was thought to be a kind of perfume itself. Clearly, breath is as important as the actual words it forms. Breath is a powerful form of nonverbal communication (see John 20:22)

As for the human body, each person has a distinct body odor, depending upon diet, drinking water, mood, living habits, race, gender, age, reproductive state, health, exercise, hygiene, emotional state, and even the time of day or month. In addition, environmental odors are absorbed by human skin, hair, and clothing. The sightless Isaac depended on Esau's and Jacob's distinctive body odor to tell them apart. Jacob lived in tents and was a smooth-skinned person who sometimes made bread and cooked pottage of lentils. Esau was a hairy man who loved the outdoors, a skillful hunter who enjoyed eating game. The lifestyle of each twin nuanced his distinctively personal body odor.

The Song of Solomon is replete with references to scents and aromas. The maid describes her lover as a "bag of myrrh that lies between my breasts" (Song 1:13). This likely refers, not to his body scent, but rather to the protective or "medicinal" function of certain spices worn in a cloth bag around one's neck. The aroma of the spice warded off evil spirits, customary carriers of illness or misfortune. She felt confident that her friend would protect her against the most powerful of enemies. The majority of the scents described in these poems appear to be garden scents, albeit a utopian or fantasy garden the likes of which would hardly be found in any single garden of the ancient Middle East. As the Song of Solomon demonstrates, scents communicate more than the simple words express.

Martial (ca. 40–105 C.E.?), a Roman poet born in Spain, described some of his (and his culture's) favorite scents: "The scent of an apple as a young girl bites it, the fragrance that comes from Corycian saffron, the smell of a silvery vineyard flowering with the first clusters of grass that a sheep has freshly cropped, the odor of myrtle, of an Arabian harvester, of rubbed amber, of fire pallid with Eastern incense, of turf lightly sprinkled with summer rain, of a garland that has rested on tresses wet with nard . . ." (III.65). He considered Thais, a semilegendary Athenian courtesan, to represent the most revolting smells. "Thais smells worse than the veteran crock [full of stale urine] of a stingy fuller, recently broken in the middle of the road, or a billy goat fresh from his amours, or a lion's mouth, or a hide from beyond the Tiber torn from a dog, or a chicken rotting in an aborted egg, or a jar polluted with putrid fish-sauce" (VI.93).

PERFUMES

Practically all the perfumes mentioned in the Bible are imports and not native to ancient Palestine. Only the wealthy could afford to be lavish with them. The queen of Sheba brought an impressive quantity of spices to Solomon as a gift. It was an amount never again matched by anyone (1 Kgs 10:2, 10). Modern readers should note that spices mentioned in the Bible are never used as seasoning for food; they are rather associated with fragrant oils, perfumes, incense, embalming fluid, and serve other purposes.

The Book of Exodus (30:22-25) gives the recipe for a special anointing oil. The ingredients are myrrh (from Arabia), sweet-smelling cinnamon (Sri Lanka), aromatic cane (central Asia), and cassia (Sri Lanka), all pulverized and then mixed with olive oil. Objects of anointment were the tent of meeting, the ark of the testimony, the table and utensils, the lampstand and utensils, the altar of incense, the altar of burnt offering with its utensils, the laver and its base, and Aaron and his sons.

The intent was to concoct a distinctive oil that should not be imitated or used by ordinary people because it rendered its objects holy. It very likely also made them slippery to the touch and difficult to grasp, but it especially bestowed a distinctive fragrance. "The precious oil upon the head, running down upon the beard of Aaron, onto the collar of his robes" (Ps 133:2) conjures up an olfactory memory more than a visual one. This is the smell of the "holy," which could not be confused with any other scent. Modern science has learned that memories evoked by smells are usually more pleasant and emotional than those evoked by visual or oral cues. Imagine the sensory memories created by a visit to the holy place. "I rejoiced when they said to me, 'Let us go to the house of the LORD!'" (Ps 122:1).

THE SENSE OF TASTE

No doubt many are familiar with the simple experiment that demonstrates how much the sense of taste relies upon the sense of smell. A blindfolded person whose nose is pinched to disable the sense of smell will be unable to identify a mashed banana given as a taste test. It is impossible to identify the banana by taste alone. In general, most food tastes like nothing at all. The human sense of taste can detect sourness, sweetness, bitterness, and saltiness. But unassisted by smell, taste cannot appreciate the full flavors of meats, fruits, butter, or coffee. Scent creates flavors; smell defines taste.

This information helps to understand and interpret in a culturally plausible way the psalmist's exhortation: "Taste and see that the LORD is good" (Ps 34:8). Commentators correctly interpret this as a call for a concrete human experience of God. The question still remains: What human taste experience would suggest this imagery? The origin of individual psalms is almost impossible to trace, but scholars acknowledge that even when composed or recited by an individual, the setting is always communal. Fr. Carroll Stuhlmueller, C.P., mused that even when not sung at a sacred service, traditional songs were likely sung around the communal campfire.

Some of these campfires and certainly all sacred services involved burnt offerings or sacrifices. Biblical guidelines invariably required that some of these offerings should be sprinkled or burnt with frankincense (e.g., Lev 24:5-7). The aroma associated with prayers, i.e., communication with God, that were recited at these gatherings combined to form a complex sensory memory involving at least sound and smell. The modern saying "That smells so good I can almost taste it" reminds us to connect taste to smell and sound. This sensory scenario seems well suited to interpret Psalm 34. The psalmist "sought the Lord" (v. 4) quite likely where the Lord camped among the people. Here the psalmist smelled the fire and the sacrifice, communicated and sometimes ate (the burnt sacrifice) with the Lord. It was easy to imagine and know how the Lord's goodness might "taste" to the palate.

When adapted by the author of 1 Peter, Psalm 34:8 manifests yet another aspect of human smell and taste. Modern science has learned that human beings begin to develop a keen sense of smell very early in life. Babies respond to the scent of their own mother's breasts but not to that of a strange mother. The author writes: "Like newborn babes, long for the pure milk of the word [traditional rendition: "spiritual milk"], that by it you may grow up to salvation; for you have tasted the goodness of the Lord [Jesus the Messiah]" (1 Peter 2:2-3).

THE SWEET-TASTING WORDS OF THE LAW

In reflecting on the Law, the psalmist once again draws on the sense of taste for imagery: "Oh, how I love thy law! . . . How sweet are thy words to my taste, sweeter than honey to my mouth" (Ps 119:97, 103; see also Ps 19:11). Even the written words of God can taste sweet: "I ate [the scroll] and it was in my mouth as sweet as honey" (Ezek 3:3; see also Rev 10:9). What human experience prompted the sacred writers to imagine words (spoken and written) as sweet-tasting?

A number of explanations are possible. One ancient strategy for teaching young boys good behavior was to rub their palates with chewed dates to accompany demanding instructions, thus associating sweet taste with difficult rules. But another more probable explanation is suggested by the ancient concept of speech. Words are formed with breath (spirit, soul), which was considered pleasing enough to be acceptable when another person blew into your face. The lover in the Song of Solomon considers his beloved's voice to be sweet (Song 2:14). Since God's personal spirit/breath enlivened the first earthlings, and human breath/speech is sweet, surely God's speech/words/Law is even sweeter.

Finally, cultures conceive of sound and smell as similar in nature. Scents of flowers are often described as their "voices." Perhaps this intricate connection between the senses (sound-smell/breath-taste) explains why the basically unlettered Francis of Assisi believed that he shared the "sweet-smelling words of the Lord" with fellow believers. God's word exudes sweet smells, which in turn create sweet tastes and, when spoken, make sweet sounds in the ear.

CONCLUSION

Some of the Church Fathers banned perfumes and roses because they were associated with Roman idolatry. Origen said that incense did more harm than good because demons feed on smoke. Paul's view of ministry expressed in sensory imagery is worth pondering and adopting as a corrective (2 Cor 2:14-17). Believers are, or should be, an aroma of Christ to God, just as ancient Hebrew offerings were tranquilizing scents to God. The scent can be death-dealing or life-giving, depending upon the dispositions of those who inhale it. What a refreshing perspective in our world of largely artificial, scratch-and-sniff scents!

FOR FURTHER READING

Classen, Constance. *Worlds of Sense: Exploring the Senses in History and Across Cultures*. London and New York: Routledge, 1993.

Dayagi-Mendels, Michal. *Perfume and Cosmetics in the Ancient World*. Jerusalem: Israel Museum, 1989. Exhibition catalogue.

Falk, Pasi. "Towards a Historical Anthropology of Taste." Chap. 4 in *The Consuming Body*. London: Sage Publications, 1994.

Le Guérer, Annick. *Scent: The Mysterious and Essential Powers of Smell*. Trans. Richard Miller. New York: Turtle Bay Books, 1992.

Matthew, Victor H. "Perfumes and Spices." *Anchor Bible Dictionary* 5:226–228.

SPIRITS

In the Bible, a variety of spirits both good and bad readily intervene in the daily life of human beings. An angel visited and chatted with Mary (Luke 1:26), and she conceived a child by the power of a holy spirit, the Most High (Luke 1:35). Jesus was led by a good spirit into the wilderness, where a malicious spirit, the devil, tempted him (Luke 4:1-13) in order to attack his honorable reputation as "beloved and pleasing Son" (Luke 3:21-22).

In the synagogue at Capernaum, Jesus cast an unclean spirit, a demon, out of a man (Luke 4:31-37). And who can forget the humorous story of Jesus casting demons out of a human being and into a herd of pigs, which then race to the sea, where they drown (Luke 8:32)? Almost every chapter of the Gospels tells of some kind of spirit interfering in human life. In other words, our ancestors in the faith recognized numerous kinds of spirits and regularly blamed them for their misfortunes as well as their blessings.

Modern, scientifically sophisticated believers are left in a quandary when they read these stories. They know the biological facts of conception. They know that germs and viruses and not malicious spirits cause human sickness. They know how weather patterns develop and even how to predict the weather for the next day or two. Modern believers rarely if ever blame spirits for anything. For many, spirits play little or no role in daily life. What can a contemporary Western believer make of all these stories from their ancestors in which spirits are believed to be responsible for so many human experiences of blessing and misfortune?

READING SCENARIOS

Here is another way to state this problem. What kind of reading scenario is culturally most plausible for these stories? Which reading scenario would help a reader make the best sense of biblical reports? In the modern Western world, science holds a central place in every reading scenario. Even youngsters learn at an early age what is and what is not scientifically plausible. Most of the events involving spirits in the biblical world have a different, plausible scientific explanation in the modern world. But this reading scenario is unsuited to the ancient Mediterranean culture. It is inappropriate for interpreting biblical texts.

In the Mediterranean world, everyone believes in spirits. Good and bad spirits are an integral part of human experience in that world and play a critical role in normal everyday life there. A variety of amulets, charms, and incantations are available to thwart or minimize spirit interference in that human world, but one can never be certain that they will work effectively. An appropriate reading scenario for biblical texts must therefore include the existence and activity of spirits.

THEORIES OF ILLNESS

But why do some spirits behave maliciously toward human beings while others are benevolent? Specialists in cross-cultural interpretations of human sickness propose a plausible explanation. Utilizing the extensive cross-cultural data gathered and analyzed in the Human Relations Area Files (HRAF) at Yale University, George P. Murdock (39) noticed the following pattern: "Without exception, every society in the sample [139 societies] which depends primarily on *animal husbandry* for its economic livelihood regards spirit aggression as either the predominant or an important secondary cause of illness" (*Theories of Illness,* 39). He further observed that the tendency toward this belief is especially strong in societies that keep large domestic animals such as horses, cattle, water buffaloes, camels, reindeer, *sheep, goats* (my emphasis), and llamas, but not pigs, dogs, or household pets. This tendency is also evident in agricultural societies that harness their animals to the plow.

Such cross-cultural insights are very valuable, particularly because they have been based on hundreds of societies. This kind of information places a healthy restraint on Bible readers, who too often tend to interpret the Mediterranean characters they read about in Scripture as if they were members of their own culture. Viewing the rest of the world exclusively from the perspective of one's own culture is known as "ethnocentrism." This often results from asking the question: "What does this text from the Mediterranean world mean to me in the United States?" Such an approach is never a helpful perspective for interpreting the Bible.

Murdock's insight about aggressive spirits, coupled with the Mediterranean understanding of sheep and goats (see pp. 135–140), sheds new light on the Gospel stories of spirit aggression and spirit-related illnesses.

SHEEP, GOATS, AND SPIRIT AGGRESSION

Why is the raising of animals like sheep and goats associated with spirit aggression? Both involve risk and caprice. Life in general in the ancient world was full of risks. Good people often suffered and failed despite their best efforts. On the other side, "good luck" frequently brought prosperity and fortune to those who least deserved it. These seemed to get "something for nothing."

Raising animals for a livelihood is always risky, but it was especially so in antiquity, which did not possess scientific insight or remedies. Sudden and sometimes fatal sickness took its toll on animals just as it did on human beings.

In addition, flocks were also subject to aggression from both animal and human predators. Shepherds had to be equal to the task and capable of responding with similar aggression to ward off those attacks or to strike back in retaliation (see 1 Sam 17:34-36). This is certainly part of the background imagery for the psalmist's assertion: "The LORD is my shepherd." The traditional reputation for violence that characterized shepherds makes their appearance in Luke's infancy stories as recipients of a message of peace rather unusual.

Moreover, the ancient and contemporary circum-Mediterranean world also holds a strong belief in the existence of a very sophisticated spirit world. The apocryphal literature is replete with information about spirits, their names, their hierarchies, and the functions they play in the cosmos, as well as the effect they have on human life. In general, these spirits behave capriciously and very unpredictably.

This world also believes that everything that happens has a personal cause. The question is never "What happened?" but rather "Who did it?" When a human being is not readily available for blame, then a capricious spirit must be the agent of the misfortune.

Thus, according to our ancestors in the faith, capricious spirits were believed to regularly meddle in their affairs. Some spirits caused all sorts of misfortunes to human beings and their beasts (see Job 1–2); other spirits were a source of blessing (see Tobit 5:4). They could take possession of or control human beings, as the New Testament bears witness (e.g., Mark 9:17-18). Even good spirits could sometimes behave very violently (see Acts 12:23).

PETER'S MOTHER-IN-LAW

According to Matthew (8:14-17) and Mark (1:29-31), Peter's mother-in-law was confined to bed by a fever. Jesus took her by the hand and the fever left her. According to Luke (4:38-39), it seems that she was afflicted by a demon named "Fever." This is implied by Jesus' "rebuking" the fever. Luke uses this very same word in Greek to describe Jesus' rebuke to demons (4:35), to the windstorm (8:24), and to an unclean spirit (9:42).

Scholars generally agree that our ancestors in the faith did not distinguish clearly between human sickness, demon possessions, and calamities of nature. All were misfortunes completely beyond human control. Many if not all these misfortunes were viewed as the result of spirit aggression. In each instance, the human victim either did not know of, or possessed no effective weapon with which to fight against, the aggression.

The apocrypha and pseudepigrapha offer additional insight into this world. Though probably to be dated in the third century C.E., *The Testament of Solomon* is recognized by scholars as accurately reflecting first-century Palestinian Judaism. The author's interest was predominantly in the sickness problems of that time. These are associated with heavenly bodies or spirits of various kinds, and the author provides the readers with assorted remedies or exorcistic words that could prove helpful.

Thus, "The sixteenth [heavenly body, or demon] said: 'I am Katrax. I inflict incurable fevers on [human beings]. If anyone wants to regain health, let [that one] pulverize coriander and rub it on the lips, saying, "I adjure you by Zeus, retreat from the image of God," and I retreat immediately.'" (*Testament of Solomon*, 18:20). And again: "The nineteenth said, 'I am called Mardero. I inflict incurable fevers; write my name in some such way in the house, and I retreat immediately.'" (*Testament of Solomon*, 18:23).

While Matthew and Mark report Peter's mother-in-law's fever as a sickness, Luke appears to report it as an act of aggression from a demon. Luke's Jesus rebuked the demon named "Fever" in the same way that he rebuked unclean spirits and winds (also a type of spirit). The New Testament authors give two different interpretations of one and the same event.

WOMEN AND SPIRITS

In the article on sheep and goats (see pp. 135–140), it was noted that Mediterranean culture in general associates goats with women and the devil. Generally speaking, both men and women in the Gospels are subjected to spirit intervention or demon aggression and possession (see Luke 4:31-37; 8:26-34; 9:37-43a; 11:14-23 for the possessed men), but in Luke's Gospel five of the six specific reports of women's problems or sicknesses involve spirits.

Elizabeth (Luke 1:13, 24) and Mary (Luke 1:35) both conceived children through spirit involvement, the power of the Most High. A cluster of women cured by Jesus of evil spirits and infirmities followed him: Mary Magdalene, Joanna, the wife of Herod's steward Chuza, Susanna, and many others (Luke 8:2-3). The daughter of Jairus, whose life-spirit abandoned her, was restored to life when "her spirit returned" (Luke 8:55). And the woman crippled by a spirit for eighteen years was made to stand straight again by Jesus (Luke 13:10-16).

The general Mediterranean association of women, goats, and the devil is reflected in the interpretation of sickness as well. The Gospel reports of healed women focus on those who suffered from ills caused by spirit intervention or aggression. There are no reports of women who suffered from paralysis, deafness, muteness, blindness, etc., though we know for a fact that women did indeed experience these same problems in antiquity. The Gospel reports seem to reflect a different aspect of women's cultural context.

THE GOOD SHEPHERD AND SPIRITS

In the Gospel stories, Jesus generally had no power at all in his social world except in his exorcisms. Power was important in Jesus' world, because it is the ability to enforce conformity and proper behavior based on what is necessary for the good of the group. No one in the Gospels denied that Jesus had this power, though they did argue about its source (see Luke 11:15; 20:2).

This concern about Jesus' authority for exorcism reflected political interests and fears. Politics in part refers to the ways in which members of a group achieve and use power to implement public goals. Jesus' exercise of power in exorcisms caused his healings to be interpreted as political acts. From this perspective, Jesus' healing ministry involved much more than doing good and helping other people. It was a very real threat to the political powers, and this impression was not lost on anyone.

When Jesus identified himself as the "good" shepherd (John 10:11, 14), it was perhaps more than coincidental that some said: "He has a demon and is out of his mind" (John 10:19). The Mediterranean cultural association of goats with the devil, the prominence of belief in spirit aggression among societies that depend on sheep and goats for their livelihood, and the shepherds' reputation for violence came together in some people's minds to the detriment of Jesus. While the beneficiaries of his healing abilities applauded and revered Jesus, unaffected onlookers, particularly those in authority, saw rather political threat.

CONCLUSION

The Persian Gulf War in 1991 highlighted how very different circum-Mediterranean culture is from other cultures. In the article on sheep and goats (see pp. 135–140), we learned to appreciate the distinctive gender-based symbolism attached to sheep and goats and the importance of hospitality. In this article on spirits, we have discovered the association of experiences involved in raising small livestock for personal sustenance with the experience of spirit aggression. These cultural insights have cast Jesus and his ministry in a new light. He was quite at home in this circum-Mediterranean world, which some Westerners would describe as bizarre and grotesque. Blessed is the one who refuses to be an "ugly American" but elects instead to grow in understanding and respect for Jesus the Mediterranean man who "pitched his tent among us" (John 1:14)

FOR FURTHER READING

Barton, John. "Eisegesis." *A Dictionary of Biblical Interpretation.* Ed. R. J. Coggins and J. L. Houlden. London and Philadelphia: SCM Press and Trinity Press International, 1990.

Murdock, George P. *Theories of Illness: A World Survey.* Pittsburgh: University of Pittsburgh Press, 1980.

The Old Testament Pseudepigrapha. Vol. 1: *Apocalyptic Literature and Testaments.* Ed. James H. Charlesworth. Garden City, N.Y.: Doubleday, 1983.

Pilch, John J. "Sickness and Healing in Luke–Acts." *The Social World of Luke–Acts.* Ed. Jerome H. Neyrey. Peabody, Mass.: Hendrickson Publishers, 1991.

_____. *Introducing the Cultural Context of the New Testament.* New York/Mahwah, N.J.: Paulist Press, 1991. Session One: "How Do You Read?"

SYMBOLISM

The Constitution on Divine Revelation issued by the Second Vatican Council urged interpreters of the Bible to pay due attention "to the customary and characteristic patterns of perception, speech, and narrative which prevailed in their time, and to the conventions which people then observed in their dealings with one another" (no. 12). Scholars have generally fulfilled this exhortation by concentrating on the literary form of biblical passages. Often studies of the literary form of a passage tend to avoid the attempt to explain what might have actually happened in a given situation.

Investigations of literary form have sometimes neglected to notice that "patterns of perception" vary from culture to culture. The sociology of knowledge has demonstrated that "reality" as conceived and perceived can and does differ in different circumstances as well as from one historical period to another. Consider the different perceptions through time of the reality known as the cosmos or the universe. And the different "conventions" that people follow in their various relationships with one another are also clearly recognized, e.g., marriage customs. Cultural anthropology and related disciplines have investigated these dimensions of human experience and have provided helpful insights. Let us consider the symbolic actions and so-called "confessions" of Jeremiah to explore these various insights.

LITERARY FORMS

The Book of Jeremiah records certain deeds of that prophet that resemble deeds of other prophets (Elijah, 1 Kgs 19:19; Elisha, 2 Kgs 13:14; Ezek 4:1; Hos 1); those deeds are usually identified as "prophetic symbolic actions" (Jer 13:1-11; 16:1-4, 5-6, 8-9; 19:1-2, 10-11; 27:1-3, 12; 28:10-11; 32:1-15; 48:8-13; 51:59-64). They are all reported in a fairly consistent tripartite literary pattern or form: (a) there is a divine command (Jer 13:1, 4, 6); (b) the prophet executes the command (Jer 13:2, 5, 7); and (c) the performed action is explained (Jer 13:8-11).

Sometimes the narrative mentions witnesses to the deed (Jer 19:1-2, 10-11: elders and priests). At other times the narrative explicitly points out the connection between the deed and the real life of the people (Jer 13:9-11; 19:10-11; Jer 32:15 as the explanation of vv. 1-14).

In brief, this is the literary form of the prophetic symbolic action. Each of these actions is understood as a "visible" word of God, therefore a word with power to effect what is represented. In each case, the deed is never directed to occasional and merely personal ends but is intended to fulfill God's plans and purposes concerning Israel.

Scholars, however, are divided as to whether these deeds were ever actually done. Fr. Guy Couturier (*New Jerome Biblical Commentary,* 13:45) comments on Jer 13:1-11: "It seems much simpler to hold that the symbolic action is purely a literary device; therefore the discourse is to be interpreted as a parable." Fr. Larry Boadt makes a similar judgment about Ezekiel's symbolic actions: "It is not necessary to assume that Ezekiel acted out fully each symbolic gesture. Many of these may have been preached or described rhetorically more than performed" (*New Jerome Biblical Commentary,* 20:240).

Others such as Johannes Lindblom and Luis Alonso-Schökel see no compelling reason to deny the reality of the deeds. The late Fr. Bruce Vawter's introduction to prophetic literature in the *New Jerome Biblical Commentary* (11:24) makes that point explicitly. Sometimes they are interpreted as acted similes or clever illustrations even when acknowledged as symbols.

SYMBOLS

Our knowledge of symbols has grown in recent years and provided a better understanding of the activity of some of the prophets. Symbol is a means of indirect communication in that there is no intrinsic prior relationship between the reality and its symbol. That relationship is established creatively, by choice, and has to be communicated in some way for the relationship to be understood and appreciated. Any action, person, or thing can be a symbol.

The various deeds of Jeremiah mentioned above were symbols creatively chosen to communicate a message. The written text indicates that God made the choice, since God gave the command. That is also why the explanation was important. Without it, no one would know that he or she was witnessing symbolic communication. Without the explanation, the act would simply have been clever or eccentric.

Moreover, the symbol is concrete, focused, and effective, and points beyond itself. God's command to Jeremiah not to marry or raise a family (Jer 16:2) was a creatively chosen fact in Jeremiah's life that pointed beyond itself to the fate of the people: children and their parents will die of a deadly disease.

Second, the symbol participates in the reality to which it points. It creates or makes the reality happen. The symbol is the first step, the first phase as it were. Thus Jeremiah's single state of life had already set in motion the single state to which those already married would be reduced. Both single states heightened the sense of the community's jeopardy.

Thirdly, symbols open up dimensions of reality that cannot otherwise be attained by human beings. A simple sermon or proclamation would hardly have been as effective as the actual living out of a message. Not only did Jeremiah live the fact, but he lived and experienced all its consequences and implications for his fellow ethnics to see. Not only did the fellow ethnics see, but they also experienced or felt a gut reaction.

Finally, symbols possess an integrating and sometimes disintegrating power. In this instance, the symbol is disintegration and prefigures a disintegration that is yet to come in full. Later in his life, Jeremiah performed an integrating symbolic action: he purchased a plot of land to bear witness that Judah will indeed be restored (Jer 21:1-14).

STRONG-GROUP SYMBOLS

Anthropologist Mary Douglas (*Natural Symbols,* 1973) has demonstrated, on the basis of extensive field studies, that it is possible to classify groups (nations, societies, cultures) along a continuum extending from "weak group" on one end to "strong group" on the other. Jeremiah, a Mediterranean person living in Judea around 650 B.C.E., lived in a strong group.

A strong group is characterized by high pressure to conform to well-defined corporate identity. Clear sets of boundaries separate the insiders (observant members of "our" group) from the outsiders (nonobservant members of "our" group and people who are not of "our" group). Indeed, Jeremiah's initial prophetic activity relative to Josiah's reform around 620 B.C.E. helped to make the group even stronger.

In the strong-group world of Jeremiah, there was always a clear but limited and select set of normative symbols that defined, expressed, and replicated group identity. A prophet in Israel was a symbol. The prophet was creatively chosen by God (see Jeremiah's call: 1:4-10) as a vehicle of indirect communication to God's people. The prophet represented in his person God's plan for and relationship with Israel. (See Jeremiah 13, his underwear; or Hosea 1 and 3, his marriages).

Symbols in a strong group are perceived as functioning independently of the consent of members of society. The society neither elected nor legitimated the prophet. Like it or not, he was a prophet.

In addition, strong-group symbols are believed to be effective by themselves, *ex opere operato*. If executed faithfully and accurately as prescribed, symbolic actions are believed to be infallibly effective. They really create the reality to which they point. That is why Jeremiah and other prophets were so infuriating at times. They could not simply be ignored or disparaged.

Strong-group symbolic actions are, in part, rituals of power, that is, they possess a generalized capacity to make others do what one says (abandon idolatry) for effective collective action (that the people of God truly please God) with implied negative sanctions (if you don't obey, God will punish you).

IMPLICATIONS

If these anthropologically based understandings of symbol are accurate and appropriate for application to the Hebrew prophets, then it is difficult to believe that they are purely literary devices, or simply parables. That would make no sense in a strong-group culture. The actions must be carried out.

Weak-group individuals, for example native-born citizens of the United States, find this difficult to appreciate. A weak group exerts next to no pressure for group conformity, since it does not have a strong corporate identity. A weak group prizes and promotes individuality.

In a weak group, as in the United States in general, there are either too few or too many nonnormative symbols defining, expressing, and replicating group identity. Individuals are free to choose what they like; everything depends on the individual's consent. We half-humorously yet half-seriously point to baseball, motherhood, and apple pie as symbols. But second-generation Polish Americans would sooner rally to soccer, motherhood, and pierogi.

Weak-group symbols are rituals of status (that is, prestige, inducement, wealth—"Here's what's in it for YOU singular!") or of influence ("Here's what *I* can do for YOU singular!"). In other words, Bible study groups of individuals in a weak-group society would like Jeremiah to persuade people that his symbolic actions would be personally advantageous to each individual. Jeremiah would have to earn the support and consent of individuals in order to be effective. Thus in a weak-group society, Jeremiah's symbols would be effective by dint of his personal charm and persuasiveness, providing he can deliver the goods. This is effectiveness *ex opere operantis*. It would not be difficult to disparage or ignore such a prophet. Consider how the contemporary American society views prophets on behalf of the environment, etc.

JESUS AND SYMBOLIC ACTION

This social scientific understanding of symbol illuminates not only Jeremiah's deeds but Jesus' as well. Jesus' taking of the bread, breaking it, and giving it to his disciples with explanatory words ("This is my body/myself") can be accurately understood as an efficacious symbolic act very much like the symbolic acts of Jeremiah and other prophets.

The action not only prefigured what was soon to happen in actual fact but it set that reality in motion. Jesus' action at the Supper produced what it represented. Of course, this understanding is very old, but repeated requests by contemporary Western believers to make the Eucharistic liturgy more "relevant" attests to the fact that strong-group symbolism (biblical) is understood and appreciated only with difficulty and great effort in a weak-group society like that of the United States.

INDIVIDUALISM

Weak-group societies foster individualism. In our culture, we are brought up to stand on our own two feet, as distinct wholes, as distinct individuals, male and female. This sort of individualism is rare in the world's cultures, and perhaps totally absent from the Bible. To read the "Confessions of Jeremiah" (11:18–12:5; 15:10-21; 17:14-18; 18:18-23; 20:7-18) from the perspective of weak-group individualism is to distort Jeremiah and his experience. What Jeremiah's strong-group society viewed as important is technically called "dyadic (from the Greek word for 'pair') personality." Such a person always needs the opinion of another in order to know who she or he is. Such a person might be described as "other-directed." The "other" is always the group (or its representative) and its opinions, norms, and values. The pivotal values, of course, are honor and shame. Honor is a claim to worth and public acknowledgment of that worth. Shame is an attitude of sensitivity to what others think of self.

Jeremiah's confessions are rooted in and reflect these honor and shame values. "I have become a laughingstock all the day; everyone mocks me" (20:7). In a weak-group society, a person would reply:

"Sticks and stones will break my bones, but names (= shame) will never hurt me." Not so in a strong-group society.

In each confession Jeremiah includes the shame he feels: "name be remembered no more" (11:19); "I bear reproach" (15:15); "let me not be put to shame" (17:18); "let us smite him with the tongue" (18:18); "laughingstock, . . . word of the LORD has become for me a reproach and derision all day long" (20:7-8); "why did I come forth from the womb . . . and spend my days in shame?" (20:18).

His consolation is his prayer and confidence that his detractors be put to shame instead. "Let those be put to shame who persecute me . . . let them be dismayed . . . . They will be greatly shamed, for they will not succeed; their eternal dishonor will never be forgotten" (17:18; 20:11).

In Jeremiah's strong-group society the "conventions which people then observed in their dealings with one another" were governed by honor and shame, and not from introspectively generated motives that are personally and uniquely individualistic.

CONCLUSION

The value of a social-science approach to interpreting the Bible is that it helps a reader move beyond a simple literary approach (literary forms) and keeps a reader out of the text. Technically speaking, this approach reduces the danger of eisegesis, that is, reading into the text information that is not there because it is culturally implausible or impossible. Applying such insights to Jeremiah's symbols, actions, and confessions helps us to understand him from *his* perspective.

FOR FURTHER READING

Holladay, William L. *Jeremiah 1*. Hermeneia; Philadelphia: Fortress, 1986. *Jeremiah 2*. Hermeneia; Philadelphia: Fortress, 1989.

Malina, Bruce J. "First-Century Mediterranean Persons: A Preliminary View." Chap. 2 in *The Social World of Jesus and the Gospels*. New York and London: Routledge, 1996.

TRAVEL

Travel in the ancient world was very difficult and never a pleasure. The enterprise was fraught with risk and danger. It was safer to stay home. If travel was necessary, the wisest and safest course was to travel in a group.

How, then, did Abraham and his family manage to travel from Ur of the Chaldees (in modern Iraq) to Canaan (modern Israel)? How did Paul make those extensive journeys on land and sea, visiting Palestine, Syria, Asia Minor, and Greece, with plans to go to Italy and Spain? How did Jesus and the Twelve get around the regions of Palestine? Did they walk or ride? What animals did they ride? Did they have wagons or chariots? Were maps available? Could they buy food and supplies on the way? Were there inns for lodging? There are interesting answers for most of these questions.

THE DEVIANCE OF TRAVEL

Because the family was a central social institution among our ancestors in the faith and because families tended to live together in the same place, the idea of travel was considered deviant. The family supported life and offered security to such a great extent that it was nearly impossible to develop a "spirit of adventure" or a "desire to see the world." One person who did soon discovered the error of his ways (see Luke 15:13-17).

REASONS FOR TRAVEL

Nevertheless, there were good reasons for travel. One was commercial (Ezek 27:25). Merchants were interested in buying, trading, or selling goods, particularly those that were not native to the Ancient Near East, such as tin, amber, cloves, cinnamon, spikenard, silk, and cotton (see, for example, Rev 18:11-13).

Another reason was military: war or conquest. Armies traveled only at the right season, "in the spring [the dry season] of the year, the time when kings go out to battle" (2 Sam 11:1). Not only were the roads dry but newly grown grain was available to feed the troops.

A third reason for travel was communication. All travelers carried gossip and news (Job 21:28-30), but rulers and governments needed to communicate more expeditiously. Suetonius notes that the emperor Augustus arranged for one courier to carry a message by carriage with a regular change of horses. Such a courier could relate the circumstances of the dispatch and add supplementary information from first-hand experience (*Life of Augustus*, 49.3).

Pilgrimages (Luke 2:41, 44) and missionary motivation (Matt 10:1-6; Paul) provided yet a fourth reason for travel.

And finally, deportations (2 Kgs 17:5-6) and migrations (for example, Abraham) provided a fifth reason for travel.

MODE OF TRAVEL

Implied in the reasons for travel was the common mode of travel: in groups, that is, caravans (Gen 37:25; 1 Kgs 10:2; Luke 2:41-45). The reasons for this were many. By cultural preference, Middle Easterners are sociocentric, that is, they are group-focused and other-directed. The general preference is for group activity rather than solo work. Even Paul, the apparently "solo" evangelist, depended upon others for assistance in travel.

A second reason for traveling in groups was that travel was dangerous (see 2 Cor 11:25-27). Travelers feared bandits (Judg 9:25; Luke 10:30) and wild beasts (1 Sam 17:34-36; 2 Kgs 2:23-25; Mark 1:13). In Palestine lions prowled the valleys (Isa 30:6; Jer 50:44). Skeletal remains of bears have been excavated in Jordan's flood plain. It is not surprising that Jesus rarely traveled without his disciples.

Mary's apparently "solo" trip to visit her kinswoman Elizabeth is a shocking anomaly (Luke 1:39). In their *Social Science Commentary on the Synoptic Gospels,* Malina and Rohrbaugh quite plausibly suggest that Mary's experience of Jesus leaping or stirring in her womb led her to believe the child had apotropaic power, that is, the ability to ward off evil. Earlier travelers in the Ancient Near East often carried with them a statuette of the Egyptian deity Amun as a protection against robbery and other dangers.

Caravans were very large (one to two hundred donkeys) and were expected to stick to the predetermined route. When dangers were suspected, they did seek a detour (Judg 5:6-7). Often they were escorted by security guards armed by the central government.

LAND TRAVEL

Walking was the most common means of travel because it was cheap and convenient. In Syro-Palestine, a walking stick or staff would be very helpful, given the difficult terrain and the danger of beasts and bandits. Yet in Matthew (10:10) and Luke (9:3), Jesus prohibited his "walking" disciples from taking a staff, while in Mark (6:8) they were allowed a staff. Some scholars think that Mark misunderstood the Aramaic original. Others think that Matthew and Luke deliberately made Mark's sensible instruction more challenging for followers of Jesus.

How far could one walk in a day? Obviously this depended upon people and circumstances. Malnourished peasants would not have had the stamina of well-provisioned soldiers. Moreover, a soldier was allowed by Roman law to compel a civilian to carry his pack from one milestone to the next (Matt 5:41). The nature of the terrain, the purpose of the trip, and climatic conditions would also enter into consideration. Generally speaking, experts believe that the average person on a journey could walk between seventeen and twenty-three miles a day.

TIME OF TRAVEL

It was possible to travel by day or night (Exod 13:21), each time having its advantages and its drawbacks. Travel in the day reduced the risk of attacks by bandits but subjected travelers to the punishing heat of summer, unless one stopped until the sun began to decline. Thus it was (and in the Middle East still is) most unusual to travel at midday (Acts 26:13). Travel at night was much more comfortable for humans and their animals (Matt 2:9).

FOOD AND LODGING ON THE ROAD

Limited water supplies kept travel in check in this part of the world, where the heat causes rapid dehydration. The traveler took bread, parched grain, and dried fruit to last about two days. Inns or caravansaries developed in Persian times, but they were not secure places. Better to rely on hospitality (Matt 10:11-15).

Stabling for animals was at courtyard level, with accommodations for the travelers located above. In theory, accommodations, food, and provender were free at the inns, but other services had a price. The traveler had to take a good amount of money to pay the various tolls on goods, wheels, axles, and persons as the trip passed through each tax district. Matthew was a toll collector in Capernaum (9:1, 9)

ANIMALS AND TRAVEL

The basic pack animal was the donkey or ass, used since about 3000 B.C.E. The donkey was well suited for caravan travel because it was a strong yet not costly beast, with an even temper and surefootedness. It carried both goods (Gen 42:26-27; 1 Sam 16:20; 25:18) and people (1 Sam 25:20). Abraham used the donkey on his way to sacrifice Isaac (Gen 22:3).

The camel was domesticated around 2000 B.C.E. and began to replace the donkey (Gen 12:16; 24:35; 30:43). Abraham and Jacob used camels, especially for longer journeys (Gen 24:10; 31:17, 34). The dromedary (single-humped camel) was the most common. Though it had little fat for storing water, its speed (nearly ten miles an hour) compensated for this deficiency. Moreover, the camel could hold more cargo than the donkey could (see the reference to "camel load" in 2 Kings 8:9).

Horses were still faster but required much more forage, water, and care than the donkey. Perhaps only someone as wealthy as Solomon could afford to trade in horses and chariots (1 Kgs 10:26-29). This king's behavior and the use of horses for military purposes (see also Exod 14:9; Rev 19:11, 19) may have prompted the Deuteronomist's caution against the Israelites' owning horses (17:16).

VEHICLES AND TRAVEL

Wheeled vehicles appeared in lower Mesopotamia in about the third millennium B.C.E. Primitive models had solid wheels attached to axles, which rotated under the bed of the cart. This made for a noisy and rough ride. It also left ridges in dirt roads, especially when they were muddy.

Later a lighter wheel with spokes radiating from a hub was invented. This wheel rotated around the axle and improved travel considerably. Carts were able to maneuver better, carry more cargo, and get longer range than the earlier model. But vehicles required improved roads.

ROADS

In antiquity, roads were very poor and sometimes difficult to discern (Ps 107:4-7). Initially, a road was no more than a track where the stones had been removed (Isa 62:10), the bumps flattened, and the holes filled in. The Hebrew word usually translated "highway" or "main road" literally means "heaped-up dirt" (Judg 20:31, 45; 21:19).

When an important person was scheduled to visit, local inhabitants were expected to "prepare the way for the lord." Along this track, as Isaiah observed, "every valley shall be lifted up [ruts from wheels and potholes will be filled], and every mountain and hill [bumps] be made low; the uneven ground shall become level, and the rough places a plain" (40:3-4; Luke 3:4-6).

The Persians may have been the first to develop a decent road system. The Persian Royal Road connected Sardis (in modern Turkey) to Susa (in modern western Iran), covering a distance of fifteen hundred miles. It had a network of places to lodge and approximately 111 staging posts with fresh horses. A traveler could cover it on foot in three months. Speedy couriers traveling by horse could cover it in nine days (Herodotus 8:98; Est 3:13-15; 8:10, 13-14). The south branch of this highway went past Tarsus on to Syrian Antioch and may have been familiar and useful to Paul in his travels.

ROADS IN PALESTINE

Some scholars have described Palestine as a bridge with the Mediterranean Sea on one side and the sea of Sand on the other. Over this bridge, all travel, trade, and communication between the north and the south had to pass. Two very old and important north-south roads were the Great Trunk Road and the King's Highway.

The Great Trunk Road was known by many names. The Bible refers to it as "the way of the sea" (Isa 8:23 [9:1]) or "the way to the land of the Philistines" (Exod 13:17). The Egyptians, who used it

Young Palestinians make use of a very traditional form of travel: a faithful donkey.

extensively, called it "the way of Horus." It ran from the east to Damascus down toward the Sea of Galilee, across the Plain of Esdraelon, to the Mediterranean, along the coast to Gaza and Egypt.

The King's (or Royal) Highway is mentioned in the Bible in Numbers 20:17; 21:22. Outside the Bible it is known as the Sultan's highway or Trajan's highway (the emperor Trajan made it into a paved Roman highway in the second century C.E.). It ran in a fairly straight direction along the Transjordan plateau.

The Romans, the best road-builders in antiquity, improved existing roads in Palestine and built others. The Roman road had four layers: sand; stone and rock pieces in concrete; crushed stone in concrete; a paved surface. Drainage was provided, and in cities a raised sidewalk was provided for pedestrians.

SEA TRAVEL

Use of the Mediterranean Sea for travel dates back at least to about 2700 B.C.E., when the Egyptians traded with Byblos on the coast of modern Lebanon. Special craft called Byblites transported goods and passengers along the coast.

The Phoenicians mastered travel on the open sea and developed extensive trade. They went beyond the Strait of Gibraltar as far as the western coast of modern Morocco and called at Cyprus, Greece, Italy, Sardinia, the Spanish coast, Malta, and Crete. Solomon relied on them (1 Kgs 9:26-28) to help his young country get started in navigating the Mediterranean.

Though initially these vessels were sail-powered, the Greeks, Persians, and Romans developed human-powered ships. For instance, Persia developed the trireme (a vessel with three tiers of rowers on each side of the vessel) but was defeated by the Greeks at the battle of Salamis in 480 B.C.E.

Even with progress in shipbuilding during Greek and Roman times, sea travel was always difficult. Cargo was more important than the passengers, who had to bring along their own provisions and find lodging at the port each night, since there was no place for them aboard the vessel (Acts 21:3, 7, 8). The account of Paul's sea journey from Caesarea to Italy in Acts 27–28 presents an accurate picture of sea travel at that time.

Roman law prohibited sailings between November 20 and March 10. The truly safe period was from about May 26 to September 14. As Acts 28:11 indicates, Paul was already at sea when the dangerous travel period set in. It is small wonder that the Seer in Revelation (21:1) reports: "I saw a new heaven and a new earth; for the first heaven and the first earth had passed away, and the sea was no more."

CONCLUSION

The difficulties of travel in the ancient Mediterranean world prompted the symbolic use of straight and smooth roads to describe a good way of life. The Hebrews sought to follow *halakah*, from the word "to walk," which were prescriptions for a proper way of life, and Christians were first identified as followers of "the Way" (Acts 9:2), a distinctive path to salvation or meaning in life.

FOR FURTHER READING

Bruce, Frederick F. "Travel and Communication." *Anchor Bible Dictionary* 6:644–653.

Graf, David F., Benjamin Isaac, Israel Roll. "Roads and Highways." *Anchor Bible Dictionary* 5:776–787.

Pritchard, James B., ed. *The Harper Atlas of the Bible*. New York: Harper & Row, 1987.

Rasmussen, Carl G. *The Zondervan NIV Atlas of the Bible*. Grand Rapids, Mich.: Regency Reference Library, 1989.

Rogerson, John. *Atlas of the Bible*. New York: Facts on File Publications, 1985.

WEATHER

No radio or television news broadcast is complete without a weather report and forecast. The five-day forecast is especially helpful in planning events for those days. Our ancestors in the faith would find this amusing. They had no concept of a future as we do, and only a fool would attempt to predict the weather five days in the future. Jesus reflected his culture's firm fixation on the present when he observed: "When it is evening, you say 'It will be fair weather [tomorrow]; for the sky is red.' And in the morning, 'It will be stormy today, for the sky is red and threatening'" (Matt 16:2-3).

What was the weather like in the ancient Mediterranean world? Did they understand how it occurred or why it changed? Did the weather make a significant difference in their lives? How can we investigate this idea if the Bible actually has no word for weather? Modern insights shed interesting light on the biblical information, and an appreciation of the native point of view will explain why their limited understanding sufficed for the people of the Bible.

MODERN METEOROLOGY

In his excellent article on the climate of Palestine (see *Anchor Bible Dictionary* 5:119–126), Prof. Frank S. Frick explains how a variety of factors help one to understand the climate. In the summer months, two low-pressure systems (one over India, the other over Cyprus) produce counterclockwise air circulation that brings several weeks of etesian winds (NW to SE) over Palestine. In the winter, the system shifts southward, and Palestine is then in the area of the temperate-zone westerlies and cyclonic storm systems (about twenty-five a year) that move eastward across the Mediterranean in about four to six days and bring rains. Psalm 29 very likely describes one such storm ("the voice of the Lord" = thunder).

Palestine's location in latitude is roughly equal to that of southern California. This angle of exposure to the sun gives the country a high amount of heat and light from the sun, with moderate seasonal variations. The highest temperatures are in August (ranging from 71 to 93 degrees Fahrenheit) and the lowest in January (ranging from 46 to 55 degrees Fahrenheit), depending on location in the country. There are four distinct locations running north and south: the coastal plain, the western highlands, the Jordan Rift Valley, and the Transjordanian Plateau. Finally, Palestine, located geographically between the sea and the desert, each of which heats and cools at different rates, enjoys offshore breezes at night and onshore breezes during the day.

THE ANCIENT VIEW

Our ancestors in the faith, of course, knew nothing of this. Their macro-picture of the universe was very likely similar to that depicted by Aristotle (see *Meteorologica*, Bks. I–III). Imagine five concentric circles. The spherical earth is at the center. Surrounding it are three circles of elements in this order: water, air, and fire. The fifth circle is the celestial sphere containing the sun, moon, planets, and other elements. The heat of the sun makes the water evaporate into the air, but when it cools it falls back to the earth as rain. Aristotle is not always consistent in his explanations, but this general picture is a fair representation of his thought.

In Aristotle as well as in the Bible, it is clear that water is a key element of life. Without it vegetation will not grow, and humans cannot thrive. It is not surprising, then, that Palestine experiences its climate in two seasons, broadly speaking: a wet (rainy) season extending from about mid-October to April, and a dry season extending from about mid-June to mid-September. These seasons are separated by transitional weeks (or months). It is important to trap and store water in the rainy season for use in the dry season. Moreover, certain activities are possible only in the dry season, when roads are sturdy and passable. The Deuteronomic historian observed that it was "in the spring of the year [literally 'the turning of the year' from wet to dry season], the time when kings go forth to battle," that David sent his armies to wage war against the Ammonites (2 Sam 11:1; 1 Chr 20:1; see also 1 Kgs 20:22, 26; 2 Kgs 13:20; 2 Chr 36:10).

There is, however, a significant difference in the biblical outlook. Our ancestors in the faith did not recognize or understand impersonal or secondary causality. Every effect had to have a personal cause. Rain was not simply condensation of previously evaporated water, as Aristotle had it. Some person was responsible for it. If no human person caused it, then an other-than-human-person was responsible: an angel, a spirit, a demon, an archangel, a god, a son of a god, or God. Jeremiah phrased it pointedly as he reported God's displeasure with his faithless contemporaries: "They do not say in their hearts, 'Let us fear the LORD our God, who gives the rain in its season, the autumn rain and the spring rain, and keeps for us the weeks appointed for the harvest'" (5:24). This concept is consistent throughout the Bible. God makes it rain (Gen 2:5; 7:4; Matt 5:45; Acts 14:17; Heb 6:7) or gives rain (1 Kgs 17:14; Jer 5:24).

THE DRY SEASON (SUMMER)

The Bible actually has no word for weather or for seasons. Recall that Jesus (Matt 16:2-3) described the appearance of the sky and urged his listeners to attend to "the signs of the times." Though Vatican II and contemporary theology understand the signs to be social, the ancients (besides Jesus, see also Theophrastus, *On Weather Signs*) believed that one should read these signs in atmospheric and celestial events. There in the constellations of the sky, the God who alone is in control of all of life, has sketched his intentions since creation. As classical specialists continually remind us, the majority of ancient people lived in the countryside and knew the skies, the lands, the plants—everything we call "nature"—very well. God had control over it all.

An old olive tree in Upper Galilee.

During the dry season, days are virtually cloudless. Grapes, figs, pomegranates, melons, and other crops are ripening and are tended by the farmers. Most of the fruits are harvested in August and September, when the transitional weeks begin. Since the wheat and barley were harvested in spring, shepherds led their sheep and goats to those fields to graze on the stubble. Travel was obviously easy at this time. Armies could feed off the local produce as they marched to their destinations. The pilgrimage feasts (Passover, Pentecost, Booths) occurred in this period.

If the Synoptic story line is historically accurate, Jesus' ministry lasted for one dry season. That is the time when people could be outdoors and could easily be engaged in discussion. Labor needs were at an ebb, so disciples could leave family, farm, or boats during the dry season to be with Jesus. When the rainy season began in mid-October, everyone returned home. It was at the beginning of the next dry season, Passover time, the time of the wheat and barley harvest, that Jesus traveled to Jerusalem and met his fate.

Have you ever wondered about the foolish man who built his house on sand (Matt 7:26)? It was the dry season, the alluvial soil had hardened, and the poor fool did not scrape down deep enough to set his foundation on bedrock. When the rains came, they washed away the previously hardened surface soil and his house collapsed. Natives of this region know this very well, so only a fool would be so stupid, lazy, or careless.

TRANSITIONAL SEASONS

There really is no equivalent in Palestine to spring and fall, so familiar in temperate zones. The rainy season proper is sandwiched between two transitional periods lasting about six weeks each. One extends from early April to mid-June; the other, from mid-September to the end of October. Winds blow in from the eastern and southern deserts. These winds are variously known as sirocco (from *sharqiyyeh*, meaning an "east wind"), and in Egypt as *khamsin*, and in modern Israel as *sharav* (though they do not describe the exact same conditions). These may last three days to three weeks. They blow fine dust around and dry up the vegetation. "The grass withers, the flower fades; when the breath of the LORD blows upon it" (Isa 40:7; see also 27:8; Ezek 17:10; Luke 12:55).

THE RAINY SEASON (WINTER)

The rainy season (see Song 2:11) is actually characterized by occasional rainstorms (three days of rain) followed by several days of dry weather. About 70 percent of the rainfall occurs between November and February. January is ordinarily the wettest and coldest month, averaging about six inches of rainfall. Travel is treacherous at this time. Recall Paul's experiences in Acts 27–28 and Jesus' warning about the destruction of the Temple (Mark 13:18).

The Bible speaks of "early" *(yoreh; proimon)* and "late" *(malqoš; opsimon)* rains. If Israel obeys God's commandments, "he will give the rain [December to February] to your land in its season, the early rain [October to December] and the later rain [March to April] , that you may gather in your grain and your wine and oil" (Deut 11:14, featuring three different Hebrew words for "rain"; see also Jas 5:7). The farmer plows the fields and plants the seeds in late summer and autumn, but the seeds cannot germinate until the early rains fall. The crops, mostly wheat and barley, grow throughout the winter but need the later rains of March and April to produce a good harvest.

Stormy weather on the Sea of Galilee.

If the late rains fall too late, this can spell disaster for the crops. Barley in particular is susceptible to rain damage in the harvest season. Such rain is rather rare. Because of the importance of rain at the right time, the Israelites were easily swayed to turn to Baal, the Canaanite storm god, to guarantee fertility to the land if Yahweh did not seem to be delivering it. When Israel forced the prophet Samuel to help them select a king who would rule over them like kings over other nations, Samuel reluctantly agreed to their requests. But to demonstrate the continuing validity of his credentials and credibility as a spokesperson for Yahweh, he caused rain to fall during the harvest. "'Is it not the wheat harvest today? I will call upon the LORD, that he may send thunder and rain; and you shall know and see that your wickedness is great, which you have done in the sight of the LORD, in asking for yourselves a king.' So Samuel called upon the LORD, and the LORD sent thunder and rain that day; and all the people greatly feared the LORD and Samuel" (1 Sam 12:17-18).

Nevertheless, rainy seasons with insufficient rain were and still are not uncommon. An occasional dry year is not very damaging, but a series of dry years can wreak havoc. Modern studies indicate that three consecutive dry years are part of the experience of every farmer in Palestine. Interestingly, this is the number that describes a drought in the time of Elijah (1 Kgs 18:1), while the one with which Joseph had to deal was particularly harsh (Gen 41:54).

CONCLUSION

Water, so essential to life, derived mainly from rains. Even though the ancients knew from experience what weather pattern to expect in general, they could not predict anything beyond the next day's condition. Rains that came when unexpected or not wanted, or that did not come as expected, were a matter of life and death. Fidelity to the Lord of creation was the only sensible course of action. The modern dictum seems to be as true for the past as for the present: "Weather. Everybody talks about it, but no one can do anything about it."

FOR FURTHER READING

Frick, Frank S. "Palestine, Climate of." *Anchor Bible Dictionary* 4:119–126.
Rasmussen, Carl G. *The Zondervan NIV Atlas of the Bible*. Grand Rapids, Mich.: Regency Reference Library, 1989. Pp. 24–26.

WORK

How did our ancestors in the faith make a living? What kind of jobs did they have? Questions like these reflect life in a modern, industrialized culture, where money is the medium of exchange. In such a culture, everyone needs money to survive, to acquire the basics of life. Of the many ways to obtain money, perhaps the most basic, traditional, and acceptable method is selling goods or services. This is a narrow but ordinary understanding of work or a job.

From this cultural perspective, it is easy to misinterpret the observation of the Sage that "the appetite of workers works for them; their hunger urges them on" (Prov 16:26). The context in which such wisdom arose was chiefly agricultural; the culture was agrarian. This insight offers the best entrée into exploring what people did for a living in biblical times.

AGRICULTURE

Without a doubt, no human activity is as prevalent in the Bible as farming, beginning with the first earthling (Gen 2:15) and extending through the parables of Jesus (e.g., Matt 13). Many aspects of farming were regulated by Mosaic Law (Lev 19:9-10; Deut 22:9-10). Some of the basic crops were discussed above (see pp. 56–58), allowing us to focus here on the work of farming.

When hunters and gatherers learned how to domesticate plants and animals around 7000 B.C.E., they made settled life a possibility. This indeed is the date assigned to the beginnings of Jericho, the oldest town on earth. The powerful, perennial spring at Tel es-Sultan gushes a thousand gallons a minute, providing irrigation that produces abundant fruit, flowers, and spices.

Unfortunately, this condition was not common throughout Palestine. Natural water sources like the spring just mentioned were scarce. Farmers depended heavily on rain (Deut 11:10-12), but the wet season is relatively short (October to April). Droughts were common (Gen 41:25-36; Amos 4:7-9). The variety of soils and conditions has always made agriculture a challenging enterprise. Rocky and uneven soil predominates, and farmers had to clear land to make arable ground (Isa 5:2; Josh 17:17-18).

Sowing. For winter crops, plowing began after the early fall rains had softened the baked soil. The plow was made of wood with a metal tip (copper, bronze, and iron as they were discovered). Usually oxen pulled the plow (Deut 22:10). Sowing was customarily done by broadcasting either before or after plowing. Sometimes sowing was performed by a seed drill attached to the plow.

Even so, planting was done according to a divinely ordered pattern: "Do they not scatter dill, sow cumin, and plant wheat in rows, and barley in its proper place, and spelt as the border? For they are well instructed; their God teaches them" (Isa 28:25-26).

A farmer prepares what he hopes will be the "rich soil" that produces a bountiful harvest.

Harvesting. When the rains ended in mid-March or April, barley was ready for harvesting (Ruth 2:23; 2 Sam 21:9). Wheat matured about three or four weeks later (Exod 34:22; Gen 30:14; Judg 15:1). Then followed the harvesting of grapes (and winemaking), olives (and pressing oil), and finally the autumn festival of Tabernacles or Booths. Harvesting covered about seven months, and in a good year one harvest followed another without interruption (Amos 9:13).

Grains were harvested by being pulled out by hand or cut by a sickle (Deut 16:9; Jer 50:16). The stalks were then threshed, that is, the stalks, chaff, and grain were cut apart and separated at a threshing floor. Threshing was done by having animals trample the stalks (Deut 25:4), or by flails (Ruth 2:17), or by threshing sledges (Isa 41:15) or wheel-threshers.

Winnowing, that is, separating the grain from the chaff and straw, was done by throwing the materials into the air with a shovel or fork (Isa 30:24), where the wind performed the task. A more intense cleaning was accomplished by sifting grain through a sieve (Isa 30:28; Amos 9:9).

Animal husbandry. Agriculture also included animal husbandry, chiefly sheep and goats. Abraham likely brought Asiatic moufflon from Sumeria, and returning exiles brought the long-legged Egyptian sheep in the Exodus. The most common species of sheep in ancient Palestine was the fat-tailed sheep, so called because the tail is enclosed in a cushion of fat from which the last joints stick out like a claw. It was considered a delicacy (Exod 29:22; Lev 3:9).

It is difficult to determine the species of goat common in ancient Palestine, but the color of its hair was generally black (Song 1:5), though the Bible mentions speckled goats as well (Gen 30:32; 31:10). The goat was kept especially for its milk (Deut 32:14; Prov 27:27), but kid was a delicacy (Gen 27:9; Judg 15:1; 1 Sam 16:20; Luke 15:29).

Whose jobs? Were these agricultural tasks performed by males, females, or both? The answer is yes! In general, honor and shame, the core values of Mediterranean culture, determine the proper roles

A shepherd tends his flock near the Sea of Galilee.

and behavior for each gender. All life in the Middle Eastern world is divided along gender lines.

As a rule, the area outside the home is the men's domain, while the home is the woman's domain. Some areas outside the home, such as the village square, are available to both genders, but not at the same time. Women who come to the field to assist in the harvest cluster by gender and do their tasks as a group (Ruth 2:8). Thus, while plowing and sowing are ordinarily tasks performed by men, harvesting may be performed by women and men, but in separate groups. (Similarly, after Moses sang his song of praise to the Lord, Miriam, Aaron's sister, led the women with tambourines and dancing [Exod 15:1, 20-21]).

Shepherding can be performed by men or women (Gen 29:6, 9), but the animals have been linked symbolically in Mediterranean culture with specific genders: sheep with men (Isa 53:7) and goats with women (Song 1:8). Typically the family's milk goat (Prov 27:27) is kept like a pet within the house complex, the women's domain. The symbolism of these animals replicates the culture's core values of honor (sheep: males) and shame (goats: females).

Indeed, agriculture was such a dominant occupation in the ancient Middle East that nearly every aspect of that work also had a figurative meaning in the minds of the ancients (e.g., Isa 21:10; Luke 9:62; Matt 9:36-38). Moreover, it served as the major expression of God's satisfaction with his chosen people's compliance with the covenant. "If you will only obey the LORD your God by diligently observing all his commandments . . . . The LORD will open for you his rich storehouse, the heavens, to give the rain of your land in its season and to bless all your undertakings" (Deut 28:1, 12; see also vv. 15, 22-24).

FISHING

During the biblical period, when Israelite access to the Mediterranean was limited, fish had to be purchased (Neh 13:16). In the Greek period (after 300 B.C.E.), fishing at the Sea of Galilee became a government-regulated activity that involved catching, preparing, and distributing the fish. Fish became a more frequent item in the first-century diet.

Jesus fed the crowd, properly divided along gender lines ("not counting the women and children": Matt 14:21), with very likely fresh fish. John's account (6:9) appears to describe processed fish, already cooked and ready for shipping and marketing.

In 1986 the level of the Sea of Galilee was unusually low. Marine archaeologists discovered an ancient fishing boat in the mud along its northwest shore, a little north of ancient Magdala. Scientific tests convinced the experts that this boat was built between 40 B.C.E. and 70 C.E. It is very likely the kind of boat mentioned in the Synoptic Gospels, the one used by the Jonah-Zebedee fishing syndicate or corporation (Luke 5:10), which included their sons Peter, Andrew, James and John, and hired hands (Mark 1:16-20). The boat was 26.5 feet long, 7.5 feet wide, and 4.5 feet deep. Originally it had a sail. There were places for four oarsmen and a tiller man. This size boat could hold a crew of five and ten passengers (Matt 14:22).

Sometimes fishermen used lines with fishhooks (Matt 17:27), but the corporations would use one of two kinds of nets. The sweepnet was circular and weighted along the edges, and was used mostly for fishing in deep water (Matt 4:18; Mark 1:16). The dragnet was weighted at one end but had floats on the other, and was used for surface fishing or fishing from shore (Matt 13:47).

The government regulated the fishing industry by selling fishing rights to tax collectors or publicans (brokers). They contracted with fishermen and frequently had to capitalize them. Since Matthew the toll collector had his office in Capernaum (Matt 9:1, 9), an important fishing center, it is quite likely that Matthew brokered the government's fishing rights to fellow citizens.

Ever at the mercy of the brokers (toll collectors) who financed their operations, first-century Mediterranean fishermen were far from middle class. They had no control over their activities because of storms (Matt 8:23-27) or unfavorable conditions (Luke 5:5) and were nearly always in debt. Jesus' promise to make these fishermen

Faithful to a long tradition, fishermen cast their nets for a catch in the Sea of Galilee.

"fishers of men" meant that he was leading them to rich fishing grounds (Luke 5:10). It was the dry season (April to October), when human beings were out and about and easily "caught" by wandering teachers and preachers.

ARTISANS

The Bible mentions a wide array of artisans: barber (Ezek 5:1), armorer (1 Sam 13:19), embroiderer (Exod 35:35), engraver of precious stones (Exod 28:9), goldsmith (Isa 40:19), among many others. Here the topic of occupations becomes a bit complicated.

From the beginning and throughout the biblical period, agricultural tasks dominated life. At periods of high taxation, when landowners lost their land, they might have become tenant farmers. If they fell too deeply in debt, they lost their land. Many of these became artisans. Scholars conjecture that since Joseph took Mary to Bethlehem to register for the census (Luke 2:4) but was himself an artisan living in Nazareth, at some earlier period in the family history Joseph's family probably lost ancestral land in Bethlehem.

Carpenter. Tradition says that Jesus was a carpenter (Mark 6:3) or a carpenter's son (Matt 13:55). The Greek word here, like its Hebrew equivalent in the Old Testament, means simply "artisan," "skilled workman." In Hebrew texts, the context specifies the material in which the workman was skilled: for example, wood (Isa 44:13-17; Jer 10:3); metal (1 Sam 13:19; Isa 40:19); stone (2 Sam 5:11), etc.

Like many other biblical scholars, Fr. Xavier Léon-Dufour, S.J., believes that the word "carpenter" is a mistranslation. He asserts that woodworkers were almost unknown in Palestine. This was certainly true in the time of David and Solomon, because carpenters were imported from Tyre to help build David's palace (2 Sam 5:11) and Solomon's Temple (1 Kgs 5:6). But some native artisans returned from the Exile (537 B.C.E.) and were able to assist in the restoration of Jerusalem and its Temple (Jer 24:1; 29:2).

Influenced particularly by excavations at Sepphoris, a city about three and a half miles from Nazareth, scholars propose that Joseph and Jesus were artisans who worked with varied materials but perhaps mostly stone. When Jesus was a young man, Herod Antipas ("that fox": Luke 13:31-32) was building the government seat at Sepphoris, including a recently excavated four-thousand-seat theater.

Though a second-century tradition claims that Jesus made plows and yokes, given the limited market for these items, it is plausible to imagine that Joseph and Jesus packed a lunch each day, walked to Sepphoris, and worked on the projects there, whether in wood or stone, and returned to their hamlet each evening.

In support of the claim that Jesus likely worked in stone, scholars note that in Matthew's Gospel Jesus' favorite degrading title for his opponents, the Pharisees, is "hypocrites." In Greek this word means "actor," and most of Jesus' references reflect an awareness of the theater and acting. The conjecture is that if Jesus did not work on constructing the theater, he became very familiar with it.

CONCLUSION

In the ancient Middle East, trades and skills were geared for the needs of the times and were handed down from father to son and from mother to daughter. At least part of the reason why Jesus scandalized the residents of his hamlet is that he did not seem to be following in his artisan-father's footsteps.

But perhaps most important for Western or American readers of the Bible on the topic of work or occupation is this observation: American men and women spend as much time "on the job" as Middle Eastern men and women spend meeting people and building networks of friendships. And they are both engaged in the same activity: making a living. In the Middle East, family and friends help family and friends.

The paralyzed man had no family or friends to help him into the pool (John 5:7). The first hired workers in the vineyard learned to their dismay that they were only hired hands, not friends (Matt 20:1-16). Making friends is the most important job the Bible knows. It was the only way to make a living in the biblical world.

FOR FURTHER READING

Hanson, K. C. "The Galilean Fishing Economy and the Jesus Tradition." *Biblical Theology Bulletin* 27 (1997) 99–111.

Hanson, K. C., and Douglas E. Oakman. *Palestine in the Time of Jesus: Social Institutions and Social Conflicts.* Minneapolis: Fortress, 1998.

Basic Resources

The following resources provide additional information on the topics in this Cultural Dictionary. The list is representative and not exhaustive. Other dictionaries, atlases, and similar books can also be helpful. These are the sources to which a novice might turn for basic and supplemental information.

Achtemeier, Paul, ed. *Harper's Bible Dictionary*. San Francisco: Harper & Row, 1985.

De Vaux, Roland. *Ancient Israel: Its Life and Institutions*. Trans. John McHugh. New York and Toronto: McGraw-Hill, 1961.

Freedman, David Noel, ed. *Anchor Bible Dictionary*. 6 vols. New York: Doubleday, 1992.

Gower, Ralph. *The New Manners and Customs of Bible Times*. Chicago: Moody Press, 1987.

Hartman, Louis F., C.SS.R., ed. *Encyclopedic Dictionary of the Bible*. 2nd rev. ed. Translation and adaptation of A. Van den Born's *Bijbels Woordenboek*. New York and Toronto: McGraw-Hill, 1963.

Matthews, Victor H. *Manners and Customs in the Bible*. Rev. ed. Peabody, Mass.: Hendrickson Publishers, 1991.

Malina, Bruce J. *Window on the World of Jesus: Time Travel to Ancient Judea*. Louisville: Westminster/John Knox Press, 1993.

Pilch, John J., and Bruce J. Malina, eds. *Biblical Social Values and Their Meaning: A Handbook*. Peabody, Mass.: Hendrickson Publishers, 1993.

Pritchard, James B., ed. *The Harper Atlas of the Bible*. New York: Harper & Row, 1987.

Rasmussen, Carl G. *The Zondervan NIV Atlas of the Bible*. Grand Rapids, Mich.: Regency Reference Library, 1989.

Rogerson, John. *Atlas of the Bible*. New York: Facts on File Publications, 1985.

Rousseau, John J., and Rami Arav. *Jesus and His World: An Archaeological and Cultural Dictionary*. Minneapolis: Fortress, 1995.

Stuhlmueller, Carroll, C.P., ed. *The Collegeville Pastoral Dictionary of Biblical Theology*. Collegeville, Minn.: The Liturgical Press, 1996.

Index

This index lists the words and ideas defined in this Dictionary as they appear in the Sunday Gospel reading for the full three-year Liturgical Cycle. Additional cultural information about these gospel readings is available in the three-volume series, *The Cultural World of Jesus Sunday by Sunday, Cycle A, B, and C* (The Liturgical Press).

Pertinent illustrations and other insights can be found on my web-page: http://www.georgetown.edu/faculty/pilchj, click on "Mediterranean Culture."

CYCLE A: MATTHEW

220.3
P637

100235

LINCOLN CHRISTIAN COLLEGE AND SEMINARY

3 4711 00154 2986